Something *Inside*

Something *Inside*

Conversations
with
Gay Fiction Writers

Philip Gambone

With Photographs by
Robert Giard

THE UNIVERSITY OF WISCONSIN PRESS

The University of Wisconsin Press
2537 Daniels Street
Madison, Wisconsin 53718

3 Henrietta Street
London WC2E 8LU, England

2   4   5   3   1

Printed in the United States of America

Library of Congress Cataloging-in-Publication Data
Something inside : conversations with gay fiction writers /
compiled and edited by Philip Gambone.
354 pp.   cm.
Includes index.
ISBN 0-299-16130-7 (alk. paper)
1. Novelists, American—20th century—Interviews.
2. Homosexuality and literature—United States—History—
20th century. 3. American fiction—20th century—History and
criticism—Theory, etc. 4. Gay men's writings, American—History
and criticism—Theory, etc. 5. Gay men—United States—
Interviews. 6. Gay men in literature. I. Gambone, Philip.
PS374.H63S66   1999
813´.54099206642—dc21   98-48765

Some of Robert Giard's photos have previously appeared in
Particular Voices: Portraits of Gay and Lesbian Writers (MIT Press, 1997).

For
my mother
Nancy DeVita Gambone
who gave me my first books

and for
Frank Bidart
and in memory of
Reuben Arthur Brower

two great teachers
who showed me how to read

Contents

Foreword

I n his introduction to Something Inside: *Conversations with Gay Fiction Writers,* the short story writer Philip Gambone fills us in on some of the things he has hoped to achieve, and others he hopes to avoid, in the interviews he has assembled here:

> Every interviewer, like every writer, learns as he or she goes along, but in general my method has followed a fairly standard procedure. I've always tried to read as much of the writer's work as I could before our meeting and to prepare a set of questions—some biographical, some thematic, some about the writing process, some about the general issues that stem from being a gay or lesbian writer today—but to allow the flow of the conversation to suggest other questions and to determine the general drift. My aim has never been to grind an ax or to be confrontational. I simply want to engage some writers whom I've read and admired in a dialogue about their work and the writing life. Nor have I been much interested in what might be called "literary gossip." That several of the interviews included in this collection are not the latest, up-to-the-minute briefings from the authors seems irrelevant to me.

He adds that if he has a model to follow it is "the superb interviews that have been published for years in the *Paris Review.*"

It is easy to underestimate interviews like Gambone's because they *haven't* appeared in the *Paris Review,* but instead in unpretentious gay newspapers and magazines such as *Bay Windows, Gay Community News,* and *Frontiers*; or as a featured program on WOMR, a "small, community radio station in Provincetown, Massachusetts." Indeed, I often wonder if gay readers are aware of the sheer quality of the work—for which the authors are generally so poorly paid—that appears so regularly in the journals they pick up and throw away, for these pieces would do credit to the *Paris Re-*

view, or any other literary publication. Like these, Gambone's interviews are long enough to be the "extended conversations" he says he finds his talks with writers have become; long enough to allow both himself and his interviewee the chance to spin out ideas that at first may not have been fully formed, long enough, therefore, to allow both conversationalists to say things they may not have known they wanted to say.

Gambone in no way eggs his writers on, however. He does not seduce them with opportunities for backbiting or self-pity, nor with demands for flashy, provocative overstatements. What he *does* is suggest topics that might be of interest to *the writers themselves.* This is tricky enough, involving a risk right from the beginning. (One can hardly ask Dennis Cooper, for instance, what one might ask David Leavitt, an author whose work Cooper "hate[s]" and "reject[s] . . . on every level.") Gambone also has the even rarer gift of knowing how to listen to the answers; this, too, is easier said than done. It is fatally easy, especially when interviewing authors one respects, to sit slack jawed while they brilliantly carry on; the author likes it, and so, in a sense, does the interviewer, for the author does everything but write the interview, asking his own questions, switching topics at will, and in general projecting to the back row. But Gambone, while highly sympathetic, is not uncritical. He will return to a topic that the author has treated too superficially—as he does when he persuades Alan Hollinghurst to say more about why, if it's gay men's nature to "wander" sexually, the protagonist of Hollinghurst's *The Folding Star* doesn't. It is equally easy for interviewers to turn the conversation into a theater for their own surpassing brilliance. Anyone who has ever attended a learned convention and heard the eight-minute questions posed by assistant professors up for tenure will recognize such self-promoting rhetoric. Fortunately this trope is not to be found in Gambone's book: the brightest light is always turned on the writer, not his interlocutor.

Thus, though Gambone tells us that these interviews reflect a "growing sense of myself as a writer talking to fellow writers," he means, I think, that as he became a more experienced writer of fiction, he began to know what to ask other fiction writers, and how to ask it. He shrewdly asks Hollinghurst about the Belgian setting of *The Folding Star.* Was it chosen, he wonders, "in order to get around [the] problem"—both legal and literary—of desire between an adult and a teenager? For, had the book been set in England (where the age of consent is higher than in Belgium), the novel might have struck English readers as a deliberate provocation and turned the story, willy-nilly, into one of sexual abuse. This would have obscured the real topic of the novel, which is (as Gambone also saw) "obsessive love," not the breaking of some sexual law.

In asking this sort of question, Gambone shows his own experience as a writer of fiction, and joins the category of critics who are themselves practitioners of the art they criticize. In fact, these interviews, for all of their personal charm, seem to me works of criticism in unexpected form. The most obvious sense in which they are critical is that they provide the writer with the chance to give an account of his work, to say what he feels to be its main preoccupations, its successes and failures. How illuminating, for instance, to hear Andrew Holleran confirm that for him homosexuality implies an almost *necessary* disconnection between a gay man and his family: "I think the cities are still necessary for gay life, in part because of that anonymity and that detachment from your familial origins. It's very hard, still, to integrate gayness with family life." Second, by asking questions an interested reader might ask as well, the interviewer helps define what the important questions are and will be. An anthology like this one thus transcends what Gore Vidal has witheringly called "book chat" (and Gambone "literary gossip") to become a contribution to an ongoing critical conversation.

As in all criticism, the hardest thing is knowing where to start, which demands a kind of intellectual as well as personal tact. One must have the manners to ask questions in such a way that the author responds with a minimum of defensiveness and a maximum of unegotistical engagement to a common question; one must also have an equivalent aesthetic tact in order to sift what is essential in an author's work from what is accidental; and finally, one must be accurate and knowledgable. Philip Gambone is unusually well-equipped to undertake all of these tasks. He has an exquisite sense of how to make these often touchy authors show their enthusiasms (how often in this book we hear them answering, "Yes, that's exactly what I meant"). He comes to the interviews fresh from a reading (or rereading) of an author's work, prepared with names of characters, specific incidents, favorite words or metaphors. And because his aim "has never been to grind an ax," he permits them to speak without immediately tidying up their opinions.

Something Inside will delight readers of all sexual and literary stamps. In it, we meet some of the best fiction writers of our day, writers who speak candidly, wittily, and unexpectedly about the themes they have more indirectly handled in their fiction. We also meet an interviewer of rare charm and intelligence, one who asks the questions we ourselves would like to ask if only we were clever and attentive enough to do so.

Reed Woodhouse

New York
October 1998

Acknowledgments

Thanks go first and foremost to the twenty-one writers here assembled, who, over the past eleven years, answered my questions with such gracious, thoughtful, candid, and generous responses.

I also want to thank the many people in Provincetown, Massachusetts, who helped make the radio series *The Word is Out* such a success. They include Len Bowen and the entire WOMR radio station staff, especially my patient audio engineer, Diana Fabri; John Skoyles, former director of the Fine Arts Work Center; the underwriters of *The Word is Out,* including the Puffin Foundation, the Massachusetts Foundation for the Humanities, the Provincetown and Wellfleet Culture Councils, the Massachusetts Cultural Council, Cape Air, and the gay and lesbian guest houses in Provincetown that put up so many of the writers; and other Provincetown friends, including Gary Coxe, Mitch Villani, and Diane Johnson, Nan Cinnater, and Stuard Derrick of Now Voyager bookstore.

I also wish to thank the editors of the publications where many of these interviews were first printed—Neil Miller at Gay Community News; David Kalmansohn at *Frontiers;* Trey Graham at the *Washington Blade;* Richard Schneider at the *Harvard Gay and Lesbian Review,* and most especially Rudy Kikel at *Bay Windows.*

Raphael Kadushin, my editor at the University of Wisconsin Press, deserves special mention, not only for his initial enthusiasm for the project but for his ongoing support and wise advice throughout the project.

I also wish to thank the Helene Wurlitzer Foundation, Taos, New Mexico, and its acting director, Ken Peterson, where, during the summer of 1996, I worked on a first draft of this book.

Thanks as well to Tom Smith, Carole Carter, and Marshall Neilson for helping me to negotiate the intricacies of cyberspace; John A. Collins, in the Government Documents Division of the Harvard College Library, for research assistance; and Paul Rehme for bibliographical help.

Finally, I owe Michael Lowenthal a tremendous debt—for his faith in this book; his unflagging encouragement; the many hours of keen and probing conversation we've shared about this and other writing projects; and, most of all, for his friendship.

Something *Inside*

Introduction

The roots of this book go back more than twenty years, to the days when I wrote for Boston's *Gay Community News*. At the time, *GCN* was the only gay and lesbian paper in New England and one of the few in the country. Under the guidance of its editor, a young journalist named Neil Miller, I covered the religion beat, mainly news stories and short features about gay men and the church. I can still remember what a terrifying and exhilarating experience it was to see my name in print for the first time, attached to an editorial that included the word "gay" in the title. It was an empowering moment, one with which I think many of the writers in this collection would identify.

The last piece I did for *GCN* was an interview with Malcolm Boyd, the rebel Episcopal priest who had recently come out in his book of prayers, *Am I Running With You, God?* In that interview, conducted in 1977, Boyd talked about the books that had helped him come to terms with his homosexuality, a list that included works by Tennessee Williams, Christopher Isherwood, and the gay football player Dave Kopay. Compare Boyd's list with the three books that Allen Barnett, in his interview with me, says he checked out of his hometown library as a gay teenager in 1971: Donn Teal's *The Gay Militants,* Dennis Altman's *Homosexual Oppression and Liberation,* and Gordon Merrick's *The Lord Won't Mind.* It's telling that neither writer mentions—because they had yet to be written—any books from that remarkable body of gay fiction that burst onto the scene beginning in the late 1970s.

The year after my interview with Malcolm Boyd, 1978, has been justly called the *annus mirabilis* of modern gay writing. That year, among several fine gay novels, two extraordinary ones—Andrew Holleran's *Dancer From the Dance* and Larry Kramer's *Faggots*—appeared on the literary landscape, ushering in a new era of gay literature, an era whose flowering we are still experiencing today.

In the twenty years since *Dancer* and *Faggots,* the evolution of the gay male novel has been, as Edmund White once put it, "breathlessly rapid."[1] The creation of specifically gay literary journals (for example, *Christopher Street* in 1975) encouraged this swift growth.[2] Likewise, the first *Men on Men* anthologies, edited by the late George Stambolían, and later the *Women on Women* series, extended the audience for serious gay and lesbian short fiction and mirrored both the diversity of talent and its slow but steady recognition by mainstream publishing houses. Gay bookstores (and serious gay sections in nongay bookstores), gay book reviews, gay literary conferences, and—perhaps most important—the rise of a gay publishing industry and the ever-increasing willingness of mainstream houses to publish gay books all played a part in the phenomenal rise of the gay literary movement that began to sweep the country. Homosexual experience, the stone rejected by other builders, had become the cornerstone in the house of gay writing.

Buoyed by this rising tide, I began to write my first stories and to contribute book reviews to a second gay and lesbian paper that had appeared on the Boston scene, *Bay Windows.* My editor, Rudy Kikel, himself a fine gay poet, encouraged me to tackle longer pieces about the emerging gay literary scene, especially through interviews and profiles. Those first interviews for *Bay Windows,* written in the late 1980s, included conversations with Edmund White, Brad Gooch, Joseph Hansen, and David Leavitt, all reprinted here.

During the next few years, I found that my interviews were evolving into extended conversations. As I read more gay fiction and thought more about the issues surrounding "minority" literature, I allowed myself a less formal, more exploratory style in my talks with gay writers. The interviews I conducted in the early 1990s—with Christopher Bram, Paul Monette, Allen Barnett, Lev Raphael, Michael Klein, Martin Duber-

---

1. Edmund White, "Out of the Closet, Onto the Bookshelf," *New York Times Magazine,* 16 June 1991, 22.

2. The importance of *Christopher Street* to the recent history of gay writing cannot be underestimated. It's the place that gave many aspiring writers (including several in this book) their start and, more importantly, the encouragement they needed to keep going. As Christopher Bram notes in our conversation, it was at the moment that *Christopher Street* published his first story that he realized, "I can write about being gay and get published. I can write about what's important to me and succeed as a writer."

man, Michael Nava, and my old *GCN* editor, Neil Miller (by then the author of two books about gay life, *In Search of Gay America* and *Out in the World*) reflect this growing sense of myself as a writer talking to fellow writers.[3]

Then, in the fall of 1992, Len Bowen, a producer for WOMR, a small, community radio station in Provincetown, Massachusetts, asked me to host a series of readings and interviews with gay and lesbian fiction writers. Thus was born *The Word is Out: Gay and Lesbian Writers and Their Work,* a series of twelve hour-long interviews that we taped over the course of the following summer and early fall. The idea was to invite gay and lesbian writers to Provincetown for a weekend where, on Friday night, they would give a public reading from their work at the Fine Arts Work Center, followed by an interview in the WOMR studio on Saturday morning. The interviews were taped and later edited for broadcast the following season. Eventually, other community and public radio stations picked up the series as well.[4]

By the end of that fall (1993), I realized that I had amassed enough interviews over the years to consider gathering them into an anthology. Although commitments to other projects kept me from immediately pursuing the idea, I nonetheless kept interviewing gay writers: Alan Hollinghurst for the *Washington Blade,* David Plante for *Frontiers,* Ed White for *Bay Windows.* When my list of interviews topped thirty, I realized it was finally time to assemble this book.

Every interviewer, like every writer, learns as he or she goes along, but in general my method has followed a fairly standard procedure. I've always tried to read as much of the writer's work as I could before our meeting and to prepare a set of questions—some biographical, some thematic, some about the writing process, some about the general issues that stem from being a gay or lesbian writer today—but to al-

---

3. This collection of interviews focuses solely on gay male fiction writers. Consequently, the interviews I conducted with poets, nonfiction writers and, later, several lesbian novelists have not been included.

4. Each broadcast began and ended with an except from a recording by The Flirtations, a gay a capella group, singing John Arterton's arrangement of the song "Something Inside So Strong." It seemed appropriate to allude to our "theme song" in the title of this book.

low the flow of the conversation to suggest other questions and to determine the general drift.[5] My aim has never been to grind an ax or to be confrontational. I simply want to engage some writers whom I've read and admired in a dialogue about their work and the writing life. Nor have I been much interested in what might be called "literary gossip." That several of the interviews included in this collection are not the latest, up-to-the-minute briefings from the authors seems irrelevant to me. I hope that the things we talked about have a value beyond the immediate and the seasonal. My models in this process are the superb interviews that have been published for years in the *Paris Review.*

I had another model, too: the wonderful public radio program, *Piano Jazz,* hosted by Marian McPartland, herself an accomplished jazz pianist. On *Piano Jazz,* McPartland invites colleagues from the jazz world to talk with her, play their music, and occasionally join her in a duet. That's the spirit I was trying for: respectful dialogues between fellow artists.

Many of these interviews, especially the ones for *Bay Windows,* were conducted and published in conjunction with my review of an author's current book. This practice brings up an important ethical question: whether linking a review with an interview sets up a conflict of interest. What are the ethics of interviewing someone whose book you are also reviewing? After years of thinking about this issue, I've come down on the side of separation of duties: a book reviewer should not also interview the author at the same time or in the same journal, as tempting as that might be.

This is an eclectic anthology. Every reader will wonder why certain writers were included or left out. When I began interviewing gay writers, I had no idea that I was assembling a book. The choice of authors—except for the WOMR interviews—was determined more by circumstance, the exigencies of the assignment, and/or my availability to meet with the author. In the case of "The WOMR Twelve," Len Bowen and I tried to put

---

5. One question that I did try to ask every writer I interviewed concerned the advice he or she would give to aspiring young gay and lesbian writers. A little booklet of these answers alone would make an inspiring, bracing, and, I think, helpful catechism for young writers (gay and straight) who are just starting out.

together as fine and diverse a group of writers as we could.[6] There are, of course, many writers I'd still love to interview. I managed to catch some people at the beginning of their careers, some late in their careers, most somewhere in mid-career. Three of the men in this collection—John Preston, Allen Barnett, and Paul Monette—have since died from AIDS.

AIDS has had an enormous impact on gay writing today. Barnett, Bram, Cunningham, Monette, and Preston all speak directly to the issues that the epidemic dropped at the doorstep of gay writers, but just about every writer in this collection brings up the subject. "The AIDS epidemic right now is the most important thing happening in our lives," Christopher Bram told me during our 1993 interview. So too Michael Nava, during that same summer: "It's part of the world we live in. It does seem to me that any gay writer cannot avoid the issue of AIDS, because it's such an overwhelming fact in our world." And Andrew Holleran: "I still think the problem of gay writing today is this: (a) you can't write about AIDS; (b) you can't *not* write about AIDS. It comes down to that."

Among other things, AIDS has allowed gay men to rethink the notion of family. *In Memory of Angel Clare, Afterlife,* and *A Home at the End of the World,* three novels that are discussed in these interviews and that include AIDS as a theme, all explore how the disease shapes and affects new family constellations. As Michael Cunningham puts it, "I've seen people mop up the vomit and mop up the shit and hold one another as they died. These are the things they told us you need your family for and—guess what?—you don't. You can make a family of your own."

On the other hand, others have seen the rise in the "gay family novel" as a retreat from AIDS. David Leavitt address this criticism: "The anxiety seems to be that gay domesticity is merely a reaction to AIDS, that it's a kind of retreat, as if gay men are saying, 'Well, AIDS is so scary, let's all just go huddle in our safe, womblike houses.' I think it's naive to see it simply as a response to AIDS. One reviewer said that [the characters] Danny and Walter's domestic life would make more sense if

---

6. The WOMR interviews with lesbian writers included Carol Anshaw, Blanche McCrary Boyd, Nisa Donnelly, Lesléa Newman, and Sarah Schulman.

it were described as a response to AIDS. To think that their life together is simply a matter of that is just the most vulgar naïveté."

Nevertheless, gay writers have felt "extraordinary pressures," as Edmund White once put it, to address AIDS in their work. "Holocaust literature, exiles' literature, convicts' literature—these are the only possible parallels that spring to mind," White wrote.[7] "The holocaust analogy actually holds true here, I think," Andrew Holleran says. "It would be like writing short stories about a concentration camp while people were being put in the box cars. I mean, would you do that? What would be the point? Art obviously has a tremendous role in everything in life, and I just haven't found the fictive mode to be useful right now."[8]

Holleran spoke those words in 1993. Four years later, a much younger writer, Brian Keith Jackson could say, "We are now getting to a point where some gay writers feel they don't need to write about AIDS." On the other hand, Jackson's contemporaries, Scott Heim and Michael Lowenthal, have each written novels (*In Awe* and *The Same Embrace,* respectively) in which AIDS, while not a major focus, does figure, though offstage. Whether, in fact, we have reached the point where AIDS is no longer an unavoidable subject in gay fiction, it's clear that AIDS has prompted an enormously significant chapter in the history of modern gay fiction.

This collection might be read as an extended inquiry into the question of who and what constitute those elusive categories, "the gay writer" and "gay literature." Are we writers who just happen to be homosexual, or is our sexuality integral and necessary to our work? What is a "gay novel" anyway, and how, if at all, is it different from any other kind of novel? Why, indeed, even attempt to posit a category like the "gay novel"? After all, as Christopher Bram points out, nowadays we rarely categorize

---

7. White, "Out of the Closet," 35.

8. David Leavitt, too, speaks of the difficulty of a kind of de rigueur adoption of AIDS as a topic for gay writers: "On a personal level it makes me crazy when I hear people saying things like, 'Well, David Leavitt *should* be writing a novel about AIDS.' I find I can't stand it anymore. It's not an atmosphere in which I'm able to do anything. From an artistic standpoint, it's not inspiring; it's the opposite."

novels by women as "women's novels." "That sounds so silly and idiotic to us now," he says. Why, then, make a distinction for novels written by gay men?

And yet we do—readers, critics, scholars, publishers, and writers alike. From time to time, all of us who are engaged in this business have used such terms—*gay writer, gay book, gay literature.* While it would be hard to imagine anyone seriously referring to Alice Munro as a "woman writer" or her work as "women's stories," very few people, including the authors themselves, would have much difficulty referring to, say, Christopher Bram as a gay writer of gay books. Does the persistent use of such terms accord less respect or dignity to the work of these writers? Does it suggest less literary merit? Does it marginalize them? What indeed are we saying when we say "gay literature"?

"I can't define it, but I know it when I see it," says Michael Lowenthal. For some of us, these categories serve as a kind of ready shorthand, a quick way to communicate, for instance, who our main characters are or what our subject matter reflects. Others of us deploy these words more discriminately and methodically, as serious and useful literary-critical terms, similar to "black literature" or "Jewish literature" or "the literature of the immigrant experience." Still others, aware of the dwindling audience for literary fiction, have tried to capitalize on such categories as a strategic marketing device, hoping to create a profitable "niche market." It's quite possible that every writer in this anthology who has ever called himself a "gay writer" has, at one time or another, intended all three of these meanings.

Many of the writers in these interviews would probably agree with David Leavitt, who says, "I don't think any writer likes adjectives in front of the word 'writer.'" Leavitt goes on to say, "If it means a writer with a so-called gay sensibility, it seems to me that that's a pretty problematic thing to define. I wouldn't deny being a gay writer, but I'd rather just be a writer who is gay. One worries about being typecast. It's like the term 'minimalism,' which has gotten thrown around a lot. It's a term which people have used a lot without anyone ever bothering to refine what it means. 'Gay writer' means ten different things if you ask ten different people."

Michael Cunningham echoes this sentiment when he says, "I'm finding the whole notion of 'gay literature,' as something distinct from other kinds of literature, to be increasingly less interesting or useful." And Joseph Hansen, the oldest writer interviewed in this book, categorically states, "I don't believe there is such a thing as gay literature. And I simply won't have anything to do with that." Nevertheless, when I asked him what it had felt like to publish his first "gay stories" (a term he did not balk at), Hansen ardently declared, "I felt that I had found what I was put on earth to do."

What seems like confusion on Hansen's part may, in fact, tell us quite a bit about how gay writers—indeed, all literary writers—experience themselves and what they do. Books about how to write fiction constantly emphasize the importance of a writer's finding his or her own voice. Rarely, however, do they mention that the discovery of specific subject matter may also be crucial to the formation of a serious writer. "Write about what you know" seems to be the last word on how to choose material.

For the gay male writer, writing about what he knows presents particular problems, not the least of which is that much of what he knows is still conventionally regarded as shameful, even immoral, and certainly not worthy of important literary treatment. Thus, in giving serious artistic attention to the full range of his experience, the gay writer (for that matter, any writer) does more than simply identify the raw material for his work. He gives witness to that experience, disclosing the value of events, desires, and emotions that might hitherto have been dismissed, ignored, or forgotten.

Indeed, until fairly recently, gay men themselves seemed to have had little hope that their lives could provide the stuff of literary fiction. "I was writing for ten years," says Andrew Holleran, "desperate to be a writer, unable to find any material or theme that mattered. . . . It wasn't until I turned to my own life and what really mattered to me that I became a writer."

Whether because of shame, fear, apathy, or lack of encouragement—all manifestations of internal and external homophobia—gay writers (perhaps at this point we should still be calling them writers who were homosexual) shied away from "material that really mattered," or developed what David Bergman has called "the E. M. Forster syndrome: queer writers' block."[9] As Michael Denneny has pointed out, in the mid-to-late seventies, the first years that *Christopher Street* magazine was in operation, the editors were surprised that so few new stories ever reached their desks. "It turned out that there wasn't all this unpublished material lying around; there was all this *unwritten* material lying around. . . ." "What is at stake," Denneny continued, is "the right to declare the reality of your own experience rather than having it defined by others."[10]

What exactly is this "gay experience" that is now the stuff of so many short stories and novels?

"I am a gay man and that profoundly affects my experience," Michael Cunningham says in his interview with me. For Cunningham, as for many of the writers in this volume, sexuality—*homosexuality*—is the bedrock of their experience in the world. As Gary Glickman puts it, "My sexuality, like everyone's, is one of the prime motivators of my life, and that's what got me to write my very first story."[11]

Gay men experience their sexuality in a multiplicity of ways, but a sense of the differences inherent in their sexuality is probably at the heart of it. Edmund White speaks of the *blessure,* the "wound," which (here he is quoting Jean Genet on Alberto Giacometti) "every man keeps inside him, which he preserves and where he withdraws when he wants to leave the world for a passing but profound solitude." In the case of gay men, the *blessure* has often been their shame of their sexuality. According to White,

> when I was young, what got me to write was that I felt such shame about being gay, and yet such a burning desire to communicate it to everybody. It was a funny impulse, be-

---

9. David Bergman, "The Gay American Novel," *The Harvard Gay and Lesbian Review* 2, no. 2 (Spring 1995): 13.

10. Michael Denneny, "Further Down the Road," in *First Love/Last Love: New Fiction from Christopher Street* (New York: G. P. Putnam, 1985), 10-11.

11. My interview with Glickman, not included in this collection, was published in *Bay Windows*, 13 April 1989.

cause, on the one hand, you'd think if you were ashamed of something, you'd just want to shut up about it, but, on the other hand, at age fourteen I was already writing my first gay novel, *The Tower Window.* So I think I was always trying to express my anguish about—no, not "about" being gay—around being gay and try to make some sense of it. It seemed to me such a crazy thing. I think I was really rather a conventional child otherwise, but it was the one thing that wrested me away from the world I thought I should be inheriting. I think that was sort of the *blessure.*

Even younger writers, those from the generation after White and Holleran, suggest that embarrassment—and the need to wrestle with that sense of confusion and dislocation—is a primary impetus to gay writing. "I write," says Scott Heim, "about the things I've always been shocked by, or embarrassed by, things from my past or things that have happened to other people that obsess me and then become exaggerated or warped into my fiction. What I can't necessarily talk about, or admit to, show up somehow in my writing. So yes, I think writing is a way of exorcising demons, or confronting things that embarrass or disturb or rattle me."

Holleran observes that while "a part of me wants to believe that every gay generation is 'an improved generation' and is further along and is more evolved and is more at ease with their homosexuality, another part of me thinks that nothing changes, that it's just as difficult for a gay man of nineteen now as it was twenty years ago. I mean, I know it's not just as difficult in certain ways, but I still think that there's a fundamental schism there."

For most gay men, this fundamental sense of difference that they experience in their sexuality and their lives prompts an eventual "coming out"—first to themselves, then perhaps to family, friends, and the world at large. Coming out is the first gay, as opposed to homosexual, experience for gay men. It defines the difference between homosexual and gay, a public declaration that initiates a specifically *gay* consciousness and, often, a gay sensibility. Since the gay liberation movement, coming out has also been, as Dorothy Allison once claimed, "the essential homosexual [literary] theme, as persistent as the romantic love story and the coming-of-age novel, containing as it does elements of both."[12]

The coming-out novel (Edmund White's *A Boy's Own Story* is a quintessential post-Stonewall example) is well represented, if not quite conventionally so, in the work of writers interviewed for this collection. Among their novels, those that might be loosely termed coming-out novels (in the sense that at least one of the main characters comes to a more conscious awareness of his sexuality) include Christopher Bram's *Surprising Myself,* Michael Cunningham's *A Home at the End of the World,* Bernard Cooper's *A Year of Rhymes,* Randall Kenan's *A Visitation of Spirits,* Michael Lowenthal's *The Same Embrace,* David Plante's Francoeur novels and Lev Raphael's *Winter Eyes.* Note, however, that the prevalent stereotype about coming-out novels—that they dwell on, as Peter Cameron says, a "very angst-ridden and torturous journey"—hardly pertains to these works. More and more, coming out is seen as an incidental, rather than focal, theme in gay fiction.

Increasingly, gay writers, even first novelists, have abandoned the coming-out theme altogether, or have linked it with other material. So, too, gay writers are more and more allowing themselves to bring in other "minority-cultural" elements into their work. "The idea that a character can't, for example, be gay and Jewish," says David Leavitt, "is a terrible thing which has nothing to do with literature, and nothing to do with art, and nothing to do with anything a writer should ever think about while writing. It's simply to do with all these cultural noisemakers sitting there bla-bla-blaing and bitching and moaning."

Michael Lowenthal iterates this idea when he says, "After a necessary period of 'gay literature' being a very specific and limited thing, it's now branching out to encompass all sorts of new possibilities." So too does Christopher Bram, when asked if he feels any limitations in gay subject matter: "I find it so rich. There are many things that haven't been explored yet." Michael Nava echoes this conviction when he says, "For me, being gay is about politics and culture. It's not about my sexuality. I mean, I know what my sexuality is, and it's just not an issue for me. For

---

12. Dorothy Allison, quoted in Michael Denneny, "Oedipus Revised," *Christopher Street* 105 (June 1986), 40.

me, the more interesting part is how the world responds to me. And that's what I write about. I don't write about sexual desire per se."

The "deproblemitization" of the gay novel—including the increasing lack of interest by gay writers in the "problem" of coming out—marks a turning point in gay fiction. "Nowadays," wrote Richard Hall in a front-page essay in the *New York Times Book Review,* "a gay novel rarely explains, complains or apologizes. It assumes that ignorance about homosexuality is a thing of the past and that bigotry signifies either a poor education or a retrograde consciousness."[13]

It is also clear that gay writers no longer feel compelled to portray exclusively positive gay images or politically correct notions. "There are of course people who don't understand what fiction or a work of art is," says Alan Hollinghurst. "They don't understand the moral complexity of a novel. Certainly some people have reviewed this second book of mine [*The Folding Star*] as if what I ought to have written was some kind of safe-sex manual combined with an upbeat homily about how to go about a gay life style. Both of which are worthy things to do, but they're not things that I'm very interested in doing myself." Joseph Hansen agrees, saying, "I try to put all kinds of homosexuals into my books—good, bad, bland and forceful, and colorful and not colorful." In short, as Richard Hall once put it, gay writers are claiming for their characters "the privilege of being no unhappier than other people."[14]

This efflorescence of diversity—in subject matter, theme, style, and portrayal of characters—both grew out of and continues to revivify the gay literary movement. "The first time I read *Men on Men,*" Allen Barnett told me, "I was startled at the diversity of our voices and thought, You don't have to write like Edmund White; you don't have to write like Andrew Holleran. You could write the way you want to write and still be a gay writer. That was a very liberating experience."

A generation younger, Brian Keith Jackson reiterates this theme: "I celebrate everyone who came before, because ultimately they opened the door for me, whatever they were writing about, whether it was for me

---

13. Richard Hall, "Gay Fiction Comes Home," *New York Times Book Review,* 19 June 1988, 25.

14. Richard Hall, quoting Eric Bentley, Ibid.

or something I liked, just by their being out there. That made me able to publish. A lot of young writers have to realize that there's been a life before us. And people have gone through the same things that we're going through now."

And yet, other young gay writers, perhaps overwhelmed by the sheer number of gay novels and stories now available, no longer feel that it's essential to be familiar with the gay classics of the Violet Quill generation.

"For me and my peers," says Michael Lowenthal, "it just can't be assumed that we've read *Dancer from the Dance,* or *Faggots,* or *A Boy's Own Story,* or Vidal or Isherwood or whoever. That kind of 'core curriculum' carries less weight. In a way it saddens me, because the commonality is diminished. On the other hand, of course, it's a sign of great political and literary progress."

One factor that perhaps does provide commonality, linking so many of the writers in these interviews, is the prevalence of the city as the setting for so much gay fiction. While that city may not always be the New York "circuit" depicted so elegiacally in Andrew Holleran's *Dancer from the Dance,* the urban landscape—the place where, as Andrew Holleran says, "you could just leave everything behind and create yourself anew"—figures prominently. And yet, here, too, we are beginning to see—in the Kansas of Scott Heim, the Tims Creek of Randall Kenan—an increasing interest in how gay men live and behave outside the urban ghetto, in "the world at large."

Ten years ago, in 1988, Brad Gooch could express the concern that "when [gay] writers return to writing about the world at large, which is what Proust was doing, they will do it in the old way: trying to hide their politics or their sexuality in traditional kinds of straight stories." Has this, in fact, happened? And if so, does it matter? "I've become annoyed by the David Leavitt thing," Dennis Cooper says, "even though I understand the significance of it: that here's this gay writer who can be just as conventional and banal as a straight writer. It means being gay has reached a point of acceptance, but I hate his work. I reject it on every level."

Cooper's words typify one side of a dichotomy that marks much of the discourse about gay fiction today. On the one hand, we have writers, like Cooper, whose work emphasizes what Edmund White has called "gay singularity,"[15] and what Richard Hall once characterized as the "separatist" strain in gay literature—"angry, polemical, and highly critical of the middle-class values."[16] On the other side are those writers who focus on, to quote Hall again, "the ordinariness of gay people."[17] Many of these nonseparatist writers are searching for, as David Plante puts it, a "context" in which to locate their sexuality.

"You know," says Plante, "one of the things that influenced me so much—and this is going back a long, long way—my mother bought me a book called *The Family of Man*. . . . And it filled me with a sense of humanity and the sufferings and joys of humanity. And so I saw sex, birth, death—all of this—in terms of this romantic, Whitmanesque sense of humanity. . . . So all this sexuality had a greater meaning than mere indulgence. It had a context."

This dichotomy between gay singularity and "ordinariness" is elaborated upon in an important essay by Reed Woodhouse that appeared in the inaugural edition of the *Harvard Gay and Lesbian Review*.[18] Rather than two camps, Woodhouse identifies five varieties—he calls them "houses"—of modern gay fiction: ghetto literature, proto-ghetto literature, "homosexual" or assimilative literature, transgressive or "queer" literature, and closet literature.

Assimilative stories, exemplified in Woodhouse's essay by Stephen McCauley's *The Object of My Affection*,[19] "are deliberately integrative and frequently concern a gay character's coming to terms with his family, living with straight friends (often women), or finding a lover and settling down in a monogamous relationship." For the transgressive writers, "queer" means "estranged" or "marginal." These writers, among them Dennis Cooper, Robert Glück, Kevin Killian, and Sam Dal-

---

15. White, "Out of the Closet," 35.

16. Hall, "Gay Fiction Comes Home," 27.

17. Ibid., 26.

18. Reed Woodhouse, "Five Houses of Gay Fiction," *Harvard Gay and Lesbian Review* 1, no. 1 (Winter 1994): 1, 22-29.

19. Other assimilative novelists in Woodhouse's taxonomy include David Leavitt, Michael Cunningham, Robert Ferro, Christopher Bram, and Armistead Maupin.

lessandro, present gay characters as "heroes of the sexual margin," even while their gayness "is not as central as their alienation."

The third "house," closet literature—more a pre-Stonewall phenomenon, and in Woodhouse's essay exemplified by James Baldwin's *Giovanni's Room*—is about shame and danger. "The closet novel focuses on that shame as its main topic and emotional effect." In the proto-ghetto novel, the protagonist, here typified by George in Christopher Isherwood's *A Single Man,* is "quite free of self-pity or self-doubt," though his isolation from other gay men or anything resembling a gay community keeps such novels from earning the distinction of being "full-blown" ghetto literature.

For Woodhouse, then, ghetto novels—"by, for, and about gay men"—represent "a gay world at its furthest point of self-definition, and are an expression of homosexuality at its most concentrated: that is, as nearly as possible without normative reference to the straight world." Andrew Holleran's *Dancer from the Dance,* a work Woodhouse calls "the best of all modern gay novels," is the quintessential ghetto novel, and ghetto fiction is, in Woodhouse's opinion, "the largest and most livable of the existing 'houses' of gay fiction."[20]

I've taken pains to outline Woodhouse's taxonomy because it moves our understanding of gay literature away from the dichotomous paradigm and toward a more elaborate and nuanced model.[21] Nevertheless, the ordinary-versus-singular debate persists, not only among read-

---

20. Four years after he published "Five Houses of Gay Fiction," Woodhouse published a book, *Unlimited Embrace: A Canon of Gay Fiction, 1945-1995* (Amherst: University of Massachusetts Press, 1998), that extended and enlarged the ideas of that original essay. In the book's introduction, "Five Houses of Gay Fiction, Revisited," Woodhouse repudiates the assimilation-versus-identity debate of the earlier essay. He writes, "I differentiated 'houses' based primarily on the kind of story they told: that is, was the gay character in the closet or out of it? . . . This was a stupid mistake because it seemed to imply that only certain kinds of stories could be told—a dogma which, *mutatis mutandis,* a homophobe like Jesse Helms would be happy to believe too. I repudiate it now" (7).

21. In his introductory essay, "Mapping the Territory: Gay Men's Writing," in Robert Giard's *Particular Voices: Portraits of Gay and Lesbian Writers* (Cambridge Mass.: MIT Press, 1997), Christopher Bram has suggested a different classification, one based more on literary style than attitude toward sexuality.

ers and critics, but, perhaps more significantly, in the conversations gay writers have with themselves. As Andrew Holleran puts it, "It's difficult when you're a writer to ask yourself, Do I see things this way because of homosexuality, or do I see things this way because I'm melancholy and pessimistic to begin with?"

Holleran remains uncertain about the answer to this question, though he adds, "It seems to me still that the fate of being homosexual or of living a homosexual life entails certain hard facts that cannot be glossed over." Among these "hard facts," Holleran identifies the "issue of infertility in gay life," which helps perhaps to explain why so much gay literature today does indeed focus on the formation of alternative families.

Another of the "hard facts" of gay experience is sex: finding it, losing it, incorporating it into one's larger life. Gay writers—even the most "ordinary" among them—have often chosen to present the rich and varied landscape of gay sexual behavior with a candor that has prompted unsympathetic critics to see their work as trivial, meretricious or outright pornographic. The issue of how many, as Edmund White puts it, "cocks and balls and all that stuff" to include is one many gay writers constantly wrestle with. "There's just no way the ordinary reader is going to read that [stuff]," White continues. "So there's kind of a confused impulse: on the one hand, the desire to be inscribed into general history, and then a kind of style that addresses so exclusively a gay reader and only a gay reader, that there's kind of a tension at the heart of this."

And that, as Christopher Bram puts it, "gets us to the dirty word: 'crossover' novel." Most gay writers, like Bram, would probably assert that they are "not out conscientiously to cover two markets—the family novel market and the gay market—with one novel." And yet, is the increasing mainstreaming of gay literature—and the concurrent pushing of more explicitly sexual writing into the niche market of "gay erotica"—creating a situation in which serious gay writers must make a choice between self-censorship and the full exploration of, as Michael Denneny once put it, "the erotic truth of their being"?[22]

"I think," says Lev Raphael, "Jews and gays share an incredible

22. Denneny, "Oedipus Revised," 42.

hypersensitivity to how we are perceived by the dominant community, and I know my gay friends see this and we talk about it. In fact, we share a lot about physical stereotypes—how we look, our sexuality. There are a lot of things that we are criticized about and I think that what it comes down to is that the minority community doesn't want the majority community to have an avenue into criticism. We have to be perfect, and perfect means straight and good and quiet."

Here we've circled back to the dichotomous model. Its persistence suggests that it is crucial to the way that *writers* conceive of and evaluate their work. The problem of how to write a novel that, as White puts it, will "insert gay experience into history" and, at the same time, as Woodhouse says, will not represent gay people as "virtually indistinguishable from straight ones" not only remains but seems to be one that gay writers are now tackling with enthusiasm and success. Indeed, White's latest novel, *The Farewell Symphony,* is one whose style (full of "cocks and balls and all that stuff") seems specifically addressed to a gay readership and yet has managed to capture plenty of more-than-respectful mainstream attention.

"I try never to 'censor' myself when I'm writing," says Michael Lowenthal, "but I did think to myself pretty explicitly when I was writing the novel that I wanted it to be something my mother could comfortably read. She's a huge supporter of mine, but has read less than half of my published work, by mutual agreement, because I've written some weird sexual stuff. . . . My hope is that the mood of the story, and the scope, will allow people like my mother to accept the sex without freaking out."

Mood and scope: these seem like particularly helpful and worthwhile criteria by which to judge *any* piece of fiction. They are aesthetic measures that open up the conversation, away from preoccupations about hierarchies of content—is a novel about a gay man who participates in the ghetto better or more authentic than a novel about a gay man who lives in the suburbs?—and toward more artistic considerations. These days there are certainly plenty of serious and successful gay writers who are beautifully negotiating the path that runs between faithfulness to the specific particularities of their characters' sexual lives and a sense of artistic responsibility about depicting those characters in the full complexity of their social and psychological being.

"Eventually," says Christopher Bram, "as we write honestly about our experience—in all its many shades and variations, the parts of our experience that are specifically gay and the parts of our experience that anyone else could connect with, too—as long as we do that, the audience is going to come to us.

Andrew Holleran's extraordinary novel, *The Beauty of Men,* is a case in point. Here the main character is an ex-ghetto dweller, a retired circuit queen, who, between visits to his mother in the nursing home, spends his days rather hopelessly and halfheartedly cruising for sex. A kind of gay *Waiting for Godot,* it is darker, sadder, and less hopeful than either of Holleran's two previous novels. Many readers, presumably those who were expecting another ghetto novel like *Dancer from the Dance,* were disappointed, indeed upset, by *The Beauty of Men.* However, Holleran's third novel may well prove to be another milestone in gay literature, because, as a work of art, it is so unrelentingly devoted to capturing the full experience, warts and all, of one particular gay man, an *older* gay man at that.[23]

Brad Gooch, himself the author of two highly charged (and mainstream-published) gay novels, foresaw this opportunity when he said during his interview with me, "We're in a period where what's possible is more of a kind of synthesis of what Tennessee Williams did as a gay writer and what people who were just writing about men-on-men situations did. Now we have the opportunity to bring all that together, which for a writer is very exciting."

Bringing it all together—our exuberance and our despair, the ghetto and the wider world, the campy and the banal, our singularity and our "ordinariness"—has always been, I think, at the heart of any serious writer's vision. Gay literature, no more nor less so than "straight" literature, must begin in the concrete particularities of the lives it portrays. The best gay writers today, as the best writers have always done, do not shy away from presenting *any* of these particularities. Just as a previous

---

23. In some respects, *The Beauty of Men* resembles Christopher Isherwood's great novel, *A Single Man,* which, in Woodhouse's schema is called a "proto-ghetto" novel. Although—as I hope this introductory essay makes clear—I'm not in favor of such a taxonomy, it might be useful to think of *The Beauty of Men* as an example of yet a sixth house, the postghetto novel.

generation of gay authors broke new ground by writing truthfully and beautifully about their reality—coming out, the ghetto, pre-AIDS sex, AIDS—a new generation of gay writers is now taking up the same task. That task, the faithful and artistic representation of human lives—in all their messy, frail, wonderful, and inconsistent uniqueness—is what great writing has always been about.

"We have to start . . . moving to that point where acceptance is based on what it is that you're doing and the quality of that work as op-posed to our sexuality," says Brian Keith Jackson. It's interesting to note that of all the writers in this collection, it's the writers who straddle two "minority camps"—writers like Jackson, Lowenthal, and Randall Ke-nan—who take particular pains to underscore the precariousness of try-ing to speak for the "community," *any* community, at large.

"Sometimes," says Kenan, "I don't even know what community I'm a part of. Not everyone's going to like you in either community. To some black people I may be too black or not black enough or bour-geois. To some gay communities I might not be doing this or not be do-ing that. I can only do what I can do and get up and deal with that in the morning."

Kenan goes on to say, "At the end of the day, I don't really say, Ah, I am a black, gay, Southern postmodern! It can't be done. I don't really think of myself in any category but as a human person who happens to have access to all these wonderful, sometimes unfortunate, but often liberating experiences."

In a letter to the *New York Times* Allen Ellenzweig, the author of *The Homoerotic Photograph,* wrote of the "unconscious bias against art with gay or lesbian themes . . . even among those with no animus toward gay men and lesbians."[24] In this case, Ellenzweig was taking exception to a remark by Ruth Caleb that the BBC film based on David Leavitt's *The Lost Language of Cranes* "is bigger, wider, more profound than just a gay film."

"If the story is good," Ellenzweig wrote, "there is no such thing as 'just a gay film,' since to be gay or lesbian certainly involves one in a rich

---

24. Allen Ellenzweig, "Gay Themes, Universal Themes," *New York Times*, 5 July 1992, sec. 2, p. 4.

web of social, political and psychological forces as complex as those in the stories of 'just' straight people."

Each of the twenty-one authors represented in this collection writes out of his own keenly particular understanding that rich web. That is why I read their work, and why I wanted to talk to them.

Philip Gambone

Boston
October 1998

Early
Bay Windows
Interviews
(1987–1990)

Joseph Hansen, Los Angeles, California, 1994

Brad Gooch, New York, New York, 1986

David Leavitt, East Hampton, New York, 1987

Dennis Cooper, New York, New York, 1986

Paul Monette, Los Angeles, California, 1988

Joseph Hansen

With the publication of *Fadeout* in 1970, Joseph Hansen launched his highly successful series of mystery novels featuring Dave Brandstetter, a gay insurance investigator. In addition to inspiring many other gay mystery writers, Michael Nava among them, Hansen's Brandstetter books are significant for being among the first gay novels to treat the protagonist's homosexuality matter-of-factly rather than as evidence of his victimization. The novels are also important in their portrayal of a gay character who is not only middle-aged but grows older as the series progresses until, in the twelfth and final volume, he collapses of a heart attack. Hansen peoples his novels with a wide variety of gay men and women, including some who commit crimes. His understated message of racial and sexual tolerance is a hallmark of Hansen's work. Reviewed favorably in both gay and nongay journals, the Dave Brandstetter novels have captured a wide mainstream readership and have been translated into several languages.

Hansen was born in Aberdeen, South Dakota, in 1923. When he was thirteen, he and his family moved to southern California, where he attended high school. Attracted to good literature at an early age, he began to write, eventually publishing stories, poetry, and nonfiction, both under his own name and, if there was any gay content to the work, under a pen name. Around 1962, Hansen took up the cause of gay liberation. Among his activities, he made frequent contributions to *ONE*, a journal that grew out of the Mattachine Society. His first novel, *Lost on Twilight Road*, was published under the pseudonym James Colton in 1964.

To date, Hansen has published over twenty-five novels. He is the recipient of numerous awards, among them a Life Achievement Award from the Private Eye Writers of America, two Lambda Literary Awards, and grants from the National Endowment for the Arts and the British Arts Council, and his teaching activities include a long stint at the University of California at Los Angeles Extension School.

In the summer of 1987, I attended the Wesleyan Writers Conference, where I enrolled in Hansen's fiction writing class; it was there that the following interview took place. (Another conference participant, Bill Mann, who would go on to become the editor of *Metroline,* Hartford, Connecticut's gay and lesbian paper, and the author of the novel *The Men From the Boys,* was also present.) Back home, as I began to transcribe the tape recording, I discovered that, because of a battery failure, some questions and answers had been lost. I wrote to Joe asking if he'd mind jotting down a few new responses. "By the way," I ended, "has anyone else ever interviewed you?"

Joe's delightfully caustic reply came five days later: "That's a stunning question," he wrote. "What am I, a potted plant? I have been interviewed more times than I can count over the past seventeen years."

The interview first appeared in *Bay Windows,* 30 June 1988.

What were you writing and publishing before the Dave Brandstetter books?

In 1961, a lover who liked my stories introduced me to Don Slater, who published a little slip of a gay magazine called *ONE.* All I'd published until that time were poems. I ended up writing story after story for Don and eventually helping to edit the magazine, whose title we changed in 1965 to *Tangents.* I've described the offices of *ONE* magazine in one of the Dave Brandstetter books. It was in a very, very old building full of lofts and ladies running sewing machines.

After I'd done enough of these stories, I figured I could use the skills I'd picked up in a novel, and I wrote a simple, short, straightforward book called *Valley Boy,* whose title the publisher unhappily changed to *Lost on Twilight Road.* It had the world's worst cover illustration. I protested loudly to the dear man, because, after all, he was a dear man and very kind and very brave to publish this book, as candid as it was. And I don't mean it was a sexy book—I just mean that it was honest—and he changed the cover then, to an abstract painting, which suited me fine.

The next novel I called *A Name for Loneliness,* and it got changed to *Strange Marriage.* That's what happened to titles in those days.

And so it went, through six more novels, some of them pretty gamy, because, let's face it, the publishers wanted sex, sex, and more sex, which gets in the way of a book being taken seriously, even when the writer wants it taken that way. All the same, the practice of the craft of writing sharpens a writer's abilities, if he has any, and eventually I did a couple of books that seemed to me better than okay. One of these was published in 1968 as *Known Homosexual,* and it was my first try at writing a mystery. It's in the book shops these days under the title *Pretty Boy Dead.* I still like it.

All of these books were written under the pen name James Colton. Why?

For their protection against the forces of law and order and decency and prudery, Don Slater insisted that all writers for his magazine use false names. I didn't want this for myself, but I did want my stories published, so I went along with it. I chose the name of a lady art teacher I remembered from junior high school, a Miss Colton, and tacked James on the front.

What did it feel like to publish those first gay stories, to call them forth?

I felt that I had found what I was put on earth to do. That sounds metaphysical and I'm not metaphysical. But nonetheless, that's exactly what I felt, and what I still feel: this was what my talent was designed for. I mean, if I was going to be a writer, this was going to be my subject. I had found my subject. I felt immensely relieved. I no longer had to blunder around in the dark. I knew what I had to write about, and I knew how to write about it. There was plenty that I understood, and knew and had learned for myself, and learned from listening to my friends that I could put on paper. I could tell people what it was like, people who didn't know. I always wanted that.

I nearly wrecked *ONE* magazine by insisting that it was no good doing a magazine for homosexuals. What we needed was a magazine *by* homosexuals for others. That didn't go down very well. With the politics of today it wouldn't go down very well. It's still the same climate. It changed a little bit in the sixties, and then it changed right back again. That's what they mean by revolution! The wheel goes all the way around and then gets *stuck.*

So creating Dave Brandstetter, a gay detective, was a continuation of what you were already doing?

I wanted to write a true detective story with a true detective in it, and it just naturally followed that my detective was going to be a homosexual. And that's how Dave Brandstetter came into being.

There are a lot of wry jokes in it: the last companies in the world to hire a detective who is a homosexual would be insurance companies, because they really don't like homosexuals. They think they're very bad risks. They don't want them as clients, and they don't want them as employees. Or, at least that's my opinion.

So what was the difference? Why did the big publishers take on the Dave Brandstetter books while they had not published your previous books?

The time was obviously right. If it had not been that—in the 1960s, there were so many other writers, of various talents and intents, writing these paperback original gay books—then this particular turnabout in the editorial offices of places like Harper and Row would never have happened. The first phase had to happen, and this was the second phase.

Do you make a distinction between your later gay novels, like A Smile in His Lifetime, Job's Year, *and your Brandstetter—what some people call "genre"—books? Is there a difference in your mind between the kinds of books they are?*

Yes, sure. Because a number of bows have to be made to certain structural conventions in a mystery book that confine what you can do. It's amusing to be able to obey all those necessary restrictions. On the other hand, they are restrictions, and when you write a novel apart from those restrictions it's liberating to your abilities, and it's an entirely new kind of challenge. It's always a thrill to be suddenly placed down with a feeling of total freedom. It's frightening, too, because when all these rules no longer get in your way, then you do have to be careful, and you feel a little at risk. But it's welcome in its way. I hope to be able to do books apart from the mysteries but I don't know whether I'll be able to.

Why?

Well, as somebody said at this conference, to writers, money is time. If I can get the money to buy the necessary time to write another book the length of *A Smile in His Lifetime* or *Job's Year,* I will write it. The question is, will I have enough money to sustain me for the eighteen months it takes me to write a book of that length and that complexity, and with the freedom of movement that it entails? This allows for exploring, which takes time, and writing and discarding.[1]

---

1. Since this interview, Hansen has published some novels not in the Dave Brandstetter series, among them *Living Upstairs* (1993) and *Jack of Hearts* (1995).

You've said several times at this conference that one of the things you're particularly proud of in the Dave Brandstetter series is the way you treat the homosexuality in such a flat-footed, understated, casual manner. Did that in any way free you up for the later novels?

I've always done that, even in the James Colton novels. They weren't sensationalistic. Except when the publishers began to demand that I put in sex scenes. There's no way to keep a sex scene from being sensational; I wish that I had been able to discover one. God knows, I tried! In the end, what happens is those scenes jars everything else in the book out of shape.

There is no way to write a serious book with these things in there. They're good for one thing, and you know what that is: it's called one-handed reading. I didn't want to write that kind of book. I wanted to write serious books about serious matters. When I came to be able to write my big books, I was able to write them without the sensationalistic stuff, and therefore they hold together. They aren't constantly shattered by these shocking, absorbing moments. I just don't like sticking sex scenes into books.

Does Dave's gayness give him a special angle on things?

Oh, of course it does! People criticize me from time to time because they feel there are too many homosexuals in those books, too many homosexual problems, too many homosexual situations. But I just say, Well, look at all the mystery novels that are written that don't have those in. It seems to me only fair that at least eight or nine little books ought to be permitted on the racks.

What particularly does Dave see differently or understand differently?

Well, of course he understands homosexuals differently, but I also think he understands any group or individual that stands outside the mainstream of society as we still rather erroneously think of it. Dave is always evenhanded in his treatment of people, whether they are foreigners, whether they are of some special racial or national group. It would never cross his mind to slur anybody.

I was particularly moved by the portrait of the boy with cerebral palsy in Fadeout. *The empathy Dave showed him was striking.*

Dave's wise: he sees that those things that can impede you in the world—whether it's cerebral palsy or homosexuality—are pretty much the same.

It's a lousy break. The point is, you have to come to terms with it and say, "It's *not* a lousy break."

What gay fiction do you read?

Almost none.

Why is that?

Most of it isn't very good. When something comes my way that I'm curious about or interested in, I read it. Generally speaking, because a book is gay does not make me read it. Nor do I read mysteries as a rule.

In class, we've talked about the mistakes that beginning writers make. What are they?

I think the tendency is to make the mistake of feeling that somehow the writer is very special and different from the whole world. Most of us know and sympathize with that feeling in young people: that they think they're the only ones. And therefore there tends to develop rather a shrillness, and a little hysteria, even after they discover, Gosh, I'm not the only one; there are two of us. I think there's a tendency toward weepiness.

And there's another tendency that I think is equally killing [for the young gay writer], which is to take everything as some kind of bitchy joke and camp it up. And that's not very attractive either. It's hard for people to come to terms with their homosexuality and it's hard for people who want to write about it, too. They cannot treat it matter-of-factly and straightforwardly. They really do feel as if they've got to apologize.

Is the term "gay fiction" a legitimate term?

Not as far as I'm concerned. Once, due to a misapprehension on my part, I ended up with a story in a gay anthology. I won't do that again. I don't believe in gay anthologies; I don't believe there is such a thing as gay literature. And I simply won't have anything to do with that.

We're all on this planet together. We'd better try to understand each other and tolerate each other and get along with the business of being human beings, because there's plenty of stuff that all of us need to improve, and one of them is not our sex lives. There are a lot of other things ahead of that.

There is too much that contributes to a feeling of "us" and

"them"—we're here and they're there, and we're different from them, and they're different from us. One of the things that made me most angry about that anthology that I contributed to was that when it came out the title was *Different*! Different is what we don't need. All-the-same is what we need.

This week you alluded to an autobiography.

It's already written, but I think it will remain sealed until the year 2023. It is next to impossible to write an honest life story if one is homosexual and not put other folk in awkward positions. I wouldn't risk that. It's not such a hell of a good book anyway. My life has been humdrum.

The other day in class, you said that it was sometimes difficult for an established, successful writer to get his editors to be honest with him about the quality of the stuff he's producing. Has this been your experience?

I think I'm doing better work than ever before, but nobody is going to tell me if I'm not.

You also mentioned in class that critics and the public have felt that Skinflick *is so far the best of the Brandstetter books. Do you have any ideas why?*

It's hard for me to say. The book is lively. It's the longest of the Brandstetter books. It's filled with life and animation and humor. And there's an outrageous transvestite. The one thing that struck me so forcefully when the book came out was the amount of fan mail it drew. And the fan mail was all for the transvestite character. Everybody loved Randy Van. I got so many letters saying, "Oh, what a wonderful thing you have done." I'm glad people liked that. On the other hand, a transvestite is a classical stereotype of homosexuals. I was not sorry I put him in, because I try to put all kinds of homosexuals into my books—good, bad, bland and forceful and colorful and not colorful. The transvestite is based on a real person I once met—though he/she was not a transvestite but a transsexual. I wanted to deal with that matter because, although it's marginal, it is a part of homosexual life.

I was just a little bit crestfallen when people became so happy with that character. I love Randy Van, too, and I particularly loved the way he sacrificed all for Dave Brandstetter by getting dressed up in a suit. He says, "'I feel ridiculous in these clothes!'"

Speaking of your readers, I was interested to learn that most of the readers of the Dave Brandstetter books are not gay.

That's very true. If I had to live on the proceeds from my gay readership only, I wouldn't be alive.

You have mentioned several times this week your "great affection for words." Do you want to comment on your early reading?

The first good adult writer I read was Carl Sandburg—his Lincoln biography, which I got hold of at age seven. Next came Jack London at age nine. And finally Mark Twain at age eleven, *Huckleberry Finn.* All through my teens, I read American novelists and short story writers: Sherwood Anderson, James T. Farrell, John Dos Passos, Sinclair Lewis, the top-flight names of their day. By age twenty, I'd discovered Floyd Dell; Frank Norris; Theodore Dreiser; Robert Herrick, the Chicago realist; Thomas Wolfe; and Hemingway, and Faulkner, of course.

Then I did a lot of Europeans, Brits, Russians: André Gide, Georges Bernanos, Jean Cocteau, Romain Rolland, the Dickens-Thackery-Eliot-Trollope canon of nineteenth-century greats, and Dostoyevsky, and Turgenev, and Chekhov. It's time to stop this list. But I didn't stop exploring novelists. I'm still at it, and I have no plans to quit.

Although you moved to California when you were still a boy, there are many indications—in your straightforward manner, your values, even the inflections in your voice—that the Midwest, where you were born, has been a major influence in your life. Do you agree?

Is it the Midwest, or simply that I had the father and mother I had? After all, their heritage was respectively Norwegian and German, solid Protestant North European. In my manner and values and in the plain way I handle language, I like to think there's something genetic. I have read some of the Scandinavian sagas. And I feel a strong kinship with those. In the approach to life, and in my approach to novel writing.

You've mentioned your father several times, and said that each burly, bald-headed man in your stories is, in some way, your father. What was he like? What influence has he had on you, especially as a writer?

My father wasn't really burly, though he loved to play football as a young man, and enjoyed all other sports. He was slight and short. But bald he was. He had a wonderful sense of humor, and though he'd only completed a fifth-grade education, he loved words and delighted when he heard new terms or new names. He liked to make up comical rhymes, too. He was the best man I ever knew. I miss him during my days; I dream about him at night. Yes, I expect I do put him into my books—notably as George Stubbs in the Hack Bohannon stories.

In class, you talked about themes in your novels, and told us that even the mystery series is organized around some big novelistic themes. You specifically pointed to secrecy and dishonesty as the major thematic concerns in the Dave Brandstetter books. Anything to add?

Nothing, except that this is a wonderful example of how the act of teaching educates the teacher. Until the particular class you mention, I'd never thought to examine the underlying theme of the Brandstetter novels. I was well aware of the themes of what I call, for want of a better term, my "big" novels, but the class discussion caused me to wonder about the mysteries and to learn something I hadn't known on a conscious level before.

As a writer, what do you see as your legacy?

I'll put it this way: A good friend from the Midwest, John R. Milton, who edits the *South Dakota Review,* once wrote me in some impatience that it was time for me to abandon my mysteries and my homosexuals and get down to the business of writing something worthy of my talent—or words to that effect. My response was that not all of us writers are up to Mahler's Third Symphony, but that I thought perhaps in the Dave Brandstetter books I had given the world a few Haydn string quartets. Would God I had done anything nearly that wonderful. I try.[2]

---

2. At the end of 1989, *Bay Windows* asked me to write a piece that surveyed gay male literature of the 1980s. In that essay, I included the Dave Brandstetter books, but failed to mention Joe's "big," nongenre books. A few weeks later, he wrote to me, "Thanks for including your *Bay Windows* article. I'll assume we're good enough friends so that I can bitch at you for leaving *A Smile in His Lifetime* (1981) and *Job's Year* (1983) off your list of the best gay novels of the past decade. These were strong books. They're still in print and still selling and people are still writing gratefully to me about them. They surely deserve more than silence from you, however unfashionable it may be among gays to praise Joseph Hansen these days."

Brad Gooch

Brad Gooch's debut novel, *Scary Kisses,* was all the rage when it came out in 1988. Set in the "modern, no-mind time" of the late seventies, it focuses on Todd Eamon, an international fashion model, and his zonked-out, "yucked-up" girlfriend Lucy. A postmodern bildungsroman, Gooch's novel portrays the deadening effect of drugs, narcissism, sex, and marketing on Todd and his friends. The author, himself a former model, was touted by his publisher and the media as an insider in the fast-track world of fashion modeling.

Gooch resented this, as well he should have, since he'd already established himself as a serious and gifted writer, a poet who had won the Woodberry Prize (1972) and the Academy of American Poets Prize (1977). With a Ph.D. from Columbia University; publishing credits in *Vanity Fair, GQ,* and the *Nation*; and a short story collection, *Jailbait and Other Stories,* that was hailed by Donald Barthelme for its "roughness and directness unequaled in contemporary fiction," Gooch was hardly just a "pretty" flash in the pan.

In my review for *Bay Windows,* which accompanied the interview, I wrote: "This is a novel that takes risks, the biggest one being its dangerous affinity with pornography. But what rescues *Scary Kisses* from being either B-novel pulp or pornography is the absence of Puritanism with regard to sex. . . . It's all about the jumble of signals—raunchy, erotic, manipulative, destructive, tender—that we give each other in our often muddled quest for intimacy."

Our interview took place on October 14, 1988, in Gooch's room at Boston's Parker House, following his appearance on a local morning television show called *Good Day!* This abridged transcript of the conversation (the full-length version has been lost) appeared a few weeks later in *Bay Windows,* in the issue for 3 November 1988.

Toward the end of Scary Kisses, *after he's turned away from the whole fast-track modeling scene, you write, "Todd feels good to have been there. It was a pastel moment in history." What did you mean by that?*

I think of *Scary Kisses* as a historical novel, really. It's about this time in the late seventies: the rise of male modeling, sexual liberation.[1] Bruce Weber was bringing out all those photographs. At this time it was very exciting. Now is a much darker time, so that period has always taken on in my mind a mythical dimension.

I was interested to learn that you're writing a biography of poet Frank O'Hara, because the style of your novel is, in some ways, like O'Hara's "I do this, I do that" poems.[2]

It's hard to swallow the conventional novel technique of getting into a character's head to show you what he's thinking. I think of *Scary Kisses* as a conceptual movie. That sets up a lot of limitations; it presented a challenge.

Many gay writers I've talked to have brought up Proust. Is Proust the author most gay writers have to come to terms with?

I don't feel that I have to pay attention to Proust, but I did. I love Proust. I'm attracted to his philosophical narrator, who is watching life and at the same time thinking about it. The narrator in *Scary Kisses* also goes off on these weird thinking tangents.

At the beginning of the novel, Lucy tells Todd that the Amish refuse to have their photo taken because they're afraid their souls will be stolen away. Is that comment emblematic of the whole novel?

Well, modeling in the novel works as a kind of metaphor. You've got these three-dimensional people in real life striving for two-dimensionality. Their goal is to turn into a picture, and the more they get into it, the more they lose themselves.

I kept thinking of Todd and his situation in terms of those classic eighteenth- and nineteenth-century novels about the evil effects of the city: Tom Jones, Candide, Sister Carrie, all those Henry James novels about the innocent American abroad. Was any of that an influence on your novel?

---

1. Gooch published his second "historical" novel, *The Golden Age of Promiscuity*, in 1996.

2. The book was subsequently published as *City Poet: The Life and Times of Frank O'Hara* (Knopf, 1993).

Oh, yeah. I was aware of that as a premise for a novel. I was thinking of *The Red and the Black,* and *Great Expectations,* when Pip goes to London. In fact, the reason I picked those chapter titles was as a reference to *Candide.*

On the Good Day! *show this morning, the caption at the bottom of the screen read Brad Gooch: Model Turned Author. That amused me because you've been an author for a long time.*

Yes, the usual mainstream take on me is that here's a bimbo who wrote a book.

Who are your favorite authors?

I guess Dennis Cooper and Robert Glück.

Why?

Dennis, first of all, because he's such a master of the language. His prose came out of his poetry—the same way it did for me. I have a lot of interest and respect for the surface of his work. And the surface of his work is quite pitch-perfect. Also because he's willing to deal with darker subjects—hustlers, violence—and because there's a tenderness mixed in there. Robert Glück because he's bravely experimental: he plays around with narrative a lot, shifts in and out of real life and made-up life.

On the subject matter level—you see, I'm more interested in the way people actually write than in the subject matter—Bret Easton Ellis and Michael Chabon are both interesting because of what they're writing about: bisexual themes, for instance.

Your writing has not always met with favor within the gay community.

I first ran into that when I published *Jailbait and Other Stories,* and the Oscar Wilde bookstore refused to carry it because it had straight sex in it. That's when I realized I was up against something. The gay writers who preceded me, who coincided with gay liberation—Edmund White, Robert Ferro, Andrew Holleran—were writing about what it was like to be gay in the gay community. They liberated the whole area of stories that people had. But now a lot of people—both in the gay community and the straight community—are writing about different kinds of subjects, so that you get, for instance, people like Ellis and Chabon, who are—quote, unquote—"straight," but then are writing novels that have male prostitutes in them, straight men in love with gay men, all these crossings of lines. This seems to make some people angry in the gay community.

When I was in San Francisco, there was this whole thing about Michael Chabon, about how it was discovered that he was married, and therefore it was assumed that the publishers were trying to pass him off as a gay writer—which is such a turnaround!

Maybe there's some fear that when [gay] writers return to writing about the world at large, which is what Proust was doing, they will do it in the old way: trying to hide their politics or their sexuality in traditional kinds of straight stories. But that's not it at all. We're just free now to write about a larger world. It all has to do with defining what gay literature is and isn't.

And I think that's still really up for grabs. It would be a shame if we thought that issue had already been settled.

Right, and it seems that's the problem: people feeling that it has been settled. We're in a period where what's possible is more of a kind of synthesis of what Tennessee Williams did as a gay writer and what people who were just writing about men-on-men situations did. Now we have the opportunity to bring all that together, which for a writer is very exciting. It's just odd—and unfortunate, I think—that this kind of radical-as-conservative should be moving right now.

Lucy twice goes into a church: she goes to Sacre Coeur in Paris and then to St. Patrick's in New York. She also does therapy with a nun. Is there any kind of religious undercurrent in the novel?

Yes, there is overt religious imagery in the novel. I've always been interested in Catholicism and religion. I go to church every week.

Is there any reason why the religious imagery is relegated to Lucy in particular?

No, they're just different people. For Todd, it's his art and his scrapbooks where he finds his center of value and Lucy tries on a different kind of spirituality: psychotherapy, feminism, Catholicism. Given her personality, it just seems that she goes for those kinds of solutions. The book presents a kind of quest, just like medieval books—the Grail quest, for instance—and here it's for a kind of intimacy, and therefore seems spiritual to me.

Another very interesting side to Lucy is how very sexually aggressive she is.

Well, the reason it seems that way is that traditional novels, especially in the nineteenth century, were written by men who had an image of women that involved them not acting on desire. If Lucy seems "aggressive," she's just being human, I think

When Todd is in Europe, Lucy picks up a guy in a movie theater on Second Avenue. That kind of disloyalty seems more shocking to people than anything men can do. There's still some sense, I think, that women can't be as freewheeling, or even as weak, or even as disloyal, as men.

David Leavitt

Having published openly gay stories in the *New Yorker* while he was still an undergraduate at Yale and, soon afterwards, a critically acclaimed debut story collection, *Family Dancing* (which became a finalist for both the National Book Critics' Circle Award and the PEN/Faulkner Prize), David Leavitt emerged as the gay wunderkind of the 1980s. He extended his reputation with the publication of his first novel, *The Lost Language of Cranes* (1986), which was later made into a television movie.

Appearing three years later, Leavitt's second novel, *Equal Affections*, whose publication prompted this interview, once again set into play themes the author had explored in his previous work. The book takes a hard, unsentimental look at middle-class families and their gay children, focusing on how each member tries to wriggle out of the others' embrace while at the same time, "banging against the doors you've closed," as Walter, the lover of the novel's gay protagonist son, puts it.

Leavitt has had his detractors, many of whom have focused on the restrained sex scenes and bourgeois, "guppie" element in his work.[1] Ironically, Leavitt's most recent books—*While England Sleeps* (1995), a novel; *Arkansas* (1997), a collection of three novellas; and *The Page Turner* (1998), another novel—have each come under attack for the opposite reason: too much sexual explicitness.[2]

Our interview took place at the Four Seasons Hotel in Boston in early 1989, shortly after the publication of *Equal Affections*. Leavitt had

---

1. See, for example, James Wolcott, "Guppie Fiction," *Vanity Fair* (March 1989, 38–46), or Michael Schwartz, "David Leavitt's Inner Child," *Harvard Gay and Lesbian Review* 2, no. 1 (Winter, 1995): 1, 40–44.

2. "The Term Paper Writer," one of the three novellas in *Arkansas*, was withdrawn from publication in *Esquire* because of its sexual content; and, in a famous battle, Leavitt was forced to rewrite some of the sexually explicit parts of *While England Sleeps* after Stephen Spender, from whose autobiography Leavitt drew material that he embellished for the novel, brought legal action.

come to Boston to give a reading at the Brattle Theater in Harvard Square, part of the author's series at WordsWorth Books.

I want to start by throwing back at you some words you once wrote about Alice Munro:

> *With their sudden leaps forwards and backwards in time, their de-pendence upon ancestral inheritance as a psychological and narrative force, [Munro's stories] are about as far as you can get from the kinds of stories most often associated with the current decade. Munro's sto-ries embrace history. Few seem to have less than forty years' span. They present a kind of temporal tapestry, weaving together the histories of several different generations and charting their progress.*[3]

That seems to me to be a fairly accurate description of what you're doing in Equal Affections.

In this book, more than in anything I've ever written, I've been emulating Alice Munro. She's my favorite writer, and there are aspects of her work that I try to learn from. It's become increasingly important to me to get history and time into my work, and not to be trapped in the present mo-ment. In this book I've been trying hard for that. It's domestic history, it's family history, but it's still history.

You're very attracted to multiple points of view.

It's so important to me. Particularly in a novel, I don't think that one point of view is enough. Since point of view is all there is, to do more than one can give you such a multiperspectival sense of life. I couldn't imagine writ-ing a novel in the first person. I can write a short story in the first person, but hesitantly.

Were you even tempted to write a novel in the first person?

No. I could never write a novel entirely in the first person. I'd get too bored with just one voice. Or, if not one voice, one point of view. What I love about writing in third person with a lot of points of view is that there's a kind of overarching voice that brings all the different perspectives together harmoniously.

---

3. David Leavitt, "Telling Truths: The Fiction of Alice Munro," *Boston Review,* February 1987, 22.

At the reading, you read passages that had the audience laughing, and yet it also seems that there's a sadness at the core of this novel—you interweave the humor and the sadness.

It's a sad novel and a funny one at the same time. I don't think it's a depressing book. There's a kind of overarching optimism that has to do with a sense of regeneration, a sense that life goes on. It was important to me to give Louise the last word in the book, but despite her death, there's a baby coming, and these people will go on. I think *The Lost Language of Cranes* was more depressing, partly because it was about a family that was made up entirely of adolescents; these people are grown-ups.

At the beginning of the novel, Danny, as a boy, has a fantasy in which a stranger says to him, "'All the things you've ever worried about, all the things that make you suffer—they're nothing.'" Another way of looking at this novel is to see all the characters as trying to get to a place where that fantasy becomes an accurate description of life.

That's certainly true of Danny. Do you think it's true of the other characters as well? I think it's more true of the men in the book than the women. The men are more interested in safety; the women tend to be more adventurous. All the wildness in the book belongs to the women. The men want safety, security; they want homes.

What about Louise's interest in Catholicism?

It's a metaphor. It's a way for her to visualize something abstract that she needs, a way to make it specific. What Louise needs to recognize is that the mistake she made thirty years ago was in not trusting herself, trusting other people's versions of who she should be, and putting herself in a position of almost complete dependence on her husband. Her only way to save herself emotionally is to break away from that, and Catholicism is her odd way of trying to do that. It is a final moment of self-reliance, and a sort of breaking away from the need to be defined by other people. In an odd way, it's kind of defiance.

There seems to be, among a segment of the gay community, a tendency to deny the legitimacy of the domestic gay experience. It's either illegitimate, or it doesn't exist, or is a wrong step. It's a kind of new intolerance.

If there's a new intolerance, it may be because there is also a new interest, particularly among writers, in the domestic gay experience. The anxiety seems to be that gay domesticity is merely a reaction to AIDS, that it's a kind of retreat, as if gay men are saying, "Well, AIDS is so scary, let's all just go huddle in our safe, womblike houses." I think it's naive to see it simply as a response to AIDS. One reviewer said that Danny and Walter's domestic life would make more sense if it were described as a response to AIDS. To think that their life together is simply a matter of that is just the most vulgar naïveté.

In a sense we took the disease and used it as an excuse for what was happening anyway. If there's a response to gay domesticity, it's a fear among the gay community of the gay community disappearing into a whole bunch of little suburban houses. From a political point of view that's a perfectly valid fear, but I don't perceive that happening. Yes, the nature of the gay community is changing, but by no stretch of the imagination is it disappearing.

What about the bicoastal aspect of this book? It takes place in California and New York.

Well, since I grew up in California and came east to college, California, which to most people is the new land, is the old land; and the East Coast, which is the old land, was for me the new land. It's a funny reversal, one that I wanted to play with a little bit. It became an instantaneous metaphor for growing up.

I know that New York is associated with adulthood, but there is a sense in which New York is a place where you can be an adolescent for your entire life. You don't have to grow up in New York City, because daily life is such an effort that by the time you finish with it you just go to sleep—there's no time for self-analysis. I think that it's significant that Danny and Walter, in order to grow up, move to the suburbs.

That division between the West and the East Coast has always been something that's fascinated me, particularly the duality between the old and the new, and which is which. For Louise and Nat, of course, California is what the East Coast becomes for Danny.

How important is New York for you personality?

Well, I hate New York at the moment, so I guess that means that it's pretty important. I really have developed a kind of antipathy to New York; I almost can't stand to be there. It's been developing over a couple of years for me, and I've been spending less and less time in the city, and more and more time in East Hampton or elsewhere. It's reached a climax at this point where I almost can't be there.

I find New York physically oppressive, difficult, loud, harsh, cruel in a lot of ways. There's so much "cultural noise." Every time you turn around someone has an opinion. There's so many, so many magazines, so many newspapers. Now the *New York Post* is doing its Book World, so there'll be a whole other set of opinions; and this is just within the book world. What all this feels like to me isn't culture; it's cultural noise. This buzz, you can't escape it. There's no space to work without hearing everybody's opinion. On a personal level it makes me crazy when I hear people saying things like, "Well, David Leavitt *should* be writing a novel about AIDS." I find I can't stand it anymore. It's not an atmosphere in which I'm able to do anything. From an artistic standpoint, it's not inspiring; it's the opposite.

I find I need the quiet—the literal and the figurative quiet—of the countryside in order to get anything done. It's not city life I find so unappealing. Just being in Boston for a brief time, I get the feeling that this is a much more livable city, that there is more space to breathe, and that there isn't this New York thing of incessant yammering which, it seems to me, has found its apotheosis in *W* magazine's "in" and "out" list.

I do need the city, the interaction with the world. I just wish it wasn't New York. For all my antipathy for New York, it's still the city that I'm linked to. That's where I'm enmeshed.

Is an American writer almost obliged to be linked to New York?

No, I don't think so. I just think I've ended up being so by having lived there. It's very hard to uproot yourself, even from a place you hate. If I did, I would go a lot farther away than Boston. I'd hurl myself across the ocean, to Europe.[4] If you're going to uproot yourself you need to do it in a big way.

Let's talk about influences. Besides George Eliot, who are the big influences— the nineteenth-century influences—on you as a writer?

---

4. Leavitt has subsequently moved to Italy and written (with Mark Mitchell) a small book, *Italian Pleasures,* about his life in Tuscany.

Well, Henry James, Jane Austen. It's not going to be a very surprising list. Proust, to a certain extent.

Does every gay writer have to come to terms with Proust?

That's a kind of provocative question, but I don't know what it means. Does a gay novelist have to read Proust? I don't know if you *have* to do anything. I certainly found it thrilling, reading Proust. This phrase, "coming to terms," it sounds like wrestling. I found Proust a sort of ecstatic experience. Even when I was annoyed by parts of it. But it was never something that I felt I had to "come to terms with." I would never use that phrase.

And, as far as contemporary writers go, whom do you admire? At the Brattle reading, you mentioned Alice Munro and Amy Hempel.

A book that I read recently that I love is Margaret Drabble's *The Radiant Way.* Cynthia Ozick is a writer who is very important to me; Deborah Eisenberg is another writer I love a lot.

What does the term "gay writer" mean to you?

Well, it means a lot of things. I don't think any writer likes adjectives in front of the word "writer." But if it means a writer who is gay, then it's simply a statement. If it means a writer with a so-called gay sensibility, it seems to me that that's a pretty problematic thing to define. I wouldn't deny being a gay writer, but I'd rather just be a writer who is gay. One worries about being typecast.

It's like the term "minimalism," which has gotten thrown around a lot. It's a term which people have used a lot without anyone ever bothering to refine what it means. "Gay writer" means ten different things if you ask ten different people.

Do you think it's worth exploring the idea of gay sensibility?

Sure, it's fascinating. I had a professor at Yale who said something that struck me as so smart about his whole theory of gay style, which he said was a style based on concealment, and concealment particularly within humor. He used as his major example the Philip Barry play like *The Philadelphia Story,* which he said is a play with an incredibly gay style, even though there is no gay content. His theory was that as gay content becomes more and more explicit, and the need for concealment disappears, the gay style will disappear. And that when you finally get to a point where you have completely explicit gay content, there won't be such a thing as gay style, or gay sensibility. That gay style and gay sensibility are entirely responses to having to conceal the fact of homosexuality.

Style is such a personal thing, that to have any kind of a style which can be defined in terms of an aspect of that person rather than of that person as an individual—to say "gay style" as opposed to David Leavitt's style—it has to be a matter of something like my Yale professor's theory. What was called gay sensibility has already become, more or less, an anachronism in the present age. There are a lot of gay writers, but they are all writing in very different styles with all sorts of very different influences. And the influences tend to come from all sorts of different places, and usually from extra-sexual areas.

The days of the Lavender [i.e., Violet] Quill, which was so much a response to living in the middle of a gay community forming in reaction to a homophobic exterior, those days seem to me to have past. Which doesn't mean that we don't still live in a very homophobic society, but the publishing community, the literary community, to a certain extent, has opened up enough so that there isn't that need to inbreed. All those writers were writing very explicitly about gay experience, but with a kind of extreme consciousness of themselves as outsiders.

Whom are you thinking of?

Well, the members of the Lavender Quill: Robert Ferro and Michael Grumley, Edmund White, Andrew Holleran, and Felice Picano. I can't think of the other members now, but they were the most well-known. They were all friends and read each other's work and got together periodically to discuss it. You do see a sort of stylistic link and a social link among all those writers.[5]

Do you have any nostalgia to be a part of something like that?

No. In terms of my life, I have a lot of nostalgia about the days of sexual wildness and liberation and the days before AIDS. But it's not a literary

---

5. See, for example, *The Violet Quill Reader: The Emergence of Gay Writing After Stonewall*, ed. David Bergman (New York: St. Martin's Press, 1994).

nostalgia. As a writer, I think I'm much more content with the way things are now, because I don't want to be strictly limited by that adjective. I want to be a gay writer, but I want to be a lot of other kinds of writers as well, and to be completely beyond the idea of gay style.

Are there any gay writers in particular whom you do admire or have learned from?

I read this [Alan Hollinghurst] novel recently called *The Swimming-Pool Library* that I really loved. I'm not sure that I'd say I learned from it, but I certainly admired it a lot. And I've always been an admirer of Edmund White's prose, though there are things about his books that trouble me. And then there was a book called *I Look Divine* by Christopher Coe that I loved. I must be forgetting something crucial.

What about Forster?

Oh, Forster I love, obviously. But, for me, it's hard to think of Forster as a gay writer. I was thinking of books that have explicitly gay content, and the fact is that of all of Forster's novels *Maurice* is the one that I find the least interesting.

At the Brattle Theater someone asked you how much of your own life is in Equal Affections, *and you replied, "Aha, the autobiography question!" I'm not going to ask the autobiography question, but I would like to ask "The Gary Question."*[6]

You mean, what's it like living with another writer? Well, like everything, sometimes it's great and sometimes it's not so great. All marriages are compromises. There are wonderful aspects about it. The fact that we're both writers and that we live together means that our lives have the same structure. We're both able to travel, for instance. Neither of us is attached to a job, so that means we can go places together, which is very nice. There's certain aesthetic commonality. We talk about books a lot. We don't so often show each other our work, but when we do it's always very nice. It's much more a shared sense of a common goal, a belief in the value of writing no matter what, whether you're doing well or not doing well.

---

6. At the time of this interview Leavitt's partner was the novelist and composer Gary Glickman. Leavitt's and Glickman's fiction and their life together were the subject of James Wolcott's scathing Vanity Fair article, "Guppie Fiction."

At the same time there's a certain element—I wouldn't say so much of competitiveness—but it's hard when you have two egos in the same field, living in the same house. There's bound to be problems, there's bound to be clashes. I'd say we deal with it pretty well. I think it's harder for Gary than for me because he's not as well-known as I am. I think I make him insecure in ways that he might not be.

You have to weigh the good things and the bad things that the relationship brings you. Ultimately, in these kinds of situations, you don't have a hell of a lot of choice. It's not as if you pick your partner through computer dating services; some machine is not going to create the perfect person for you. It seems to me that often you end up, for reasons that are inexplicable, bound to someone.[7]

Are you ever tempted to take out the Jewish element in your work? Do you ever get the sense that writing about Jewish gays is putting in too much "local color"?

See, this is what I meant by all the cultural noise, that idea that writers can't have more than one thing that makes your character a minority, that

---

7. In 1989, I interviewed Glickman in conjunction with the publication of his novel, *Years From Now.* At that time, I asked him the "David Question." In part, here is his reply:

> We've lived together for three years, and of course he is a major dynamic in my life. I think, being the dark horse, it's more a major factor in my life as a writer than in David's. Whereas for David it stops at the parameters of our marriage, for me it completely infuses my career and my identity as a writer. I have to think about it all the time.
>
> I feel that, for me as a writer and for me as a spouse, we both must do our work as best we can, in good faith. It's really not for us to judge but we're both admirers, of each other's work. With that supporting us, we then can say, Okay, now our job is to ignore the response in terms of each other.
>
> The most common experience for writers is that they don't show their work to their lovers: you don't want to make your relationship vulnerable to those tensions. David and I slug it out sometimes, and I'm just coming to understand how much bad there is in that. But what I'm doing is trying to correct that rather than avoid it, because as two writers we just can't avoid the fact of each other's work.

The Glickman interview has not been included in this book. It appeared, in an abridged version, in *Bay Windows,* 13 April 1989.

if your character is Jewish then he can't be gay. I think that's ridiculous, though I do worry about the same thing. The one I'm always tempted to drop is the gay part simply because that's the part that everybody gets up in arms about. In Gary's book the homosexual element "liberated" the reviewers to be anti-Semetic. It was all right to say nasty things about Jews if in the same breath you were saying nasty things about homosexuals.

The idea that a character can't, for example, be gay and Jewish is a terrible thing which has nothing to do with literature, and nothing to do with art, and nothing to do with anything a writer should ever think about while writing. It's simply to do with all these cultural noise-makers sitting there blah-blah-blahing and bitching and moaning.

And don't think that I'm an enemy of book reviewing, or an enemy of criticism, because I write a lot of book reviews. And I'm a great admirer of a lot of book reviewers and a lot of critics. There are brilliant book reviewers, people who have made an art out of it; and there are people who have made an art out of cultural commentary. But there are other people who have made a nightmare out of it. A lot of reviewers are crotchety complainers who seem to have made a business out of complaining.

What kind of advice do you have for a young writer?

Perseverance is very important. Also, always maintaining a sense of privacy about your work. You have to keep the work separate from everything else. You have to shut the door in the room where you write and not let either the good reviews or the bad reviews in. Because if you let the good stuff in you just get complacent; and if you let the bad stuff in you get crazy or start writing for an audience, which I think is a very bad thing to do. Finally, the only people who count in an act of reading are the writer and the reader. It's important to think of your reader not as some book reviewer ready to launch his own opinion, which probably has to do with a thousand other things outside the book, but to think of your reader as someone smart and coming to the book without prior judgments, who just wants to learn and to know and to experience.

That's one piece of advice. You also have to be career conscious, you have to be pragmatic. You have to do what you need to do in order to promote yourself. But the thing to do is to compartmentalize your life, to say *this* is the time for that, and *this* is the time for writing.

Dennis Cooper

Admired for his astringent, polished, lapidary style and, at times, excoriated for his fascination with dark plots about "blank generation" teenagers and predatory older men, Dennis Cooper has been dubbed the "'boys, sex, and gore' queen" of gay literature.[1] His dark subject matter, including scenes of depersonalized sex, torture, and murder, belies the exquisite lyrical surface of his work, which no less a writer and critic than Brad Gooch has called "quite pitch-perfect." Indeed, so unsettling and repugnant are some of Cooper's novels that he has even been the recipient of a death threat.

Born in 1953, Cooper grew up in California. During his years in private school (he was expelled in eleventh grade), he became, according to biographer Earl Jackson, Jr., "the leader of a group of outcasts: budding poets, druggies, and punks, who eventually would provide the models for the wayward youths who populate his fiction."[2] He attended Pasadena City College for two years and Pitzer College for one, where he studied poetry and poetry writing. In 1976, he founded *Little Caesar Magazine*; two years later he created Little Caesar Press, which published his collection *Tiger Beat*. In addition to his poetry and fiction writing, Cooper has worked at a variety of jobs that have promoted punk music, alternative art, and performance artists. He has also written for *Artforum* magazine.

I interviewed Cooper in 1989, when he came to Boston to read from his novel *Closer*. During our conversation, Cooper kept shifting between "high" and "low" idioms of speech. One minute he would employ the vocabulary of deconstructionism; the next he would punctuate a sentence with throwaway words—"like," "kind of," "really"—that sounded like the voice of one of his teenage-punk characters. He seemed

---

1. See, for example, Craig Allen Seymour II, "Refusing Compromise: Cooper's Discontents," *Lambda Book Report*, 3, no. 6 (September/October, 1992): 28–29.

2. Earl Jackson, Jr., "Dennis Cooper," in *Contemporary Gay American Novelists: A Bio-Bibliographical Critical Sourcebook*, ed. Emmanuel S. Nelson (Westport, Conn.: Greenwood, 1993), 77.

equally comfortable, or uncomfortable, in both worlds. I got the feeling that the usual distinctions between high and low, whether in terms of conversation or aesthetics, didn't mean much to him.

Closer went on to receive the first Ferro-Grumley Award for gay literature.

Can we start with some biographical questions?

I was born in Pasadena, California, and grew up in the neighboring city, Arcadia. Schoolwise, before college, I was mostly at boys' school and then I was kicked out and went to public school for my last year. I went to Claremont College for one year and then I quit.

Why did you get kicked out of your prep school?

The official reason was that my grade average wasn't high enough—it was a B plus—the actual reason was because I had a sort of gang of people. We were doing a lot of drugs; I had a lot of influence on the kids. I was arty, too arty for them. They caught everyone else in my gang with drugs, but I was too smart; they could never catch me. So they threw me out for other reasons.

How did you get started writing?

I've been writing since I was young, thirteen or fourteen.

You started out as a poet first, right?

Well, I always wrote prose, too, but poetry was most interesting to me. They eventually merged into one thing; I started writing paragraphs, and they got longer and longer, and then I got interested in narrative. I don't write poetry anymore.

Have you studied formally with anyone?

I went to City College for a couple of years, and I studied there with a couple of poetry teachers. When I went to the university [Pitzer College], I went specifically to study with this one poet, but he's the one who told me to leave school. He said it was stupid to be in school if you wanted to be a writer, so I did. Other than that, I've just read a lot.

Anybody in particular who has influenced you a lot?

I could mention a lot of people. The main one is [the Marquis] de Sade. I read him when I was very young, and that was the big thing for me. Rimbaud was really influential, and Genet.

What specifically about Rimbaud and Genet?

Rimbaud, I guess, because I was a teenager, and he was, like, this genius. He really believed that language could transcend itself, and that writing should do more than just map out what you do every day, that it could get to some secret truth. I guess I believed that, and still believe it in some way. And he was, like, you know, gay; but he was this outsider gay guy. Just about everything about him was appealing.

    With Genet the language was really interesting. I also leaned toward him because he was writing about the same thing all the time; and I'm interested in this one area, and I think that if I keep exploring it in different ways I'll get something really, really important out of it. Genet obviously felt the same way since he wrote these four or five books always basically about the same thing: kind of a religious interpretation of sex and desire.

I'm interested to hear you bring up the religious dimension of Genet, because a lot of people have talked about Closer *as a portrait of the so-called blank generation, which I suppose it is, but it seems to me that it goes well beyond that. A lot of the reviewers seem to focus on the specific content of your novel and miss the larger issues.*

Yeah, a lot of the critics have found the book interesting and they want to justify their interest in the book so they have to say, Well, it's about how the world is so screwed up and how it creates these little monsters. But I never think about that.

    To me, it's just about these characters who want something—to connect with another person. They don't have any rules; they don't really believe in anything. They feel as if the only thing they're going to get any information out of is another person. And specifically another male, a beautiful male. At the same time, they're terrified to feel anything. Although I'm not religious at all, it does seem to me that that's a religious thing. Beauty is a kind of religion.

You and Robert Glück are often linked as "experimental writers" or "new narrative" writers. What does that mean to you?

I don't know. It's one of those terms of convenience. I think George Stambolian started using it to collect together those people who were doing something that was a little different from what Ed White and Bob Ferro were doing. We're playing around with narrative. I'm very conscious of what narrative can and can't do. I'm not interested in representing what it's like to be gay. Writers like Ed did allow the kind of freedom for what we're doing.

At the beginning of the novel you write, "Punk's bluntness had edited tons of pretentious shit out of American culture." To what extent, then, do you admire these kids' punk culture, and to what extent are you critical of it?

Well, I came of age with punk, and it's still a scene I'm very involved in. The characters are just configurations of the prose, but they're also based on people I know. I really don't feel as if I'm criticizing at all. I really hate moralisms. I think they're a total obstruction toward trying to understand anything. Of course, people shouldn't be cruel to each other, so when there are acts of cruelty in the novel I suppose I'm condemning those, but I still think you should look at them clearly and fairly. For instance, I'm really interested in serial murderers; I think it's interesting to study that rather than just condemn it.

Everybody has ideas like that: I mean, most people would like to kill someone; or people who when they're having sex with someone imagine them dead, or imagine them an object. I'm trying to use the language to get into that, into the feeling, without giving it these really boring things they do in most fiction: you know, motivations. They're so false.

My characters talk to each other like they want to get information from each other. And I want to understand them: the characters and all the action are just sort of like information.

And what is that "information" that they're wanting? They can't quite articulate it, can they?

No, and I can't either. That's why it takes me so long to get it right, I guess. It's just like everybody is so completely separate from each other, so isolated; it's about trying to get outside your own body somehow—but you can't—and trying to get inside someone else's body, because you think maybe you'll feel something there—but you can't—because the body is just this sack full of junk, right? And even if you killed them, which is what some of my characters want to do, you still have a bunch of junk.

So if you don't believe in God and religion, and you don't believe in the heterosexual family, but you want to find some kind of meaning . . . so they're really completely confused. They're living in chaos, trying to find some sort of order.

Your characters try desperately not to use the word "love," yet toward the end that word does emerge.

Right.

And it seems like love is the thing they're embarrassed about, but is that also the thing they're getting—to quote the title of your novel—closer to?

I don't know. That last character is sort of a savior character, I guess. When he finds he can say the word "love," it's like some kind of ridiculous salvation. Yeah, I mean, it's with great difficulty that he uses the word "love," but after that he deconstructs what he really means, which is this convoluted idea about perfection.

The boredom your characters keep experiencing comes from the fact that whatever they keep thinking is "it" isn't really it.

Right.

And then they get to a point where they automatically anticipate that whatever they're going to experience isn't going to be it.

Right.

They're bored before they even begin.

There are incredible ways in which they keep themselves from doing anything. They're almost catatonic. I've been heavily influenced by [Arthur J.] Bressan's films. His characters all speak in these very flat voices, and very little goes on in them. But I get the feeling that the less that happens the more resonance there is. So that even the slightest bit of feeling takes on this incredible significance.

My father was like that: he was really distant, and the little amount of affection he showed was so incredible.

You almost seem to be exploring different kinds of distractions: there are the distractions, like drugs, that have a numbing effect, but there are also the distractions that are unexpected intrusions into the world of these characters. In bouncing around, looking for something, the distractions they least expect may act like . . .

That's true. Like ghosts of some kind of answer. Absolutely. If that's where I want to get closer to when I write, it's those things. Getting over the embarrassment about those things. For me it's about creating elaborate systems of language to, like, not deal with that stuff. That's the stuff that's really important, but it's how to frame it in a way that doesn't seem stupid or banal.

What are your writing habits like?

I work all the time. All the time. I'm completely obsessed about writing. When I write, it takes forty or fifty drafts. It takes me forever and forever and forever to get it right. At some point, I usually realize where the thing is, and then I start trying to focus it, clear the language away from it as much as I can, but not go too far because then it will become some sort of fake thing.

Do you start from an outline?

Not really, because I don't write in order; I write out of sequence. With *Closer,* I wanted to divide my voice up into different voices, so I did a series of cutups based on other texts, like Nijinsky's diaries and Verlaine's letters and a bunch of stuff. Then I used those voices as the basis to construct the voices in my novel.

Besides Robert Glück and Gary Indiana, which writers writing today do you admire?

Well, let's see. I like Kevin Killian. Bruce Broome. Brad Gooch I really like. There's a whole bunch of people you wouldn't know yet. When Gary and I were on tour, we were running into these kids who were writing this fantastic stuff. I'd love to do an anthology. For this magazine called *Farm,* I'm bringing out a bunch of new gay writers. Most of them are in their early twenties. I like a lot of French writers, too.

What do you think is going to happen to gay writing in the next, say, ten years or so?

There's a lot of stuff going on right now that's really exciting. I've become annoyed by the David Leavitt thing, even though I understand the significance of it: that here's this gay writer who can be just as conventional and banal as a straight writer. It means being gay has reached a point of acceptance, but I hate his work. I reject it on every level. There's a lot of that kind of writing going on right now.

On the other hand, that kind of work has allowed the kind of writing we're beginning to see now: it allows the kind of freedom that allowed for great artists all through time to be gay, a kind of outsiderness. You can experiment. Not just with sex, but in other ways, too. Emotionally, and relationship-wise. Homosexuality itself is an experiment.

So I see a lot of these writers using the freedom of being gay to do things with language that are really interesting. And if there are publishers who are brave enough to publish the stuff, we'll see some interesting things in the experimental writing tradition.

Paul Monette

Better known for his poetry and nonfiction, Paul Monette was also the author of several novels, among them *The Gold Diggers, Afterlife,* and *Halfway Home.* While not as commercially successful as his memoirs, Monette's novels have been admired (and criticized) for their inclusion of elements from popular genres like melodrama and romance, their portrayal of women and gay men of color, and, in the case of the later novels, their unsparing attention to the AIDS epidemic.

Monette was born in Lawrence, Massachusetts, in 1945. He attended Phillips Academy (Andover) and Yale, where he received his B.A. in 1967. After college, he taught English and writing at Milton Academy and Pine Manor College, writing and publishing poetry on the side. In the mid-1970s, he turned his attention to fiction writing. His first novel, *Taking Care of Mrs. Carroll,* was published in 1978. During the late seventies and early eighties, other novels and a volume of poems appeared. During this time, Monette also wrote screenplays and novelizations of films.

I interviewed Monette in the early spring of 1990. Two years before, he had published *Borrowed Time,* a harrowing memoir chronicling his lover Roger Horwitz's battle with AIDS. But on this occasion, we talked about his latest book, *Afterlife,* a novel about AIDS widowers, which at least one gay reviewer, Jesse Monteagudo, has called, "the greatest novel ever written about AIDS."[1]

For our interview, Monette and I met in the South End apartment of his friend Craig Rowland. Monette was eager to know what I thought of his new novel. He hadn't published fiction in a while. Did I think it held up against the best of the gay novels published in recent years? It seemed like an unusually anxious question to come from a writer of his stature.

At the end of the interview, Monette said that he expected to be re-

---

1. Jesse Monteagudo, review of Paul Monette's *Afterlife, TWN,* 25 April 1990, 6; cited in David Román, "Paul Monette," in *Contemporary Gay American Novelists: A Bio-Bibliographical Critical Sourcebook,* ed. Emmanuel S. Nelson (Westport, Conn.: Greenwood, 1993), 280.

membered best for *Borrowed Time*. This was a few years before he published *Becoming a Man*, a book that matches, if not surpasses, *Borrowed Time* for its power, eloquence, and honesty.

The tape of this interview has been lost. The following transcript was pieced together from the profile I wrote for *Bay Windows* (April 26, 1990) that incorporated excerpts from that now lost tape. All of Monette's words are direct quotations.

I had hoped to interview Monette more extensively for the WOMR radio series *The Word is Out*. I wrote to him in the spring of 1993, inviting him to be one of the twelve gay and lesbian fiction writers I would be interviewing that summer on the radio.

He wrote back, "The WOMR series sounds marvelous, and I wish I could be part of it (and see P'town again), but unhappily my health is too precarious right now. I did make it to Washington for the March, but spent a lot of that time in bed because I'm just starting chemo for KS and battling toxo—well, you know all the rest. If I can stabilize all this, I might feel more inclined to travel at the end of the summer, but you can't count on me."

Paul Monette died of complications from AIDS on 10 February 1995.

You've published three books in two years. That would be a sizable accomplishment for any writer, but given the fact that you've also been diagnosed with HIV, producing three books in so short a period seems like an even more stunning achievement.

The war is where I belong. I wish to leave a proper testament of what my people have gone through. When Roger died, I assumed that I would be dead in six months to a year. The burden of the poems that I wrote in those next six months—well, they were written truly as if I were going to be dead the next day.

When I started *Borrowed Time*, I think I had gotten my breath enough to say that there was no way I was going to die before I finished it. It was hammeringly difficult to pull it off: the last hundred pages was like Roger dying all over again. So that after a year and a half, I was very brutalized by the demands of the work. But it went with what it meant to be in the war.

When I started *Afterlife*, I thought that maybe I could take a break from that war, even though I was writing about the same world, because I would write something that would be ironic. But as I worked, I realized that this was everybody's story, *everybody's*.

But why did you tackle another enormous project, especially while you were just beginning a new relationship, with Stephen Kolzak, who also has AIDS?

The center of me seems to have to do with work. One of the things that Roger released me to be able to do in my life was to work. I take immense pleasure in writing.

Writing is what I do best to effect the gravity of the situation. I really have lived with AIDS long enough to be able to see two prongs to the gravity of the situation: the holocaust and this mind-boggling world of hate that we face. The longer I have a chance to live, the more I feel like facing that other thing while I talk about AIDS.

And yet, Afterlife *is a very romantic book, a love story, really.*

I feel as if love stories are suspect these days. Not that we as gay people can't write them, even in the middle of the holocaust. We can and we must do that.

It is in the nature of modern life to be ironic about love. Irony has been the only way that people in the culture at large have known to respond to the simplistic edge of love. Some of the writers that I respect the most, the books that I respect the most—*Dancer From the Dance,* for example, which I think is just a masterpiece—can only be ironic about love. The characters wish to be romantics, they wish to find somebody, but they don't, and that is the story that is told.

It's fine to tell that story, but I happen to be interested in telling the other story, even if I must, in the process, idealize it. I am interested in two people getting together and what that's like. I'm not interested in writing about a relationship that doesn't work. I'm really interested in how people come to know they love and what it feels like to feel love, because that was the thing that was missing in my life for twenty-five years.

Having experienced love so deeply with Roger for twelve years . . . , boy, was I conscious that what was going to happen in *Afterlife* was that Steven and Mark were going to fall in love. In the course of writing *Afterlife,* I fell in love with Stephen Kolzak. And so Stephen and I really helped Mark and Steven in the novel get together.

Among other things in Afterlife, *I was impressed by your creation of Margaret Kirkham, a straight woman who tends to a dying character named Ray Lee.*

Margaret is the one who has the AIDS experience in the novel. All the widowers in this novel do not want another AIDS experience. I understood how they felt. When I proposed the novel, I said, No one is actually going to get AIDS. They're all seropositive; I want to talk about what that's like. And yet Ray Lee just crept up on me, and Margaret crept up on me. The image of Ray and Margaret watching forties noir thrillers on an afternoon—when people read my novel, I hope they think, What a great couple!

There's another interesting character in Afterlife, *Linda Espinoza, a woman who late in the novel discovers she's a lesbian.*

In my gay and lesbian writers circle in Los Angeles, one of the lesbian writers recently said, "One of the things I think we need to do is to have each other in our books." It seemed like a wonderful notion, and I realized that I was doing that, both in the book I'm writing now and in *Afterlife.* We need to reach across to each other. It's not a false thing. The fact is we have achieved that union in the last five or ten years, and one way to celebrate that union is to do it in a book.

Afterlife *is also a very sexy, very erotic book. Did you worry about how that was going to go over with your readership?*

Ever since I finished the book, I've wondered how people are going to be about handling all the sex. We live in a sex-phobic culture. If the sex is hot, straight people can't handle it. When I was writing this novel, everyone I knew was talking about how abstracted they were from sex. That twenty-page sequence about not being able to get it up came out of that.

Christopher Bram has just published In Memory of Angel Clare, *another novel about "AIDS widowers." Are we entering a period of AIDS widower novels?*

It doesn't surprise me that there's a lot of work coming out now about AIDS survivorship, because any sentient person who lives a life with any kind of larger view knows someone who has died of AIDS. Every gay or lesbian person—it's actually a larger group than that—but certainly every gay or lesbian person is an AIDS survivor currently. Everyone still alive is an AIDS survivor. I do see the profound effect on every gay and lesbian person I know. AIDS survival requires that we be strong, and that we be highly alert to our politics, and that we do not waste a minute, and that we suffer fools badly: so many of those things that one might call post-widowhood.

Are AIDS widowers different from straight widowers?

It is certainly true that grief is a great leveler. People who have loved greatly and have lost greatly probably have a better sense of live-and-let-live than most people. A lot of the great hatred we have from the heterosexual majority comes from people who cannot love or have not loved; people who are so cold and withheld that they haven't experienced loss either. So no, everyone who has lost a great love is the same.

What's particular to the AIDS situation is that we find ourselves—so many of us—young and vital and in a war. We see it as a war; we have a political response to it. And since widowhood fills you with pain, the rage has a political edge to it. Anyone who is dealing with grief is wailing at the wrongness of things, but we who are dealing with AIDS are dealing with it in the context of what our government allowed to happen.

I can scarcely read fiction by straight people. It seems so irrelevant, not just to the world of AIDS, but to what AIDS has focused us on in the last ten years: the loss of free speech in this country; the seething, foaming hatred that boils in this society. I keep seeing the heterosexual, white, male subculture in this country backed against the wall like Afrikaners. Their last gasp involves barbaric dogs like Jesse Helms. But it's so much bigger even than Jesse Helms.

This country is going down the tubes. My hope—beyond the fact that the holocaust will be over for gay people and that AIDS will end—I want gay and lesbian people to be strong for what's going to happen in the next twenty years, for the millennial earthquake that's going to happen. It's going to be a tough, hard place. The very rich are going to have all the money and everyone else is going to be poor. The lack of civilization will become like cavemen. There are real dark forces out there.

Where do you find the optimism to go forth and develop a new relationship?

In a world where so much of what is called the "point of life" seems like ashes and nonsense, the urgency of living in the face of death makes you go after your most urgent feelings. I don't say that love is possible for everyone. People have different levels of difficulty with relationships. It takes a whole life to really work that out.

A year after Roger died, I knew I wanted to be involved with someone. I tried for a while dating someone who was seronegative, and there was something so weird about it, about the unstated matters. When I met

Stephen, he didn't know what he was doing with his life. He was doing a lot of AIDS politics and otherwise basically freaking out. We danced around this relationship for a few months, having a good time and making each other laugh, so that it didn't feel like chronicles of wasted time. But it was not until we went to Washington for the FDA demonstration and the Quilt—four days of very powerful stuff—and we took a ride into the Shenandoah Valley, that we realized, yes, we were in love and that this is what we had a chance for. There was no need to discuss how provisional it was. That was just so obvious. We had a real flowering of love in the next four or five months. It was not difficult to maintain optimism in that at all.

I have a kind of belief in the way men bond in foxholes. One of the ironic things we learned during our ten years of flagrant openness that followed the revolution that Stonewall began was that a night with someone, or a week with someone, could be deeply profound after several hundred years of repression. Yes, it was a kind of postadolescent or late adolescent reaching back for something we didn't have, but it was also dazzling what intimacy could teach us. I find that being in a relationship is full of all the lessons of intimacy.

What are your working on now?

I expect that I will be best remembered for *Borrowed Time*, and that's as it should be, but if I have stuff that I want to keep saying, then I want to find a form to say it. I hadn't written a novel in a long time. When I finished this one—and it was a lot of work—I thought, Ooh, I've got my fingers back; now I'd really like to write a novel. That's why I've already started my next book, *Halfway Home.*[2]

---

2. *Halfway Home* was published in 1991, a year after this interview.

Allen Barnett

Allen Barnett lived to see only one book to completion, but that book, *The Body and Its Dangers*, lives on not only as a clear witness to the author's great talent and promise, but also as a superb literary achievement, one of the finest collections of modern gay short stories.

"Everything about Allen Barnett's work suggests nothing but *lived* life," wrote Ilene Raymond in the *Washington Post*. "The details and emotions of these stories are so immediate, so explicit, so heartfelt, that often there is nothing left but to release a shocked sigh of recognition and admiration for the honest power of Barnett's prose."[1] Joseph Olshan, in *New York Newsday*, singled out Barnett's voice, calling it "at once sultry with image and suggestion and cool and objective in its analysis of interpersonal relationships."[2] And Robert Dawidoff, writing in the *Lambda Book Report*, noted, "We'll be reading these stories for many reasons for a long time to come."[3]

Like the bird in Robert Frost's poem "The Oven Bird," Barnett's stories pose the question, What to make of a diminished thing? "What do you make of the present, the condensed, the concentrated moment?" the cancer-ridden narrator asks in the title story. The pull in each story is toward some kind of "unquestioning faith in the present tense," toward some accommodation of "This is you now," even though the present world may be unacceptable, and past unhappiness and the dread of what's to come continue to haunt. In avoiding making AIDS a metaphor and, at the same time, finding in his stories a language to describe the dreadful urgency of *every* moment, Barnett made an enormous and beautiful contribution to contemporary gay literature.

The Body and Its Dangers won a Lambda Literary Award, the Ferro-Grumley Award, and a citation from the Ernest Hemingway Foundation

---

1. Ilene Raymond, "Alarms and Confusions," *Washington Post Book World* 20, no. 32 (12 August 1990): 10.
2. Joseph Olshan, "Love and Death," *New York Newsday*, 12 August 1990, 17.
3. Robert Dawidoff, "Bodily Dangers," *Lambda Book Report* 2, no. 6 (August/September, 1990): 42.

recognizing it as one of the best first-published books of fiction by an American writer in 1990.[4]

Late in the summer of 1990, Barnett came to Boston to do a reading. Afterward, in Provincetown, we taped the following conversation. An abridged version appeared in *Bay Windows*, 22 November 1990.

Barnett died on 14 August 1991, at age thirty-six.

Tell me about your early life.

I grew up in a small town in Illinois with two brothers and four sisters. I'm the oldest. The jargon is "dysfunctional," but I don't think that's descriptive enough for what my family was. There was nothing much there that resembled a family. My mother's first husband—who was not my father, actually—was a truck driver who was working on the road for long stretches of time. He would come home and get her pregnant and then go off again. Usually there was no money for rent and no money for food, and yet this man owned three trucks and had people working for him. I remember us being dependent on neighbors and friends for groceries. When you grow up poor and hungry, you learn very early what desire is.

I understand that you spent some time in an orphanage.

We were in the orphanage a couple of months. That really started my life-long approach-avoidance thing with Catholicism. I found it horrendous. The nuns were bitches on wheels. Not to mention those masses that we were yanked out of bed for, sitting there, nauseated by that horrible incense and not knowing what they were saying. To me it was as exotic and frightening as the witches in *Macbeth*.

And then you moved to a new subdivision in Joliet?

There were so many of us in such a cramped space that I found ways of retreating and having privacy. At first, I was a slow reader, but once I caught on, I started reading a lot. Reading was a form of escape and fantasy.

Earlier you told me about a man who was very important to you in your teenage years, a poet named Thomas James.

---

4. In a letter to me dated 27 March 1991, Barnett wrote, "Did not get PEN/Hemingway. I'm shattered. Got Miss Runner Up, the 1st loser."

I was fifteen years old. My family was trying to make the tentative leap into the middle class. My friend Dean told me about this crazy man down the street, a poet. At first I avoided him. He lived in one of the duplexes where a lot of poor white trash lived, and we were trying not to be that. He was effeminate, as well. But then one day I saw him in the park with Dean. They were swinging golf clubs. He was drunk, even then. But he was it, the real thing: laughing and talking about literature and poetry, reciting poetry, talking about *Alice in Wonderland,* talking about why March hares are crazy. I was just overwhelmed. I went back to my house and wrote a poem about him. That night he took me to see a production of *Picnic* done by a local theater group. A few days later, I was back at the Tangerine Tent auditioning for the children's theater company.

And this guy was Thomas James?

I think that Tom started writing a novel that summer because he said that art is cheaper than therapy. Well, art is not therapeutic and it did not solve his problems. But a few days later, my friend Dean gave me a copy of two poems, one that Tom had written for Dean and one called "Letters to a Stranger." I read the poem and I knew that it was very, very good. It had a voice that to me was lovely and mysterious. Tom used to give me a ride home from those rehearsals. We would sit in his car and talk.

Were you in love with him?

No, no. In many ways he appalled me. And frightened me. Eventually he left Joliet and moved to Chicago. When I was still in high school, he came back once to do a reading from a book of poems called *Letters to a Stranger.* He read a poem called "Reasons," and that's where I got the title for my book, *The Body and Its Dangers.*

What happened to him?

In 1973, I entered Loyola University as a theater major. In January of my freshman year, while I was rehearsing for a production of *Endgame,* I got a phone call from a friend who told me that Thomas James was dead.

I knew right away that he had killed himself. At Tom's funeral, I was compared with him three times. People called me his protégé. He was the first person I tried to write like. His language—his patterns, his rhythms, his metaphors—were shaping me. Of course, what I first wrote was horrible.

I spent my sophomore and junior years in Rome, wandering through cemeteries, being depressed, crying over Tom. Senior year, I began to write stories. I wrote a story called "Roxy" about a girl who was named after the movie theater where she was conceived. The story was told as a monologue in the Il Gesù church in Rome. Even in my first story, the Catholic architecture was there.

My years as an aspiring actor contributed to my writing career. Drama is crucial to me—plot, people interacting, the what-happens-next. I had a mime teacher in college who always said, "What is the drama here?" That is the question I've always relied on whenever I get stuck with a story: What is the drama here? It's the crowbar that opens it all up for me.

Tell me more about your development as a writer.

I met a teacher who was the first to teach me that what I took for granted was important. I loved reading poetry and I loved reading poetry aloud, so he always called on me to answer his questions and to read the poems aloud. When I got my first A for a paper, I just assumed that he was an easy teacher and that everybody else got As in the class as well, which turned out not to be the case. So I ended up taking every course I could take from this man. At the end of four years of college, I had as many English credits as I did theater. Seems to me the emphasis was on poetry; at least that was the education I got.

How did you get to New York?

I tried to find work in the theater. But, as a friend of mine said to me, "Allen, there are lots of pretty boys in New York, and you know what I mean"—meaning, I wasn't one of them.

Initially when I came to New York, I was going to the New School for their master's degree in liberal studies because I was absolutely certain that I had to landfill gaps in my education. I got there and realized that the education I'd gotten at Loyola was a lot better than I was giving myself credit for. And another thing, I didn't want to read St. Augustine's *Confessions* again. I'd read it three times already. I didn't have to do it again.

I was just unhappy there. I wanted to take writing courses, but the writing courses were not in the graduate program, they were over at the New School—the contemporary New School—the Sears-Roebuck catalog of classes. I tried to take a writing class, but there were, like, thirty-five people in the room. That wasn't a writing workshop. So that didn't last. At the

New School I realized I did not enjoy being in the class with people who were just out of college and people who were coming back after twenty-eight years away. If the teacher would say, "Troilus and Cressida," someone would say, "Shakespeare's or Chaucer's?" And I just wanted to say, "Shut up! Use your head!" So that's when I tried to get into Columbia.

I turned in "Roxy" and a couple of other stories that I wrote very quickly. Two days later, they called me and I was in. I started at Columbia in January of 1979 and finished in '81. I wasn't long at Columbia before I realized that I couldn't write—I could write some beautiful, pretty sentences, but I didn't know anything about fiction. In fact, if I had had my druthers, I would have gone to Columbia for poetry and not for fiction, but I didn't have any poems. I studied with Elizabeth Hardwick and Daniel Halpren.

I spent the winter and spring of 1981 in Provincetown writing my thesis collection.

How many of the stories in The Body and Its Dangers *are from that thesis collection?*

None. I had worked on [the story] "The Body and Its Dangers" here. It was a story I had started working on while I was at Columbia, and I didn't show it to many teachers. I didn't show it in the classes at all. I didn't show it to my fellow students. But it was about that time that I became very interested in the novella as a form, because of reading Andre Dubus, especially his amazing book *Separate Flights*. Whew!

So I started writing that story because of something that Dubus had written, something about abortion in one of the stories. I realized that even as late as 1979 I had never read anything about abortion. And it makes you realize how historical that book is, finally. So I wanted to write a story about abortion, and I started "The Body and Its Dangers" and wrote the story about the boy who has the affair with the two women who become lovers. The story never really quite worked. I knew it was a good story, but I knew that it didn't work, itself.

So a year ago, after I had been operated on,[5] I was trying to figure out how I was going to finish my collection of stories, which I had a contract

---

5. Barnett didn't elaborate on the reasons for his operation, and I didn't pursue it. Most likely, his surgery was related to the HIV infection that eventually took his life. In a letter to me dated 5 May 1991, he wrote, "I'm not doing at all well. I have a hard time breath-

for and [for] which I was already several months past my deadline, and the end of the tunnel was nowhere in sight, and I didn't know how to get back to writing. I was having a hard time regaining myself, because I had almost died, and not only had I almost died, but I realized how easy that was going to be in the emergency room at NYU. I said, Well, okay, this is it. Goodbye, child. The final curtain. I had a good time but I don't want to stick around. The world just isn't what we thought we were growing up into.

A month later, when I was getting my physical strength back, my mental self said, Okay, let's deal with what just happened. I was just overwhelmed with that realization that I had almost died and that it was going to be easy. It wasn't going to be painless, but it was going to be easy. And I wasn't terrified at that death. It just wasn't frightening. I wasn't *excited* about the prospect, and I certainly wasn't imagining walking through a curtain and being somewhere else, like James Merrill's *The Changing Light at Sandover*, which I hope is what it's all about.

Anyway, I was on the dunes—it was dusk—and I was walking, trying to think how I was going to write again and I thought, Well maybe I could start with rewriting "The Body and Its Dangers," which I knew I had to do. St. Martin's [Press] loved it as it was, but I didn't. Richard Howard had urged me not to publish it. And I just heard this voice in my head that said, "My name is Sara. My daughter thinks that lesbianism is next to laziness."

Actually I kind of based that premise on a woman friend of mine whose mother became a lesbian when she herself [the friend] was sixteen. There was always kind of a resentment that my friend had for this aspect of her mother. Not that all of us don't have problems with our mothers. I started thinking about that. It was also shocking to me as well that in the original version of the story Sara had had an abortion. And I thought, Well, wait a minute. If this is sixteen years later, she's got this kid and that kid wants to know who her father is. So suddenly I knew that I had a snapshot, and another way of looking at that story. And by having Sara dealing with her own illness, plus the betrayal of Sara, by her body as well as by her own lover, and by her daughter, I was able—I don't like the word "heal" so much—but it helped me make a transition from being in recovery [from surgery] and then getting over it.

---

ing, and have a pain across my chest. The tests came back; it looks like KS in the lungs. I'm meeting with a pulmonary specialist and an oncologist. Scary. Looks like chemo."

I also wrote faster writing that story. I knew I had to finish the book in the summer, and I let go of a lot and I also let myself be a little more lyrical.

You spent the summer on Fire Island finishing the book?

Yeah. I wrote a lot of the book on Fire Island, during the week when everybody was gone. Last summer [1989] on the weekends I would come back into the city so I could stay in my head. Because what was happening, even last summer, I'd go into town and everything was being transformed in to fiction. I was writing "The Body and Its Dangers." There's that scene at the end where she talks about her mother wanting her sister to leave the room so she could die. I got that story from a boy who was all by himself, who begged me to come into his room and sit with him. He told me that story about his father. I thought [at the time], This would be better if it was a woman; I'll put it into "The Body and Its Dangers." That boy actually turned up in one of the other stories as well. And just everything was, like, Oops, take that, take that. And finally I said, I gotta put wax in my ears or something, because it's all coming in and it's all coming out, instantly.

I want to fill in the chronology a bit. Between '81, when you came to Province-town to finish your thesis collection and the summer of '89, when you were on Fire Island finishing the book, what happened?

I'm sorry, I have to say something else. Because another kind of accident happened. I was writing that story, and I was about two-thirds of the way through it and I realized I had this woman talking about Gordon but she herself had dropped out of the story and I couldn't figure out how to get her back in. And I was on a ferry going back to the Island and I was sitting next to a woman friend who said—she was very upset about the Supreme Court decision reversing, you know, the initial attack on *Roe v Wade*—and she said, "It just made me start thinking about the early seventies when abortion was illegal," and she told me this story about going to an abortionist and being molested. I just grabbed her wrist and said, "I have to have this." And I went back and was able to finish the story. It all connected. So, over ten years ago I began this story on the impulse of abortion and was able to finish it.

Writing is finally accident, but as Elizabeth Bishop says, "You have to be on the road to have an accident." And that was happening.

Okay, what did you want to know?

Your life between '81 and '89.

When I was at Columbia, I wanted to write a novel called *Margaret's Pearl*, the classic American story about the young woman getting pregnant and being abandoned and making do, doing what she had to do. And I remember Elizabeth Hardwick once said to me—she turned to me one day while we were talking and said—"The story you're trying to write is not the story that you're going to tell or that is the story worth telling: the story is what happens after your mother—or, this woman—gets married." I don't know how she knew that but she was absolutely right. I'll never write that story, I don't think, but I think that would be the right story.

When I graduated I wanted to write the crossover gay novel. I wanted to write the funny gay novel that was going to be read by everybody. And Steven McCauley wrote it and I'm glad he did and he did very well. But I wanted to write about the gay man living with the two straight women. It was going to be funny and they were going to be so much in love and all that. I started writing it. I wrote several chapters. I think I've destroyed them because they weren't very good. There were some funny lines which I managed to salvage, but one of the things I said to myself—it wasn't last summer but the summer before that I said to myself—why don't you consider that material again but from your new vantage? What is it, ten years later? Let's look back and write from now. I was also very angry at straight women friends who I felt had abandoned me, who refused to recognize the epidemic because they would not take the issues of gay men seriously. So I wrote that story really out of anger.

This is "Philostorgy, Now Obscure"?

Yeah. I wanted in the original version of the story for them to give him a ticket back to Italy as a present and as a way of connecting again their past lives. And then I realized that that ending was very, very sentimental. I took that stuff out. But I had initially planned on that being a much longer story. It was a story called "Equal Affections."[6] The second part of that story would be that character back in Rome.

So I wanted to write that funny novel. I turned in my thesis in 1981

---

6. Here Barnett changed the inflection in his voice and paused, indicating he was aware that David Leavitt had subsequently published a novel entitled *Equal Affections* in 1989.

and what happens next? There's AIDS. And my theme was always "the body and its dangers." And I just realized I could not write that novel about the girls, the three of them.

I thought, How in the hell do I write that book when all my themes—early pregnancy, the dangers of intimacy, unwanted intimacy—when the ante had been raised on all that stuff? How do you write about sex when your friend is dying across the street? I just thought, I can't do this.

I started at that time to write "Snapshot." I had written a four-page version of that story for a writing workshop with Manuel Puig, and I taught myself how to write with that story. I wanted to write a story without lyrical, pretty sentences. Which actually—I don't think I even realized it at the time—was going to become the prevailing literary mode of the eighties. And I also wanted to do something different with that story, which is to have that very tight surface control—because it was appropriate for that character—and the absolute abyss beneath that surface. And I think there's a point in that story where it goes from Raymond Carver to Allen Barnett.

It was also a time of thinking about what I was doing aesthetically. Which I think is an important thing, to finally make that leap. I exercised tight control over all that and just went at it word by word. It took me two years to write it. I remember writing one part of it here in Provincetown—not the first time but several years later—and knowing that I had done it, that I had achieved what I'd set out to do. When I look down at the manuscript and see that sentence and am proud of that sentence, knowing that it's *exactly* what I wanted to say. There were times writing that story when I'd write a scene of dialogue and run to the toilet and vomit. Especially that scene between the two men where the older man asks him to [move out?].[7] That to me was a very painful scene.

I sent that story out for a year before it was accepted and indeed I had decided to give up writing altogether when a friend of mine gave the story to Sandra McCormick at St. Martin's and she gave it to Michael Denneny. They both took me out for drinks and Sandra said, "We're going to change your life." They said, "We'd like a book from you."

That was in 1986. It was the same year I was awarded a fellowship from the New York Foundation for the Arts. All that came together at one time to make me think, Okay, maybe you can do this.

---

7. The tape recording from the interview is unclear here.

How did you feel when you got a story published in the New Yorker?

I didn't send them that story. I wrote that story for myself, probably more so than any of the stories in the collection. I never think about sending things out because I figure my stories are too long so they'll never get published. I write gay stories—there's no place to send them anyway. And then I get this phone call. Michael [Denneny, Barnett's editor at St. Martin's Press] was sending the stories out. I didn't know he was sending them out. There's this emergency message on my answering machine: Michael was calling me from Los Angeles. I thought, *Hollywood! Movies!* Oh, my God, somebody's going to make a movie out of my book. I'm so excited! And then somebody said, "Do you mind if we delay publication of your book? The *New Yorker* is interested in publishing one of the stories." I was a little let down. But not too much.

He said, "They want to publish one of the stories. Guess which one." I didn't have the faintest idea. He said, "'Philostorgy.' " I said, "That's terrific." And it became a long ordeal—not ordeal, but process.

You mention in the acknowledgments that it appeared in a very different form.

It did.

You're happier with the New Yorker *version?*

I am. It's cleaner, and I think it's even more powerful. It's the difference between what a gay sensibility thinks something should be and what an outside look might suggest. We're so, Oh, this is gay and this is the way we are. And you start thinking, Wait a minute. For me it was a good moment. Not all gay people act alike, and not all moments are going to force the same behavior on different people.

The difference between the two stories is that the men who meet—Preston and Jim, the old boyfriends—in the book go home and have sex. And the *New Yorker* said, This is not a story about sex; it's a story about affection, and secondly they said, "If you have these two men go to bed together it will take away from the reconciliation between Preston and Nor-ma at the end of the book." Well, I'm not sure that Preston and Norma are reconciled, but, okay, that's the way you feel about it. This was Bob Gottlieb's doing. Now listen, if somebody who has been editing longer than you've been alive says change something and they're paying you a dollar a word, you listen.

They had already done about two weeks' worth of editing on the story—maybe a week's worth—and then together we did a week's worth of editing. And they called me up and said, "Well, this is the last thing we want you to do." I wasn't going to say, "Oh, listen, Mr. Gottlieb, I am a gay man and I know what these people would be doing." I'm supposed to defend a finally indefensible point? I left my office, I went out to lunch, I thought, What am I going to do? How am I going to rewrite this? I don't know. I picked up *Friend of My Youth* by Alice Munro, read about two paragraphs—she's a lovely writer—and *click*, something happened in my head.

It was the Paul Taylor season, a choreographer I'm crazy for, and he was doing his signature piece, *Esplanade*, which is a very glorious piece on the surface. But I remember the first time I saw it, it broke my heart—I don't know why. I talked to a friend at Taylor's, and Taylor had said it was a piece about the difficulty of love. And I went home, I put Bach on—the violin concertos—and what I thought would take hours of writing took ten minutes. I called up the *New Yorker* and said, "I've got the rewrites," and they said, "You did that too quickly. Sleep on it." I slept on it. I rearranged two lines and turned it in. And that's all it was.

As soon as I realized that those two men weren't on the bed together, stuff came pouring out—and stuff that I had taken out of the original, that's not in the book, I put back in. Things that I feared being too sentimental, like the line about what you've built your human life upon—the foundations crumbling below you—and then falling and being terrified at the depth of your own feeling. I put that back in. And moved some lines as well. And I made it, I think, cleaner; and I think I made it sadder. And more acceptance on the part of Preston of his illness, and the fact that, finally, things happen in the past and that's why they happen and that's it. They don't change.

What gay writers do you read? Earlier you mentioned to me Thom Gunn and Robert Ferro.

Well, I knew Robert. I don't think any of us—we're still such a young movement—I don't think yet that we're looking at one another for influence. The first time I read *Men on Men*, I was startled at the diversity of our voices and thought, You don't have to write like Edmund White; you don't have to write like Andrew Holleran. You could write the way you want to write and still be a gay writer. That was a very liberating experience. I try to read us all, but, Jesus, go into a gay bookstore anymore and try to find a book to read. There are so many you don't know where to start. So you don't read any of them. Read Alice Munro.

I think that Gunn is a gay writer, but he's also one of the best poets of this last half of the century. Auden. We all read Isherwood, I hope. I don't know. I can't say that I steal a lot from my gay brothers.

What are your writing habits like?

When I write full-time, when I can do that, that's what I do. I don't even like to eat. I mean, I love to eat, but I don't take the time. I wrote a lot of the book on Fire Island during the week when everybody was gone. Last summer, on the weekends I would come back into the city so that I could stay in my head, because . . . so many voices! And everything can crowd out what you've got up here [*points to his head*].

You took a house with friends?

Friends? Ah, use that term loosely! I just wrote constantly. Last summer, at the end of the summer, when I felt that I was finished with the book, and I'd walk along the beach, people would say, "Oh, are you out for the weekend?" Been here all summer. I just holed up to finish the book. I want to do that again. Reclusion. Total. I just found that I like that. I've told this to other friends—people I went to Columbia with who never wrote anything—I said, "Well, you just never created that time and that space to write, to create." You've got to close out everybody. Initially it's a painful thing to do. Finally, it's an extremely rewarding thing.

How about a sketch of your emergence as a gay person?

I was sixteen years old. I knew what I was, but there wasn't anything to do about it. Right? And I went to a local public library, and there were three books on the shelf, and I took them out. Unfortunately, I had forgotten my library card, so I had to sign for them. I put my name on three gay books. I remember when I put the books down on the counter, the librarian, a young woman who was very brittle and I never liked anyway, looked at the books, and her face snapped at me, and then back to the books, and then she became very nervous. I took out Donn Teal's *The Gay Militants*, Dennis Altman's *[Homosexual] Oppression and Liberation*, and

Gordon Merrick's *The Lord Won't Mind*. That's all that was available. That was '71, I guess. Yeah, '71.

I took them home and learned in one weekend that gay was a political thing, and that a political movement had started with Stonewall, and that a man could fuck another man and that the man who was getting fucked could like it. So that was a lot to learn in one weekend. And I've never forgotten those two lessons.

What did you do with that information at age sixteen?

Not a whole hell of a lot. I turned seventeen weeks later and went to the University of Iowa for a drama workshop for high school students. There were two girls in the workshop who were obviously lesbians, who . . . This wave of nostalgia! It was in many ways so much sweeter than it is now with everybody being an activist and all this self-righteous anger.

But Kitty—what was her name? Kit? And what was the other one? I can't remember—wore Keds and they had drawn with Bic pens the feminist symbols on their shoes. We were talking about feminism and liberation. At sixteen, seventeen, right? I think Kit was probably thirteen. I said, "Well, if you're really interested in liberation you should read *Homosexual Oppression and Liberation,* by Dennis Altman," and the table went absolutely silent. And I thought, Maybe I've gone too far.

A few days later, the RA—you know, the resident advisor of the boys' floor—knocked on my door. This was a man I had a big crush on. He was ancient to me; he was twenty-six years old. He had a beautiful smile, mustache, sun tan. Oh, I just wanted him so much. I was so horny, as we all were. He said, "I just wanted to tell you that there are people who are talking and saying that you're gay." And I said, "I don't care what they're talking about me behind my back. I'll never see these people again." You know, the bravura of the seventeen-year-old. And he said, "Well, I just want you to know that if you need anything, I'm here for you." And I thought, Yeah, you're a married man. Little good you're going to do me. And he said, "A lot of people say that they've never had a homosexual experience, and they're lying." And I said, "Well, thank you very much for your attention and I'll keep that in mind," and he closed the door.

To make a long story short, the workshop ended. I went to visit friends who lived [nearby], and then I came back to the campus because they were doing a production of *Madame Butterfly* and we high school kids had been slave labor on the scenery, and this man [i.e., the resident advisor] had invited me to spend the night with him in his room. He went out to dinner that night and I went to my first gay lib meeting.

At the University of Iowa?

Yeah. I remember going to this meeting and seeing—I haven't thought about this in years!—two of the most beautiful men I'd ever seen in my life sitting next to each other. One was obviously a football player—big, beefy, dark—God, as beautiful as the day is long; and his boyfriend was blond and not quite so handsome, but very handsome, obviously the intellectual type. And they were just together and there was a way that one had his hand resting on the other's knee. Not like *this*, you know, with the hand grasped on the knee, but just resting there, with the fingers up like a Renaissance painting, that just sank into my consciousness.

I got home that night. Larry, the RA, was asleep, naked under the sheet. I wanted to take the sheet back and just look at him. I went to sleep, and I woke up at six o'clock. He was leaving on a day trip with a friend. He was shaving at the sink. I wanted to say, "Nice ass, Larry." And I went back to sleep. Then I woke up, he was gone, it was time to go back to Joliet. I didn't have anything to do for a couple of hours before the bus came. In the room, the bookshelves were on a single shelf about a foot down from the ceiling. And I thought, Well, I'll look at his books. I climbed onto a chair, took a book, opened it up, and it was homosexual science-fiction S and M pornography.

I read it with a raging hard-on, put it back. My head just went like this [*drops forehead to table*] to his desk. I got off the chair, opened the drawer, pulled out the brown envelope. I mean, there was nothing in between. What was inside but magazines of sixteen-year-olds, bound and gagged, or posed along river streams and tree trunks, and Michelangelo sonnets. My one chance! My first chance—real chance—for sex, and I didn't get it.

He was waiting for you to make the first move?

Probably. I'm sure he's not married anymore. Unless he was married to a lesbian at that time. Which actually would not surprise me.

Now with our gay consciousness today, you'd think a man who's a camp counselor at a camp for drama kids, who's away from his wife for the summer, and comes up to a sixteen-year-old and says, "I'm here if you need me . . ."

It was all there. The other thing about the gay consciousness was that in 1985, I founded an organization called The Gay and Lesbian Alliance Against Defamation [GLAAD]. We all take credit for founding it together—a bunch of writers—but it was my idea. And I ran into Gregory Kolovakis, and knew that Gregory was a great organizer and had a lot of connections. I told Gregory my idea, because we had problems. There was a lot of crap going on, a lot of antigay feelings going on because of the epidemic. I said, "Listen, I'll have a dinner party. I'll do the kitchen, you work the room." So I called these people up and that's what happened: I'm doing the chicken and at one point I walked into my kitchen and Vito Russo was literally sitting in my sink. He wasn't sitting *on* the sink, his ass was in the sink. And he was talking about GAA [Gay Activist's Alliance]. So we decided to have a meeting, and people were going to call their friends. And there was all those people I had read about in *The Gay Militants*—there was Arnie Kantrowitz, Marty Robinson, Jim Olds—and it was one of the happiest moments of my life, to be in the same room with those men. That was really wonderful.

My early vision of GLAAD was what ACT UP would become, but I think we were a little ahead of our time. I think our one strategic mistake was, Let's have these little board meetings, let's keep the rest of the people off because we'll never get through, there'll be a lot of arguing, and we'll run this. We weren't having secret meetings or anything, but we just did not envision that mass meetings were going to be the thing of the future. Who could have known? And if you'd already lived through that, you didn't want to go through it again. That it has been as successful as it has been is extraordinary and something that nobody could have predicted.

What's the extent of your activism now?

I do a lot of stuff for GMHC. And I'm glad that ACT UP exists. I couldn't become as involved in it as others have. I suspect that a lot of the best stuff that ACT UP does is done by the committees and people working closely together. But all the time I'm thankful that there is an ACT UP and that there's a GMHC, two organizations I've railed against myself. Let me tell you, at one of our first meetings of GLAAD I said, "Let's have a demonstration at St. Pat's," and they all laughed at me. That these young kids could come along and say, "Let's have a demonstration at St. Pat's" and pull it off—what can I criticize them for? They did it. Nobody told them they couldn't.

The
WOMR
Interviews

(1993)

Christopher Bram, New York, New York, 1988

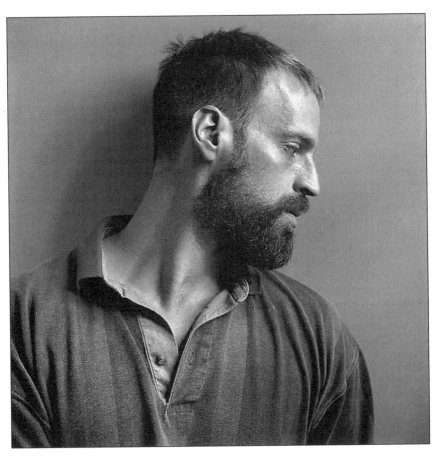

Lev Raphael, Okemos, Michigan, 1993

Michael Nava, Los Angeles, California, 1988

Michael Cunningham, New York, New York, 1991

John Preston, Boston, Massachusetts, 1988

Andrew Holleran, New York, New York, 1985

Christopher Bram

The author of six highly respected novels, Christopher Bram was born in 1952 in Buffalo, New York. When he was still young, his family settled in Norfolk, Virginia. Bram took a bachelor's degree in English at the College of William and Mary, graduating in 1974. In 1978, he moved to New York, where he still resides, in Greenwich Village. During his early years in New York, he worked at odd jobs, including typesetting for the *New York Native*, but he is now able to write full-time. He also writes occasional screenplays and book and movie reviews.

What is most impressive in Bram's fiction is the psychological and emotional accuracy with which he portrays his characters, and the complex moral vision of his stories. His novels are about ordinary gay people trying to be decent and good in a morally compromised world. He focuses on the often conflicting claims of friendship, family, love, and desire; the ways good intentions can become confused and thwarted; and the ways we learn to become vulnerable and human.

The interview that follows incorporates two conversations that I have had with Bram. The first, occasioned by his appearance in Boston to read from his novel, *In Memory of Angel Clare*, took place in the Harvard Business School office of his friend Mary Gentile, on a hot afternoon in the summer of 1989. It was, according to Bram, only the second interview he had ever given. An abridged version of the interview was published in *Bay Windows*, 18 January 1990.

The second interview was taped on 12 June 1993, in a recording studio at WOMR in Provincetown, Massachusetts. With that interview, the summer-long recording of the radio show called *The Word is Out: Gay and Lesbians Writers and Their Fiction* was launched. Each program was recorded in advance, then edited for broadcast later that season.

Bram seemed a natural choice for the inaugural program. After our first meeting, I kept reading more of his work, continuing to admire the craftsmanship, the scope, the humor, and the knack he had for finding interesting material in the lives of ordinary gay people. In the winter of

1992 and 1993, Len Bowen, the producer of *The Word is Out*, and I began kicking around names of writers we wanted to invite to participate in the series; Chris Bram's was the first I suggested.

At the time of the WOMR interview, Bram had just published his fourth novel, *Almost History*. Here his love of history found full expression in a sprawling tale that covers thirty-five years and two hemispheres, with a cast that includes Richard Nixon, and Ferdinand and Imelda Marcos, and a plot that weaves in the Vietnam War, inauguration night parties in D.C., and Philippine politics. Perhaps most significant, the novel looks at the life of an older gay man, Jim Goodall, a subject that is rarely explored in gay fiction.

Since our second interview, Bram, a prolific writer, has gone on to publish two other novels, *Father of Frankenstein* and *Gossip*. A film version of *Father of Frankenstein*, entitled *Gods and Monsters* (Regent Pictures), directed by Bill Condon and starring Ian McKellan and Brendan Fraser, was released in 1998.

I want to begin by asking you about your first novel, Surprising Myself. *In a lot of ways* Surprising Myself *could be called a "coming-out novel," but you take it one step further, following Joel's life well beyond his discovery of his gay self. Why did you make that decision to extend the novel?*

I found it more interesting. Joel has come out by page 100—it's a 400-page novel—and I wanted to explore the next steps, primarily his relationship with his first lover Corey. Nobody was really writing about this yet. The book was published in 1987. I had finished writing it in '85—it took me two years to get it published. To most publishers, gay fiction meant books like *Dancer From the Dance*, by Andrew Holleran, or *Faggots*, by Larry Kramer. These are two books that I like very much, but they weren't my life. I wanted to write about my life and the importance of developing a relationship, finding out just what sort of balance of how much you can keep of yourself and still be committed to another person. And so the focus of the novel became on that kind of life after coming out.

Do you think that coming out novels are young novels? Are they the kinds of novels that young gay novelists write? Is there a place for the coming out novel in an older, more established gay novelist's career?

I think so. It will be interesting to see what happens next. Originally, in the first gay novels—*Dancer From the Dance*, the classic of the novels that we began to see in the late seventies—the basic story line is a coming-out story. Coming out is such an important trope. Not just coming out as a gay person, it has so many parallels with other experiences of accepting yourself and discovering yourself that it's something that you can't help but write out. It's a very important experience for every gay and lesbian person. So it's inevitable that it's going to be written about. It will be interesting to see if people who have written their first novels about other things then come back and do a coming-out novel. I can't think of anyone who's done that yet, but it's very imaginable.

One thing that I find interesting in many of your novels is that there is that coming-out "trope." It's not the central focus of the novel, but it's certainly an important aspect to the novel, the discovery of oneself as a gay man.

Yeah, in some cases I wasn't aware until afterwards that I'd written a coming-out story. In my second novel, *Hold Tight,* which is set in New York City in 1942, the main character there, Hank Fayette, is a farm boy from Texas. He's in his early twenties, and sex with men is just something he does naturally. He doesn't think of himself as gay; it's just something that he likes. In effect, his coming out there is not really just his accepting himself; it's his understanding that that's not how people see him, understanding that he's a minority and he can be punished, and his friends can be punished for this. His coming-out experience is a discovery of the pain attached.

With few exceptions, you write novels almost exclusively. What attracts you to the novel as a literary form?

I find them much easier to write than short stories. I'm in awe of short story writers. I'm one of those writers who needs a couple hundred pages just to get somebody from one side of the room to the other. I'm exaggerating there, but I'm really amazed how some people can, with one line, suggest all these different aspects, where it will take me several chapters to get into a character and to make that clear to the reader.

Novels to me are like laboratories where I work out my own fears and desires, and discover them in the course of writing them. In a short story, for me there's not as much space to discover and invent; there's not as much breathing room. And I need that breathing room.

Do you continue to write short stories?

I'm not a very good short story writer. Originally, "Aphrodisiac" went on for twenty pages beyond where it stops now. It took me several drafts to realize where the story was.

Do you feel you're a more natural novel writer than short story writer?

I think I have more of the vegetative temperament a novelist needs. I work better in the "long haul," where you move in with a set of characters and a situation for a year or so. I'm stumped by how a short story works, by the quickness with which it can get something across.

What's your history as a writer, and specifically as a gay writer?

I started seriously writing fiction when I was in college. When I was in college, my original desire had been to be a movie director. I even wrote a few scripts. But I understood early on that you need a lot of money to make a movie, but to turn a script into, say, a short story, all you need is some time and a typewriter and some paper. So I began writing these stories for movies that were never made. And I was quite happy with that.

Did you major in film, or English?

In English, but if I had to do it all over again I think I'd major in history.

Why?

Well, because the way you learn to read books in a college English literature class is not the way you write. So you have to spend a couple of years unlearning all that, Oh, what sort of a network of symbols should I set up? and things like that. Of course, that sort of stuff will come up, but it comes up unconsciously, by accident.

Interestingly, I was able to write gay stories even before I could accept that I was gay. I kind of came out to myself as a gay writer before I came out to myself as a gay man. I could tell myself all these little lies like, Gee, what an interesting subject this is! Isn't this neat? And then I would publish these stories under my name in the college literary magazine, without any kind of shame or embarrassment.

Afterwards I tried sending a few stories off here and there, but I was never able to get published until *Christopher Street* published "Aphrodisiac" around 1978. Their publishing that story helped me to become a gay writer.

How so?

Well, I'd written a novel, which I was never able to publish, your standard a-bunch-of-friends-who-go-out-drinking-every-night novel, the kind of novel that almost every male seems to write. It was fairly straight, although there was a gay subtext to it that I was only half conscious of. So I told myself that, if I wasn't going to get published, in the next book I might as well write what I want to write. At the same time, "Aphrodisiac" was published and it seemed that there was a readership out there for this, and so I started *Surprising Myself*.

Had you been hiding your gayness before you wrote "Aphrodisiac"?

Not really. I was already out to most of my friends and one of my sisters, but I used the story to come out to my brother and another sister: I sent them copies. That was very convenient. I told them, "Any questions you have, just feel free to ask."

Is "Aphrodisiac" at all autobiographical?

No. At one point, it had been conceived as a dialogue about socialism. But I became much more interested in the people who were having this dialogue than the dialogue itself, and that became the center. It was basically about a young, heterosexual married couple in Richmond, Virginia, who both fall in love with a young socialist politician, and are using this love as an aphrodisiac for their marriage: as a turn on, as a new excitement.

Do you think that in turning to gay subject matter in "Aphrodisiac" you somehow unlocked your talent?

Oh, definitely. It was an unlocking. I was able to write using my unconscious self more. I was able to let things spring out of each other. [When *Christopher Street* took it], it was at that moment that I realized, I can write about being gay and get published. I can write about what's important to me and succeed as a writer.

It's really two or three publications like Christopher Street *that have given lots of aspiring gay writers their first audience and their first publication.[1] And, as you say, how important it has been for gay writers to discover that their subject*

---

1. A few years after this interview, *Christopher Street* ceased publication.

*matter and their stories are not only important to them, but do have an audi-
ence out there eagerly awaiting those stories.*

I remember once talking to Michael Denneny about that. Michael was one
of the founders of *Christopher Street* magazine. I think their first issue was
in 1976. And he was saying that, at the time, when he and Chuck Ortleb
and a couple of other people were putting it all together, they assumed that
there was going to be all sorts of gay and lesbian work out there that was
just waiting to be published. But when they started the magazine they
found out, *no*, that because there was no outlet for it, nobody was writing
it. And it was after the first few years of publication that people, now that
they had a place to publish it, seriously began to write it.

You published your first novel, Surprising Myself, *relatively late. You were—
what?—close to thirty-five when it was published?*

I was thirty-five.

*Were those early years before the publication of your first novel discouraging?
What were they like? What did you tell yourself to keep yourself going during
those years when you weren't being published?*

Oh, God! Looking back on it, I'm amazed that I was so pigheaded that
I could keep at it. I had two unpublished novels. I eventually had a third
novel that became *Hold Tight*. Sometimes I felt like I was deluding myself. I felt like I was Wile E. Coyote, who has run off the edge of the cliff
and hasn't noticed that he stands in midair. At the same time, there was
nothing else that I wanted to do as much as write fiction. I really enjoyed it even when I wasn't getting published. I would have occasional
attacks of masochism where I would even take pride in having two unpublished novels in my filing cabinet. Then there were times when it
would catch up with you. It's a tricky thing to talk about or even remember, because I'm making it sound like I was much sunnier than I
really was.

If *Surprising Myself* hadn't gotten published, I might have gone on
into something else. I'd already begun reviewing movies and books for
first the *New York Native* and later *Premier* magazine. I might be a movie
reviewer today, instead of a novelist, if *Surprising Myself* hadn't been
picked up.

What were you reading during those formative years? What gay books were you finding to read?

All the usual suspects. Many books that I reacted against or rejected. Oh, *Other Voices, Other Rooms* by Truman Capote; *The City and the Pillar* by Gore Vidal, where one man remains in love with another man for his whole life and then, at the end of the novel, when he finds the other man is straight, he kills him. This was in the original version, which I read; later Gore Vidal relented and softened it, and he only rapes him.

But then I began to stumble across books that were much closer to my own experience, that I could really respond to. One of the most important ones was a short story by Jonathan Strong called "Supperburger," which was printed in his collection, *Tyke and Five Stories*. It's about a young man in Boston, in the sixties, who becomes involved with an older man. The whole tone and world of the story—it's very much the street life of the sixties—these were people I knew; this was my life. I realized that being gay or writing about gay subjects is not a case of having to wear tuxedos, or being evil and gothic and sinister, or you don't have to be Baron Charlus—you can just be yourself.

Then I remember, later on, one of the first gay anthologies was *The Other Persuasion*, edited by Seymour Kleinberg. It was the first place I read Edmund White. He had a short story there titled "The Beautiful Room is Empty," which turned out to be no relation at all to the novel he later published on that title. More important to me was a short story by Jane Rule called "Middle Children" about two women who meet in college as roommates and immediately very easily and naturally develop a relationship and become lovers; and then they find that that's not enough—just the two of them—living alone without other people. They want more. And they try several things and eventually buy a very large house and basically kind of staff it with their friends and students—gay and straight—so they're surrounded by this wonderful mix of people. I found that genuinely exciting, really satisfying. It was both the life I wanted for myself and the type of fiction I wanted to write, too.

One of the things that impressed me very much when I read Almost History *is the voice of Jim and the character of Jim. At one point, he's reviewing his life and he says, "'I think I wanted to play a lead in* Lawrence of Arabia. *I ended up with a bit part in* The Godfather.*'" So many of your characters are ordinary people, not particularly glamorous or important. One might call them bit players in the theater of life, not the leading men and women. What attracts you to write about such ordinary, decent gay people?*

It's because it's the life I know and the life that I think most of my readers know, that most of us know. There's an antiromantic streak in my writing, so that even when I'm writing about something—like [in *Almost History*] with the state department, the Marcoses—I want to bring it down to our level of life. I'm not writing a Tom Clancy novel here. Not very many people get a chance to save the world. What they do is get trapped in these lives which are mixtures of compromise, good intentions, and sometimes good things can happen from them [but] they're going to be small things, minor things that can influence and effect the immediate community of friends around them, and sometimes, if they're lucky, a larger community, but nothing global, none of the fantastic. I want to bring things down to the level of everyday life.

What attracts you to historical themes and historical settings?

I'm not sure. I love history. I almost went to graduate school in history instead of becoming a novelist. I love to read history, I love the stories. I love the perspective of history, the sense of development and change over a long period of time. And, as a writer, I also have to admit that I feel freer when I'm writing about the past than I do about present. There's something about writing about the present that you know the reality so well, and you know what could and couldn't happen. When I'm writing about the past—even the recent past, the 1950s or 1940s—some of that knowledge lifts a little and I'll take more chances.

It's funny; in *Hold Tight*, the main character, Hank Fayette, ends up having to work for the government in a male brothel, as a male prostitute. And for some reason the fact that this happens in 1942 [meant] I was much more willing to risk doing that than if I was talking about someone who was working as a prostitute in 1993. I'd be going, Oh, God, what do I know about being a prostitute? Who can I talk to? Can I get into that person's head. But because I'm already having to make this leap back in time, questions like that become far less important. It liberates me as a writer.

One of the ways in which you do take risks and do a lot of imaginative writing is in the creation of Gus Luna, the gay Filipino, who is Imelda Marcos's hairdresser in Almost History. *You recently took some criticism for portraying a gay Filipino. The argument went that since you're not a gay Filipino, how could you possibly write about one? What response to you have to that kind of criticism?*

This criticism was made at a panel in New York City, a Center for Lesbian and Gay Studies/PEN panel. The man making them, who was Asian, respected what I was doing, but he felt I had slipped into a couple of Asian stereotypes. He cited them and I answered as best I could. The conversation continued after the panel. He came up to me and said that what his real criticism was is that there are so few presentations of gay Asians in fiction that he wanted one who was heroic, who was good. And Gus is a mess. Gus is not heroic. He's married, he has two children, he's very irresponsible. He's not a bad person, but in the situation he's in, he will always opt for the easiest way. And the man who was talking to me said he understood that, but he wanted a gay Asian hero, he wanted somebody who was Asian who was presented the way Juke, the black character in *Hold Tight,* had been presented, or, he said, even Hank in *Hold Tight.* And I can see that. I wasn't really sure how to respond to that, because there are just so few gay Asian characters in fiction.

Recently, in the most recent *Men on Men* collection, there's an amazing story called "Cultural Revolution," by Norman Wong, about a Chinese American teenager who goes with his father back to mainland China. What's exciting about it is that we're seeing the point of view and the experience of somebody we haven't heard from before, and we need to hear from them.[2]

You're touching on an even larger issue, certainly within the gay and lesbian writing community, and that is the extent to which we as gay and lesbian writers have a responsibility to portray positive images of gay and lesbian people. Is that an absolute responsibility?

No, I don't think it's an absolute. And it can be not just a limiting but a dangerous responsibility. The thing is, it becomes necessary in cases

---

2. Norman Wong went on to publish a collection of stories, entitled *Cultural Revolution,* about a gay Chinese American man.

where . . . for so long there we no representations of this at all except occasionally as villains. Those gay psycho killers: there don't seem to be many of them anymore, but in the seventies, in film and fiction, they were rampant. That was virtually the only type of gay character you ever saw—a killer. Today, there are enough more varied representations of gay and lesbian characters that . . . I mean, for many people, *Silence of the Lambs*, it didn't bother them at all. Some people still became upset, but for many it wasn't a problem.

Most of my gay characters are very problematic. Jim Goodall is a very difficult man. Joel Scherzenlieb, the narrator of my first novel, can be a real ass at times. As a writer, I'm attracted to difficult people. And I want the freedom to be able to write about difficult people.

As a writer, do you feel any limitations with your gay subject matter?

No, I don't really. I find it so rich. There are many things that haven't been explored yet. Right now I'm interested in how homosexuality interfaces with, say, a family. That gets us to the dirty word: "crossover" novel. I'm not out conscientiously to cover two markets—the family novel market and the gay market—with one novel. But it's a very interesting subject.

Do you think you might ever write a novel in which gay characters or gay themes are not predominant?

I can't really imagine it, just because for me writing about a gay person or a gay experience gives me a toehold into a story, a place to enter. And so, from the gay perspective, that gay point of view, I can look out on all manner of things around it. In *Almost History*, I get quite a bit into American foreign policy, on both its most abstract and its most practical levels. But I needed to be able to see that through gay eyes. Once I had that, I could write about any number of things.

So many gay and lesbian writers hope to write what some people call the "crossover novel," a book that will appeal to straight readers as well as gay readers. Is finding a crossover audience important to you as a writer?

Not really, I've stopped thinking about it. I think the audience is eventually going to come to us. When we deliberately go to them we lose our strengths, our material becomes diluted. Eventually, as we write honestly about our experience—in all its many shades and variations, the parts of our experience that are specifically gay and the parts of our experience that anyone else could connect with, too—as long as we do that, the audience is going to come to us.

Do you think that there is, or should be, any difference between gay fiction and so-called more mainstream fiction?

Well, lately I've begun to wonder if there really is such a thing as the "mainstream." I think, particularly in the past five, eight years, that assumption has scattered, has just broken apart. Reading reviews from the fifties and sixties—"mainstream" really meant white, male. And then there would be a couple of women included, too, that were . . . "Well, they're not women writers; they're as good as real writers." I was recently reading some reviews from the seventies and came across a review of Diane Johnson's novel *Lying Low,* which I think is a wonderful novel. It's about three women in northern California in the seventies, and it was being discussed as a "woman's novel," as if it would interest you only if you were interested in "the woman question." That sounds so silly and idiotic to us now. And this was only, like, fifteen years ago that novels by women were being discussed that way.

Now, somebody like Jane Smiley, somebody like Bharati Mukherjee—you don't even say, Oh, she's a woman writer and she's concentrating on women. It's not important to us, as we see that through this experience they're exploring all these other things as well?

Are we moving in that direction with books by gay and lesbian writers?

I hope so. It's still a ways off yet, but by the end of the century I think we might be seeing that.

You've also done some screenwriting, right?

I recently finished a screenplay for an independent producer based on David Leavitt's *The Lost Language of Cranes.* I don't know what's going to happen with it.[3] I met Leavitt while I was working on it and told him that he might not like the screenplay but that one thing I wanted him to know right off is that I really respected the book the more I worked on it. It's a

---

3. In the end, Bram's screenplay was not used for the film version of Leavitt's novel.

very gay novel. In fact, one of the strangest things about the project is that the producer wanted me to make it less gay. I thought, Hold it, he's bringing in a gay novelist to make *The Lost Language of Cranes* less gay!

You write very beautifully and honestly and accurately about gay sex. Is writing about sex hard to do? What are the pitfalls involved?

In a way, I find that's it's weirdly easy for me to write about sex. I find it might easier to write about sex than to talk about it. I can be far more confessional when I'm pretending to be somebody else than when I'm myself.

Also, in *Surprising Myself,* there's a fifteen-page sex scene between Joel and his lover Corey—at this point they've been together for four years—and to describe a scene between two people who have been together so long, there's all these other emotions and memories that are happening. It just expanded, it just kept going. As long as the sex scene was expressing something, as long as there was drama going on, it was very natural to me, both fun to write and exciting. At the time I was writing, I was thinking, My God, this is fifteen pages long! But when I read it through, it never seemed mechanical, it always seemed alive. I think in all my sex scenes, as long as something else was happening, as long as something was being expressed—whether it was love, or in a couple of cases hate—that it held together, that it was real, that it both satisfied and emotionally excited me.

It seems impossible today to talk about gay fiction without talking about AIDS and AIDS fiction. Do you think that it's possible to write a gay novel today and not have AIDS figure in it?

If it has a contemporary setting then, no, you've got to have some acknowledgment of it. It would be interesting to see a novel where AIDS is present, but not in the foreground. In Gary Indiana's new novel, *Horse Crazy,* AIDS is just in the background; it's a very thick background. I think there will be more of that.

One thinks of Jane Austen and those five novels she wrote during the Napoleonic Wars that never overtly mention them. Maybe that kind of novel, that kind of life—so insulated from the outside world and its crises—is just not possible today.

Well, there are all those naval officers that come and go in her novels, but you're right, you never hear what they're up to. It's interesting that in the nineteenth century almost no novels had contemporary settings; they were always set fifteen or twenty years before—as a cooling effect, or something like that.

What is AIDS fiction, exactly, and why do we need it?

The AIDS epidemic right now is the most important thing happening in our lives. It can't help but affect us. And we need to address it. It's very difficult to know how to address it. Do we address it head on? As I said in my essay for the *Lambda Book Report,* what can you do with this story except to redo the death of Little Nell in Dickens' *The Old Curiosity Shop?* Well, we know that's not what we need. And what we need is ways to understand how we think about it, how we confront it, how we avoid it. What sort of emotions we're letting build up when we don't talk about it. You hear a lot of gay people saying today, "Oh, I live with AIDS everyday; I don't need to read about it." And they actually have a case, they have a point, and yet I think that AIDS can be louder in fiction that pretends it's not there than when it's openly addressed. I'm still working things out about it.

Two of my novels are historical novels than have taken place pre-AIDS.[4] I've had people say to me, "Well, did you do that deliberately so you wouldn't have to write about AIDS?" No, it's just the subject, the time period would interest me. What I did find that was happening sometimes is that AIDS was entering into it; it was reaching backwards.

In *Almost History* there's a scene where Gus Luna has been tortured, and Jim has custody of him. Jim is trapped within his house. And the scars on Gus's body, Jim's feeling of helplessness—when I was writing the scene, I felt very depressed about it, and I realized only afterwards it was just so much like what I experienced with friends who'd been sick, and taking care of them. It's not just that AIDS is a metaphor; there's something else going on there that taps into and connects with feelings of helplessness as well as those of rage and fear.

---

4. *Father of Frankenstein,* which was published after this interview, was Bram's third novel to be set in a time before AIDS.

In many of your books, you depict a constellation of gay men, and sometimes their lesbian friends, that could be considered to be a family, a gay family. What does family as a theme mean to you, and why does it keep surfacing in your fiction?

Part of the reason that it keeps surfacing is that it's dramatically interesting when you have not just two people who are alone together but two people that are part of a constellation of other people, and all the different lights and shades and sparks that come off of that. And it's what I know from real life, too, from my everyday life, and I find that it's satisfying and as frustrating as your biological family. It's part of the thick cake of things.

Part of that thick cake of things is the urban landscape of New York, which figures prominently in several of your novels. In Surprising Myself, *you call New York "the capital of the twentieth century." What does New York mean for you?*

Well, it's a great subject; there's just so much of it. I've been in New York for twelve years now, and I keep seeing different aspects of it. I like the energy. I like all the bookshops that are available, I like all the movie theaters. I like the very different types of people you're able to be. New York is so wonderfully theatrical. It's an enormous stage where people accidentally run into each other all the time. And the scale of the place is so elastic. You can go from an encounter among a small circle of friends who'd be perfectly at home in any small town to a mammoth rally or dance that would be possible only in a big city. Of course, much of that is true of any urban area, but it seems more public in New York, where so few people have cars. At the same time, I've decided that I've done New York in three books and that the next one—whatever it is—I'd rather it not be in New York.[5] Sometimes you get a feeling that there are so many writers in New York, all writing *about* New York, and that the ground has been worked over with knitting needles.

At the same time, I haven't quite seen anyone writing about the New York that I know, which is a little frumpy—nothing glitzy, not exactly academic. My milieu is sort of the milieu that you'd be able to find

---

5. In fact, the next three Bram novels, *Almost History, Father of Frankenstein,* and *Gossip,* were not set in New York.

in any medium-to-large city. Except for some details, *Angel Clare* could take place in Philadelphia or Boston or Chicago.

A lot of people would say that an artist, a writer—maybe particularly a gay artist or gay writer—has to live in New York to catch the pulse, to catch what's happening currently. How do you feel about that? Is New York essential for a gay writer?

No, I don't think it is essential. I think it's even less essential now than it was fifteen years ago. I would like to read some fiction about life not even in the city but in, like, Connecticut towns where there's gay communities, where there's these incestuous little networks of friends and lovers who, even when they've had a big fight, end up having to be each other's best friend, because there's nobody else to turn to. I find that exciting.

One of the things that was very exciting about the March on Washington this year [1993] was the large numbers of openly gay people and gay organizations in places from all over the country—from Arkansas, from Georgia, even outside Atlanta. Gay life has spilled over from a few big cities into the smaller towns, these smaller cities. I find that very exciting. I'm waiting to read about it.

What are your working habits like?

I'm a workaholic. I get up, drink coffee, read until ten o'clock, and then sit down to the typewriter and work until . . . well, if the work is going badly, I'll stop at three, and, if it's going well, I'll work until five. I'm very lucky in that I'm able to write full-time. A year and a half ago, I was able to quit my part-time job, so I do nothing but write now.

And you told me earlier that you don't work from an outline.

Not anymore. I'll use notes, but I've found that if you outline it you know how it's going to end. I'll start off with a situation and the characters, and I'll kind of know where I'll be going for the next couple of chapters, and have some vague idea or something in the distance, but working without an outline makes you more interested in the writing because you want to find out how it's going to end. There are problems with that method. *Surprising Myself* was originally seven hundred pages long. Then I got smart and cut it.

David Plante said in an interview that writing a novel is like putting together something out of Lincoln Logs in the dark: you have no idea what you have until you finish and can turn on the light. And that really is what it's like. With each of my novels, I would know there were good things in there, but I didn't know if they worked as a novel until I finished, and could show them to one of my friends.

Do you think of yourself as part of a larger community of gay writers?

I don't know many; it's strange. The writer I'm friendliest with is Steve Mc-Cauley up here. Let's see, in New York, I run into Dave Feinberg all the time.[6] And Joel Redon, who wrote a very good novel called *Bloodstream*, about a man with AIDS who goes home to live with his family. I knew Joel when we were both typesetters for the *Native*.

What would you say are the primary values or qualities you look for in good writing?

A kind of emotional honesty. Emotion that's not claiming more for itself than it should. Good prose. And a certain self-critical quality: stories where the characters aren't gods or angels, but very human, flawed people. I like novels that grant everybody their say.

What advice would you give to a young gay writer today?

Oh, first off, be pigheaded. Just keep trying. Don't believe rejection letters. When somebody writes you a rejection letter, all they're saying is, "This isn't what I'm looking for right now." Any judgments they have beyond that, they're trying to be helpful, but they're not particularly sincere. And just to keep at it, that the support of a few friends, being able to have a few people who can read your work and respond to it, both critically and supportively, is very useful, is really necessary. It can help you grow as a writer.

---

6. Among McCauley's novels are *The Object of My Affection, Easy Way Out,* and *Man of the House;* David Feinberg wrote *Eighty-Sixed* and *Spontaneous Combustion.*

Lev Raphael

Lev Raphael's debut collection of stories, *Dancing on Tisha B'Av* (1990), focused on the experience of being gay and Jewish. The book received laudatory notices in both the gay and straight presses, among them the *Los Angeles Times*, which praised the author's prose for being "poetic in its simplicity,"[1] and the *Washington Blade*, which said that the collection's "greatest triumphs . . . are in drawing connections between experiences in the two communities, as well as comparing the identities of each."[2] The book went on to win a Lambda Literary Award.

In the summer of 1990, in conjunction with a review of *Dancing on Tisha B'Av*, I recorded the first of what would be two interviews I had with Raphael. An abridged transcription of that conversation was published in *Bay Windows* early the following year (31 January 1991). Three years later, we taped a second, more substantial interview, part of the WOMR series. At that time, Raphael had recently published his first novel, *Winter Eyes*, a coming-of-age story about the son of Holocaust survivors.

In his review of the novel for the *Los Angeles Times* Jonathan Kirsch applauded the "intimate human dimensions" of the novel's scale. "Raphael's book resembles a piano sonata rather than a symphony," he wrote.[3]

Since that second interview, Raphael has gone on to write two mystery novels, *Let's Get Criminal* and *The Edith Wharton Murders*. He is also the author of several nonfiction books, including a study of Edith Wharton, and, with his life partner Gershen Kaufman, *Coming Out Of Shame: Transforming Gay and Lesbian Lives*.

The following transcript incorporates the majority of both interviews, leaving out only those answers that supplied repetitious information.

---

1. Faye Kellerman, "Pariahs on Parade," *Los Angeles Times Book Review*, 11 November 1990, 8.

2. Wayne Hoffman, "Gay and Jewish: Tying Together a Dual Identity," *Washington Blade*, 21 December 1990, 31.

3. Jonathan Kirsch, "Growing Up in a Family of Dark Secrets," *Los Angeles Times*, 11 November 1992, E-6.

Let's talk about your childhood in New York.

Well, where should I start? I grew up in Washington Heights, which is north of Harlem. It was a German, Jewish, and Italian neighborhood—a lot of immigrants. A lot of people came there from Germany before the war. You had a strong sense there of the effect of Nazis in Europe, you were surrounded by people who had escaped. There are still many people who live in that neighborhood who are survivors of the Holocaust. So that was something that I was aware of from a very early age. I think that colored my outlook.

I was raised a completely secular Jew. I was more a "Yiddishist," in the sense that I went to a Yiddish Sunday school. Yiddish was my first language, not English. I never set foot inside a synagogue until I was twenty-four, which was the same year I had my first gay experience. It was a watershed year.

I was raised as a Jew but not a Jew. There was always that tension for me. The kids at the public school where I went were mostly Jewish, but I didn't quite fit in, because I didn't live in the same neighborhood they did. They were German Jews; I was Eastern European. We were lower class compared to them; they were all bourgeois. I didn't really affiliate with Jewish ideas. I resisted it.

Tell me about your parents.

Mother was born in Petrograd; her father was some minor official in the first Soviet government, the Menshivik government. When the Bolsheviks took over, they fled to Poland. My father is from the eastern mountains of what used to be Czechoslovakia and are now in the Soviet Union, in the Ukraine. Mother had a very sophisticated urban life. Her mother went to college; she went to university. My father grew up in a very religious orthodox town. After the war, he gave it all up. He had absolutely no use for religion. Oh, we lit candles on Hanukkah, but I never even had a real seder until I was twenty-three, twenty-four.

Both were in concentration camps. My mother was in the Vilno ghetto from 1941 to '42, I think. She was there when the ghetto was liquidated. Only about eleven hundred people were left. She was one of them, and they went to a concentration camp in Latvia. As the front changed, they were moved closer to Germany. And she was in a forced labor camp in Germany.

My father spent part of the war pretending not to be a Jew. He had to learn how to pray in Latin. He doesn't like talking about it. He spent part of the time hiding, part of the time as a guerrilla, part of the time as slave labor in the Hungarian Army when they were fighting the Russians, and wound up finally being captured in Budapest by the Germans at a point when he said he couldn't hide any more. He wound up in Bergen-Belsen at the end of the war. If the war had gone on three or four more months, he'd be dead, too; everyone in the camps would have been dead.

My parents met in a displaced persons camp in Germany after the war. He has a sister living; she has a brother living, and maybe a few distant cousins, but aside from that *everybody* on both sides of their families was destroyed.

That was another thing growing up—not having grandparents, not having a family. There are people with enormous ethnic families who say, "Oh, I wish I'd been an only child; I wish we didn't have sixteen cousins named Bertha." But I would have liked a little of that. It was a very isolated life: my parents didn't have a lot of friends. Most of their friends were survivors, too, of course. I think that may be one reason why I have a lot of friends, people I stay in contact with.

Is it at all fair to say that the experience of being displaced persons, such as your parents had, is at all analogous to the experience that gay people have?

Oh, I think so. This is where you get into that territory where people are offended that Larry Kramer used the word "holocaust" in *Reports from the Holocaust.* I think the experiences are analogous in the sense of being a stranger, and also the sense of terrible potential threat at any time. Here we are in Provincetown, a wonderful gay town, and yet you sit down and have coffee and you overhear people talking about being punched in the street at night. You think, This could happen at any moment. It's that same sense of terror. I think that is very real. There are parallels, certainly, between the two experiences.

You went to Fordham University?

Yes, a nice Catholic school. It was through a really strange coincidence. My brother was dating a young woman who was going to Fordham, and she had a terrific writing teacher, Kristin Lauer, and she just kept raving about this writing teacher. I already knew in high school that I wanted to do creative writing classes, so I basically applied to this school so that I could work with her. She was my writing teacher over four years. I took every course she taught. She became my mentor, and twenty years later she is my best friend.

So you were writing stories and seriously considering a career as a writer before you went to college?

I don't think I was thinking of a career. I don't think it was that concrete or formed. But I've been writing fiction since about fourth or fifth grade. I'd always loved storytelling and I loved short stories from the age of nine or ten on. I wanted to do that. I think for me it was less thinking of a career and having a book, and more imitation of being like those people. It started to take shape in college—I was seventeen—when my writing teacher said, "Well, you're going to be published some day." That doesn't impress people in New York, because at seventeen in New York City everybody thinks they're going to be famous, in eight or nine ways, at least by the age of twenty. But she had a great amount of belief in me. Another person who was in that same workshop was Kevin Killian, author of *Shy* and *Bedrooms Have Windows*; and she said the same thing to him, too, that he was going to be published some day. So I think she was a good judge of talent, because she didn't say that to many students at all.

What was it like being at a Catholic university?

I wasn't very Jewish-identified then in a positive way, so I think I wouldn't have been ready to be in a very Jewish environment. It wasn't just that it was Catholic. The liberal arts campus near Lincoln Center was an ideal place to learn. There were only eleven hundred students, so all the classes, except for one or two, were very small. You got a lot of attention from teachers. I actually enjoyed being in a Catholic environment. My knowledge of Catholicism came through the culture and some literature and some friends, but in college I was surrounded by it and I think I learned a lot. I did work-study at Campus Ministries for two years, and got to know priests. It was very valuable for me.

After Fordham, you did an M.F.A. in creative writing and English at the University of Massachusetts at Amherst, and then went on to Michigan State University?

Well, I had a brief period in graduate work at the CUNY [City University of New York] Grad Center in New York doing a Ph.D., and I decided I couldn't stand living in New York. If you've ever been to Amherst—western Massachusetts really spoiled me for living in New York City. The year and a half I was back in New York, I just couldn't stand it. I was casting around for places to go to grad school, and one of them was the alma mater of my mentor, Kristin Lauer, at Fordham. She knew a lot of people at Michigan State, she had liked it there. And it turned out that I did, too.

When you did start writing seriously, were you writing from a gay Jewish awareness?

Not at all! When I look back at my early writing, it's very, very painful. It's ultimately painful and funny, because I was writing material that was completely distant from myself. I wanted to be P. G. Wodehouse. No one bothered to explain to me there already was one, so we didn't need another! I wanted to be English, I think, and I was a *Masterpiece Theater* junkie. I was writing a gothic novel about this woman who was locked in a tower by her piano-playing evil father. You know, she wrote poetry upstairs while he played the "Appassionata" downstairs. I was writing lots of things that really didn't connect to anything that was firsthand experience. It was really all secondhand, from other people's work.

I make fun of that now. I think part of it was imitation, and I think all writers go through phases where they copy other writers consciously or not and they're learning them. There have been times in my life when I'll find a new author and I'll read all six of her books, because I need to know how that person writes and thinks and sees the world. I think that's part of what was going on.

I really got into writing about Jewish material very, very slowly. At the University of Massachusetts at Amherst, I was not encouraged to write material that was either gay or Jewish. It was a very straight program in many ways. When I did do a Jewish story about a child of survivors, people talked about the structure, and didn't really talk about the theme. The clear message there is, we don't want to talk about this, so don't write it.

So I came to it very, very slowly. Part of it was historical: in the late seventies, children of survivors were getting a lot more attention. Helen Epstein published that book, *Children of the Holocaust*, and there was another burst of writing about the Holocaust, so the times were right for me to start thinking about its impact on my own life.

Your first story, "War Stories," was about a child of survivors.

Right. And for all the writers out there who dream of revenge on their enemies or the people who don't think much of their writing, I have the perfect story. I did this story in workshop. The class hated it. The professor hated it. And two weeks later it won the Harvey Swados Prize, which was awarded by Martha Foley, founder of *Story* magazine. She had known Hemingway and Fitzgerald and all the greats. I went up to her after the ceremony and said, "They didn't like the ending of the story." And I'll never forget, she said, "Don't change a goddamn line!" So, a week later in the writing class, the professor said, "Well, it's still not a good story. I don't care if it won a prize." Then it got published in *Redbook*. So I had this enormous potential audience, and I made a lot of money on it.

It was both wonderful affirmation and also a really bad thing to happen, because for me it reinforced the New York conception of success, which is national magazine publication, and big bucks, and prizes early, fast. I'd written the story in a day and a half, so I figured, Well, that's not bad. I'm making all this money and getting all this exposure. I could probably crank out one of these a month and live. And that's not how it works.

You were how old then?

I was only twenty-four. And I didn't publish any more fiction for about five or six years.

My parents were very deeply upset by "War Stories." Here they were trying to protect me from what they went through, and I'm writing about it. Their pain about that kept me from going as deep as I could with further stories.

Careers are strange. When I wrote "War Stories," it was the deepest and best thing I could do, but it didn't necessarily mean that I was going to get better right away. A couple different things were going on during that five-to-six-year period. I was growing as a writer and also marking time.

Now, at that time were you writing gay stories as well?

I was just starting to. The themes were very separate, they were diffuse. And when I did a gay story in one of my workshops, the people didn't talk about the gay material either. They skirted around it. In fact, one person in class was so angry that he came out. No one knew he was gay, and he said, "Well, I'm gay! And it's not like that to be gay!" And there was dead silence. People shunned him after class. It was a really strange environment. For me those themes came into my work very slowly.

I think the really good stuff started coming in 1984, when I did the first version of [the story] "Dancing on Tisha B'Av." That story grew out of something that someone said to me in 1981, that they knew a lesbian who was asked to leave a congregation out in Washington. And *Boom*, I thought, *That* is an incredible story! I must write it!

So the Jewish and the gay stories were overlapping. Those years— 1984, 1985—were a turning point. When I moved to Michigan, I came out as a Jew. As a black friend of mine once told me, "When I came to Michigan, I knew I was black." I felt so isolated in Michigan that I started doing a lot more Jewish stuff and discovering my Jewish identity. Overlapping that was a coming-out phase, too. As I became more gay, I became less Jewish, because it was difficult for me to balance those two.

Does that feel like a loss, a giving up?

No, because I'm back. I'm into a third cycle now of trying to pull both sides together, finding other gay Jews and gay Jewish organizations and joining a local synagogue as an out gay man in a couple, making it unmistakable to the rabbi that that's how we're joining. The environment now in American Judaism is very positive and receptive to gay issues. Phenomenally so. It's hard to express how exciting it is, because the reform movement not only embraces but endorses gay and lesbian rabbis, who are sexually active, who are in couples. The Reform movement recognizes that a same-sex couple is as important as a family. So the climate is right now for bringing the two—being gay and being Jewish—together. I think that the stories I'm doing now will be even better.

One of the interesting things in your work is that you bring those two coming-out experiences together.

I think a lot of young Jews deal with it in high school or college. I see it with one of my stepsons, because he is claiming a positive Jewish identity. He just went to a Jewish leadership camp. He was negative before about being Jewish, but he's finding a way that's comfortable for him. I wants to go to Israel in his junior year of high school. He's coming out as a Jew. He didn't hide it before, but he's creating an identity. I think that's where we come together—Jews and gays and lesbians. We have to create what it means to be gay, what it means to be Jewish. Probably all minorities have to do it, but it's layered differently for us because we can hide if we want to: you can change your name. If you think you have a Jewish nose, you can have it fixed. It's easy to hide.

I think many of us have an understanding of why it would take someone so long to come to a positive gay identity. Why also did it take you such a long time to come to a positive Jewish identity?

Well, my earliest memory of confronting or dealing with being Jewish was in first grade. An older kid came into the class during recess or something—I think this may have been around the time of the [Adolf] Eichmann trials; that's what I've reconstructed—and she was saying to some other kids, "They threw Jewish babies up in the air and caught them on bayonets." Well, I went home and I asked what this was about, and my parents were freaked out. That's my earliest consciousness of talking about being Jewish. I think that helped open the floodgates, so that I started learning some of what happened to my parents. My grandparents had been killed, both their families had been killed by the Nazis. So I started from a very negative place: the Jews as victims, as people who were locked up, murdered.

It's not the same for everyone, but for me it was hard to feel positive about being Jewish. I had some positive elements, but I really didn't connect. So it was a long struggle. For me, what had to happen is I had to come to a place where I understood what it meant to me to be a child of survivors. Was that going to stand in the way? Was that going to be my *whole* way of being Jewish? Would that be everything to my Jewish identity? Would it mean I couldn't be Jewish, that I rejected everything that was Jewish, or did I get beyond it?

Part of the process for me was teaching a course on holocaust literature. I read hundreds of books over a period of months, and I learned a lot that I really didn't know. I came out on the other side in a strange way, because I realized that I'd been reading about how Jews had died in the thirties and forties, but I really didn't know much about how they had lived before that. I came to a place where I thought, Well, I respect my background and religion. So it was a long and very difficult process.

You began to be recognized as a gay writer when George Stambolian accepted one of your stories for Men on Men 2.

Having George Stambolian choose a story of mine made an enormous difference in my career. It gave me national exposure and I still meet people who know my name because of that story.

The crucial event was connecting with Michael Denneny, who suggested the idea of a collection mixing gay and Jewish themes. I've never had an editor so responsive to my work, able to see it from the inside, and suggest changes that are true to what I intended. When we first discussed a pile of my stories in May of '89, he said that some reminded him of Michelangelo's unfinished sculptures, not fully emerged from the stone. He was right, and every story in the book is sharper in focus because of his insight.

In so many of those stories, you identify a tension between your characters' rich Jewish heritage and the powerful need they have to claim their own reality and experience. Is that tension, between the past and the present—that "gap of comprehension," you call it, between parents and children, between survivors and others—is that tension an irresolvable one? What do you make of that?

I don't think it's irresolvable. I think people resolve it in different ways, at different times in their life. I don't think Jewish observance or identification, or even gay identification, is a constant over your life. I don't think sexual identity is a constant over your life. You go in and out of phases of intensity around certain things. There was a time in my life when I went to synagogue a great deal. For minor festivals, for everything. I found it very, very fulfilling and important. That's not where I am now. It's hard for us to give ourselves permission to do that, to say, "Well, I don't feel very observant right now," or "My Jewishness is around politics," or "My gayness is around politics," or "My gayness is around AIDS research right now," as opposed to something else. I expect to see some sorts of shifts in my writing over the years. Some books will be more or less gay, more or less Jewish. Those elements will always be there. I can't hide them, but there's going to be fluctuation. There has to be. People are not fixed entities.

Cultural assimilation seems to be a big theme in your work.

I got a triple dose of it. Not only am I a Jew in America, and not only am I gay in a straight society, but I'm also a newcomer—first generation.

There are all those levels of difference that reverberate off each other. I guess I'm reaching Jungian synthesis before I'm supposed to!

But it seems that there's more and more to write about than there used to be. I find tremendous similarities between gay and Jewish experience. When I was at a gay shabbat service in Toronto, at the World Congress of Gay and Jewish Organizations, I found it tremendously moving to read a rewritten text of the prayer service which had interpolated passages about gay and lesbian experience in with everything else. I felt such a tremendous sense of validation, but also continuity. And I think that both gays and Jews have suffered silence. Our experiences are very similar in some ways.

Have you experienced any criticism from the gay community because of your embracing of religion?

No, not anti-Semitism, and not ostracism, but what I have experienced is an incredible amount of ignorance in the gay community about what's happening in American Judaism, as far as gay rights are concerned. A year ago, the head of Reform Judaism said that not only should synagogues makes sure that no gay or lesbian Jew is denied access to the community, but they should actively reach out to them and embrace them. People are surprised to learn news like that. But why should they be surprised? Look at Jews in the civil rights movement and look at our consistently liberal attitudes. That doesn't mean that that's always been practiced. But politically, Jews are a lot more accepting of gay rights. Now, they're uncomfortable about it, because they're trying to embrace that and make sure that the family-oriented culture survives.

Do you feel pressured to write a non-Jewish or nongay book?

No, not at all. I don't have to prove anything to anyone. Nobody's asked me for a Catholic novel. It'd be interesting. There are some stories in the collection that aren't Jewish. I'll tell you, some people have noticed that there is less—quote, unquote—"Jewish content" in *Winter Eyes* than in the short stories, and to me it's clear that of course there is because his family's hiding his Jewishness from him. I know some people have been uncomfortable with that because I guess they expected *Dancing on Tisha B'Av*, part 2. That's not going to happen.

You know, when people expect things from you as a writer, that's the greatest compliment. It means they're so involved in your work and they like it so much that they want an answer. At a number of readings, people would say, "I want to know what happens to Brenda and Nat and Mark. I want to know, you have to write something. I want to see them ten years from now." And I say, "So do I!" Ten years from now I'll have a different perspective on those characters.

Speaking of Brenda, one of the stories in Dancing on Tisha B'Av *is told from Brenda's point of view. She's the sister trying to deal with her brother's gayness. Do you think that it's easier for gay men to create female characters, to write from a female point of view?*

I don't know. I wouldn't say for sure that that's the case. I think it would have to depend on any writer's ability to step outside of herself or himself and project into another consciousness. There are people I based Brenda on, and Brenda is parts of myself, too. I don't think so.

In your novel Winter Eyes, *the parents of Stefan Borowski, who is the protagonist, definitely go on a campaign to conceal his entire background. They, in fact, pretend they are Catholic, make no mention of the Holocaust whatsoever.*

They raise him as a Pole, as a Polish ethnic.

That wasn't your experience?

Not at all.

But you, in fact, do know people who were raised that way.

I have met many people whose parents—and not just in World War II— have fled, for instance, a pogrom in Russia, and by the time they got to the U.S. they had chosen another religion: "I'm not a Jew anymore, I will not have to deal with this, my children will not have to deal with this." Touring around the country, I have met dozens and dozens of people who in varying ways have had their past hidden from them. Someone came up to me after the reading yesterday and said that his mother had told him that she had been rounded up during the war even though she wasn't Jewish and then let go. He said now he's beginning to wonder why was she rounded up in her village with other Jews. So she told him something and didn't tell him something. There are a lot of these stories.

The subtitle of Winter Eyes *is "A Novel about Secrets." There are many secrets in this novel—the parents' Jewishness and their holocaust experiences during the war, Stefan's homosexual crush on his teenage friend, the parents' dissolving marriage. What drew you to this theme of secrets?*

If you grow up in a family where there is so much silence about anything, your sense of the price of admission, of making an admission, and the costs of asking questions and bridging the gap is very acute. You know there are places you do not walk, there are things you do not ask, and yet you want to. So it grows very much out of my own experience. But also it's a very common experience for gay men and lesbians. We all deal all the time with coming out and secrets and who knows what and what they do with the information and how out you are. You could be as out as possible and yet still there are environments where it happens again and you have to make a split-second decision: Well, do I say I'm here with my partner? Do I not say? You know, how do you negotiate it?

It's fascinated me, a question for Jews, because we—gays and Jews—don't have to deal with oppression in a way that African Americans do. If we want, we can hide who we are. Unless you can pass as white. But we can pretend to be anything we want to. In the U.S. you can just pick up and move across the country. No one will ever know where you came from. So I think Jews deal with this all the time, too, about how much they reveal about themselves, in many different situations. It's as simple as "Merry Christmas." Okay, it doesn't sound like a big deal. Do you say, "I don't celebrate Christmas?" Will that make the person embarrassed? Will that make the person annoyed? Do you say, "Happy Hanukkah to you"? I mean, how do you deal with that? That's just a day-to-day simple example. It comes up around questions about Israel, anti-Semitic jokes. There's a whole range of things.

Are there differences between homophobia and anti-Semitism?

I think there's a deeper level of disgust in homophobia. Both are rooted in Western culture—anti-Semitism and homophobia—but there's kind of a visceral disgust and contempt around gay issues that I don't see in anti-Semitism. On the other hand, anti-Semitism informs Western Christian culture much more. There are many more references in literature and liturgy to Jews than there are to gays. So it's more omnipresent.

A good example, the *Advocate* recently had a article on brain research on gays. The first lines [about the scientist conducting the research] said, "People call him a Judas." Well, for me as a Jew that's a very loaded image, because Judas was a Jew and people use that as the symbol of the archbetrayal. It's just as simple to use the word "traitor" as the word "Judas." So our language is corrupted by anti-Semitism.

One of the things that surprised me in Winter Eyes *was the element of bisexuality that comes into the novel. Even the ending is somewhat ambiguous as to where Stefan's sexuality lies.*

Absolutely.

What are you doing with that? What are you exploring there?

The older I've gotten, the clearer it is to me that for many gay men, and gay women, opposite-sex relationships have been a really important part of their lives, and that to be true to all of our experience, we can't write that out. We're always editing our history anyway, especially writers. We can't tell an anecdote the same way twice because it always gets better and more colorful. That's why we're good at parties, usually. I've had very positive relationships with women, sexual and emotional, and that's part of my life. That's part of the lives of many gay men that I know, and yet it's kind of a dirty secret. I can remember being at a party, and somehow getting into a conversation about how much we missed women, and the two of us were off whispering in a corner lest someone should hear us and be freaked out: you know, what does it mean? We're closeted heterosexuals? No! I am a gay man, that's really clear. That's my fantasy life, that's my commitment. I live with a man who is my life commitment, but I've had relationships with women that are important. And so, I can't leave that out of how I see the world.

The other thing is, I know I've been criticized by some people for the end of *Winter Eyes.* They said I'd sold out. Well, I didn't get anything for "selling out." Dorothy Allison once said something about, you know, "sell out to whom?" If you read the ending closely, to me it's unambiguous that he is going to bed with a gay woman. The irony there is that it's only in bed with a gay woman that he is free to talk about himself. She creates a safety, a space of comfort—whatever you want to call it—in which he can share himself. It also captures for me the ambiguity of adolescence in those sort of explosive confrontations—or conjunctions— you have where you suddenly meet someone who opens you up to yourself. I really didn't want the book to end with him going to Key West and meeting, you know, a surfer and everything working out happily. This is someone who is struggling with his identity, and it just so happens that a woman at that point in his life has something to offer to him.

Let's talk about sex. There are some explicit sex scenes . . .

Let's talk about sex, baby!

There are some explicit sex scenes . . .

I don't think of them as explicit. I think of them as passionate.

Is it difficult to write sex scenes?

It's not more difficult . . . I think with anything you are writing you have to have a clear sense of what you are trying to accomplish. I think for me, when I write sex scenes for characters, I have to step back sometimes and ask myself what is this going to say about who they are? How would this expand them as characters? The most difficult part of it is trying to avoid cliché and keeping it from being routine or boring or artificial or mechanical. I think it's something that's incumbent on me anyway as a writer to *not* leave out sex. It's important for how I see my characters. Certainly I don't see how you can write a book about a character's sexual awakening and leave it out, because I think, especially now, it's important, and it's important for me not to feel bound by the taboo, which still exists within American literature. You can write anything you want to about straight people having sex, but if it's two women or two men, suddenly people are squeamish, or we can't say what happens. Well, why not? If sexual realism works for 119 people, we can do it, too.

Do you think there is more shame attached to being gay in Jewish culture than in the prevailing culture?

I think Jews and gays share an incredible hypersensitivity to how we are perceived by the dominant community, and I know my gay friends see this and we talk about it. In fact, we share a lot about physical stereotypes—how we look, our sexuality. There are a lot of things that we are criticized about and I think that what it comes down to is that the minority community doesn't want the majority community to have an avenue into criticism. We have to be perfect, and perfect means straight and good and quiet.

My sense is that gay Jewish people are less likely to be driven out of their families. I mean, Jewish friends tell me they just never see that happen. I guess it would happen in a very Orthodox family, but they are a very small portion of American Jews anyway, and don't really determine how we are and who we are.

You mentioned that you grew up in Washington Heights, but you left New York in 1980 and haven't returned.

I *fled*!

I think many of us have an idea that gay writers are all city dwellers, and that that city should preferably be New York or maybe San Francisco. That certainly isn't the case for you. You live in Okemos, Michigan. Why?

Well, first of all, I fell in love there. That made a difference, but even before that I think I fell in love with Michigan. I really like the quiet in the town I live in. It's a wonderful place to work. I like the feel of a relaxed pace. I don't feel driven there by ideas of success. It's easier to think more about my audience and what it is that I want to say. Personally, I had to unhook from that whole New York success ethic. I think it's very hard not to be stung by it in a big city and think that everybody else is doing better than you are.

I'm interested to know who your Jewish and gay models are.

There really aren't any gay Jewish male writers who have inspired me, because hardly anyone has really brought that material together. Most of my models tend to be straight, and many of them are English.

For example?

Edith Wharton, of course, since I've written a book about her. Henry James. A lot of people will laugh and say, "Oh, another gay person influenced by Henry James," but in senior year when I read chapter 42 of *Portrait of a Lady* at three o'clock in the morning—that's the chapter where Isabel sits up, looking into the dying fire, realizing she has fallen into a trap and that the house of freedom is the house of dumbness and deafness and suffocation—that one chapter was like a bomb in my life. It opened me up completely. I never wrote the same after that. Before that, my writing was superficial and clever. I dropped all that. Afterwards, I just saw things so deeply. James helped me see.

People who have had an influence on me are sometimes people who write completely different from me. William Burroughs. Joan Didion. Don DeLillo. I could never write like them. Yet they have an impact on me. I love Anita Brookner's work. Elizabeth Taylor. I adore Philip Roth. I think he's the best Jewish writer of the century.

And gay writers?

Robert Ferro, Andrew Holleran, Edmund White. I was reading all three of them, in fact, when I wrote *Dancing on Tisha B'Av*. Michael Nava—when I read *Goldenboy*, I was on an airplane, turning pages faster and faster, thinking, This is how to write, this is wonderful. His stuff is very complex and very polished. I'm sure there are lots of other people I haven't mentioned. I like to read a variety of people. D. H. Lawrence is somebody who has opened me up.

You're in touch with a lot of gay writers?

I try to be. If I read someone's work and I like it, I write right away. For years I was too shy to do this and, to anyone I never wrote to, I'm sorry because I wish I had. The first person I got over it with was Robert Ferro after I read *Second Son*, which made me cry; just beautifully written. I wrote him and he wrote me just a wonderful letter, so friendly. I've never written an author if I've had any ambivalence about the work, because then I'd have to bullshit and this is not a high school exam, but from the heart.

I've really felt like I entered a community of writers, and that's terrific. It's wonderful to be able to call someone and talk shop. People have told me that I should have a writers' group where I live, but I have a writers' group at the end of the telephone—people who can help me through bad times, or with whom I can just chat about stories or books.

What are your writing habits like?

Chaotic, irregular, anarchic. I don't have a fixed schedule. I write when I want to, when I have something to say. If you made me get up at eight and write until one, I would die. Even with a gun to my head, I don't think I could do it. I revise as I go along, frequently. I dream a lot, I doodle. I think that because I'm writing full-time, what I've been able to do is create a space and an environment in which even when I'm out mowing the lawn I'm really working on something. Even when I'm at the gym, I'm working on a problem with a book. I think that nonwriters don't understand that writing takes place in many spaces, not just at the computer or at the desk. You're always writing, you're always thinking about it.

Michael Nava

Since the appearance of *The Little Death* in 1986, Michael Nava's mystery novels featuring Henry Rios, a gay Latino criminal defense lawyer, have earned the author a wide readership and high critical acclaim. Like his mentor Joseph Hansen, Nava has achieved a large crossover audience and praise from such mainstream publications as the *Wall Street Journal* and the *Los Angeles Times,* which said of his books that they are "set apart by their insight, compassion and sense of social justice."[1]

Elegant, complex, and, at times, disturbing, Nava's mysteries achieve much beyond the pleasures of a good whodunit. He employs the device of the mystery to explore themes normally associated with "high" literature: love, justice, sexuality, disease, humanity. Indeed, Nava's books successfully bridge the gap between popular and literary genres, and he has won several Lambda Literary Awards.

The first of the two interviews I conducted with Michael Nava took place in the fall of 1992, when the author came to Boston, a stopover on a two-week vacation he was taking through New England. At the time, he was also promoting his latest Henry Rios novel, *The Hidden Law.* We taped our conversation in the South End apartment of his friend and first publisher, Sasha Alyson. Parts of that interview were excerpted in an article entitled "From the Barrio to the Bookstore" that appeared in *Bay Windows* (3 December 1992).

The second interview took place on 7 August 1993, as part of the WOMR series, "The Word is Out." The evening before, Nava had read from the manuscript of his then forthcoming novel, *The Last Days,* the fifth in the Henry Rios series. There was a large gathering, male and female, at the Fine Arts Work Center, the location of the reading. Many were fans of the Rios mysteries, but few of us were prepared for the powerful emotional experience that Nava delivered when he read the chapter in which Josh Mandel, Henry's HIV-positive lover, dies and Henry takes his ashes home.

---

1. Victor Zonana, "Poetic Justice," *Los Angeles Times,* 6 May 1990, E-1.

I have interpolated questions and answers from both those interviews in the following conversation.

You've been sightseeing in Boston?[2]

I tramped around from nine o'clock until three o'clock today. I went to Filene's Basement. I wanted to see where Kitty Dukakis bought her dresses. Last week I went to the North End. John Mitzel, the manager of Glad Day [bookstore], gave me a tour of the cemeteries. I love cemeteries. We went to look for Cotton Mather's grave.

Boston has something that few other northern American cities have: a white underclass. That was the first thing I noticed when I was walking around today. This is the first town I've ever been in where it's the white kids who make me nervous. They walk around with those narrow, hard faces and those blue eyes that stare a hole in you.

You've lived in California your whole life?

I've lived in the West my whole life. I grew up in Sacramento and went to college in Colorado. For the past twelve years, I've lived in L.A.[3]

You grew up in the Mexican barrio of Sacramento?

I grew up among people who were not very well educated and not interested in books or ideas, and really were just struggling to stay alive on the most basic economic level. And I was this very bright child, and I needed to talk about things—about books I read, about ideas I had—and to ask those questions that bright children ask. It became pretty apparent to me pretty quickly that there was no one I could talk to. So I was filled with all of these words that I never got to express as a child, and it is one of the reasons I'm a writer.

I don't know how other writers are, but I am still extremely introverted, and I'm filled with words, but I find it very difficult frequently to express them. I don't necessarily think this is a good or healthy thing, actually. I think sometimes I would trade writing for ordinariness.

It's not such an unusual story, my story. It's really smart boy from

---

2. The first two questions and answers are from the 1992 interview. The remaining questions and answers from the earlier interview have been interpolated with questions and answers from the much longer, more substantial 1993 interview.
3. Nava has since moved to San Francisco.

poor family makes good, and in the process becomes completely estranged from his family.

Are you now completely estranged?

Yeah. My stepfather died last year, and that was the last time I saw them. It was not a happy family. Really, all I wanted was to get out of it, and having done that I don't feel any sentimentality about it.

What was your early life like?

Well, I was raised by gargoyles. God bless them! I lived in what people now call a dysfunctional family, but at the time, I didn't think about it that way, of course. It was an alcoholic family and we were very poor. It was kind of miserable, actually. Not that I, at this point, am holding anyone accountable for that. That was as it was. And it gave me particular things—some of them I like, and some of them I struggle with. It gave me this desire to escape it, which really focused my intelligence, like a laser, and permitted me to get out of there through the agency of higher education. I mean, I lived in this welfare family, and then I graduated from Stanford Law School. That trajectory would not have been possible had I not had this burning need to get out of there. So that's something that is positive that came from that experience.

From reading your piece called "Abuelo" in John Preston's anthology, A Member of the Family, *I gathered that you feel an affection for your grandfather, though it's not a sentimental affection.*

No, I don't have that kind of sentimental affection for my grandfather and my grandmother, who were the pivotal people in my childhood. You see, I never really know about families. People tell me about families and I get annoyed when the sentimentality intrudes, because that wasn't my experience. I grew up among very complicated but very unhappy people. They were very much apart from each other. My grandfather was a bigamist. He had another family—I learned this long after he died—and my grandmother found out about this early in the marriage. You know, they were married for almost fifty years, but for forty years of that . . . well, they were Catholic, so they couldn't divorce. As a child, I didn't know what was going on, but I sensed that there was a lot of distance between the two of them.

Your early teachers in elementary school and high school—were they encouraging, were they helpful?

Yeah. I remember when I was in third grade—I guess I would have been about eight years old—my mother went to an open house and my teacher told her, "You have to send him to college." My mother had a high school education, and I didn't know what college was, but when she said that, I thought, Yes, I'm going to go to college. That was really my ambition, and I was encouraged along the way by really good teachers.

I understand that you started out as a poet.

I read a lot of poetry [when I was growing up.] I read very little fiction. Joseph Hansen is trying to improve my mind. He keeps giving me these books—Chekhov short stories, whatnot. And I'm supposed to read them because I have such dramatic lapses. But I don't. I sort of accept the books and hope he doesn't ask me about them.

So I read a lot of poetry and I wrote a lot of poetry. I was a good poet except I couldn't write about the one thing that I needed to write about. I'm sure you can guess what that was. I have what my friend Robert Dawidoff calls "ambition disorder," which a lot of gay people have, that need to compensate by doing three times as much as the next person. So I graduated Phi Beta Kappa with honors.

After college you went to Argentina?

I went to Argentina, ostensibly to translate the work of a nineteenth-century Nicaraguan poet named Rubén Darío. I barely spoke Spanish! Really, I conned my way there. It was really because I was the golden boy at the school where I went. So I went to this city of nine million people at the end of the world where I knew no one, barely speaking Spanish.

What was it like living in Buenos Aires?

It was right after the military had overthrown Mrs. Perón, the second Mrs. Perón. I was staying at this YMCA hotel on a street, and there were soldiers with machine guns strapped over their shoulders guarding the streets. I had to carry my passport with me at all times, because I never knew when I would be asked for identification. I had a very hard time meeting people. It wasn't until almost the end of the year that someone I did meet explained to me that a young American who had lots of money—in those terms, in terms of the Argentines—with no visible means of support seemed awfully suspicious to them and, in fact, some of them thought I was CIA. So they kept their distance.

It was the loneliest year of my life. I spent a lot of time in bed reading Charles Dickens. I think I must have read the entire Charles Dickens library. I was so lonely for English. I learned something about myself. I had a very lonely childhood. It was a very lonely year there. I learned how to survive. I learned that loneliness wouldn't kill me. And for some reason that was important for me to know that.

What was gay life like in Buenos Aires?

It was nonexistent. It's really changed in the last few years since the civilian government has taken control of Argentina again. But when I was there in 1976 to 1977, there was no gay life. I suppose there were the usual bathrooms and bathhouses, because saunas are very popular with Argentines, but there was no visible gay life, which was also a source of considerable frustration to me.

And after Argentina?

I didn't want to teach. And I didn't want to stay in Sacramento, and I didn't have enough science for medical school, so I took the law boards. Stanford accepted me right away. I was not a very good law student. I didn't like law school; it had no reality. Even the courses in criminal law. It was all just so speculative. I thought about dropping out, but I didn't know what else to do, so I stuck with it.

What did you hope to achieve with a law degree?

I hoped to make money with a law degree! Really, at that point I was twenty-four years old, I guess, and I knew that I was not going to be able to support myself writing poetry, as much as I loved it. And I didn't want to teach, because I didn't think I had the patience for it, nor did I have the interest. I was right about that, because I've tried it since then and I'm just not that kind of a teacher. I'm a different kind of a teacher. So I needed a profession that would support me while I figured out what to do as a writer. I have a very good mind; it was easy for me to slip into that gear of legal analysis and the legal profession.

What happened after law school?

I got a job as a prosecutor in Los Angeles at a time when they were actively recruiting gay lawyers, because the then city attorney wanted the office to reflect the community. I liked that job a lot. I did a lot of trials. I've always been introverted, so it was very challenging for me to get up and make speeches to juries, but I did it and I did a good job. I stopped when it got very depressing, when I started seeing the same people coming back two years later.

The criminal justice system is broken. There is so much misery in the world, and the criminal courts are not the place to handle it, but it goes there by default because no one else is doing the job. And this was in the early eighties, before the worst effects of Reaganomics! I wouldn't want to be in the criminal courthouse now.

To some extent I feel that in the Rios novels I'm really cheating because he always has middle-class or upper-middle-class clients. And that's not how it is at all. I mean, if he were a real criminal defense lawyer, he would be handling a lot of street people.

With the themes that I want to investigate, it's easier to write a book when your characters are articulate and intelligent; it's much easier to write a book when they can say the things that you need them to say. So that's why I end up using middle-class people. I don't know what to do about that because, although I come from an extremely poor family, I've been middle class for a long time now. In aspiration, if not income. It's hard for me to write the way my family speaks without being patronizing, and I'd rather not write about them than patronize them.

Are you at all tempted to try your hand at a novel without a middle-class cast of characters?

What I've been thinking about doing for a long time now is what [I'm doing in] these pieces in *Hometowns* and *A Member of the Family*. I'd like to write a memoir of my childhood. I want to say something about that; I don't think I can say it in fiction, because I'd have to have a story, and there really is no "story" in the sense of a plot. It would introduce an element of artifice that I don't want. A lot of it will probably be fiction anyway! I guess I'll try.

You're still a practicing lawyer. What attracts you to the law?

It is a great source of material for me, and it also keeps me involved in the world in a way that I suspect I wouldn't be if I wrote full-time.

When did you start writing?

I started writing poetry when I was fourteen. It was a way of saying things I couldn't say. Until I was about twenty-six, I only wrote poetry. I wrote a lot of it.

Then when I was in law school, I was reading a lot of mysteries. It really was a case of, Oh, I could write one of those. I was going out with a man at the time and we would talk about this mystery we were going to write called *The Little Death*. After we stopped seeing each other, it lay dormant in my imagination. I started writing it when I was studying for the bar. I worked at a jail in Palo Alto from ten in the evening until six in the morning, and as the police would arrest people and bring them in I would interview them to see whether they should be released on their own recognizance or be made to stay in jail. So I had a lot of time on my hands, and it was a very evocative ambience. So I started writing one. It took me three years.

Joseph Hansen has been a pretty big influence on you?

Yeah.

When you set out to write your first novel, had you read any of the Dave Brandstetter books?

I'd read all of them up to that point, which is why I thought I could write about an openly gay character as a protagonist. So he gave me that. And also, he's pretty unsentimental.

What other mystery writers do you read?

I don't read very many mysteries any more, because it's too much like homework. I really admire Katherine Forrest's mysteries. I like Chandler, even though he's a bigot on many levels. And Ross MacDonald, because he's a great poetic writer. I like Sarah Karetsky among the new women writers. And there's an English writer named Reginald Hill who's very good. But by and large, I don't have much time to read.

How did you come to invent Henry Rios?

It never occurred to me that my protagonist would be anything other than gay or Latino. I suppose it was narcissistic.

Why was it important to make him gay?

Well, because I am. It's a part of my character that I struggled for a long time to accept and having accepted it, I wasn't about to go back into the closet as a writer.

Had you attempted to write other mysteries with a nongay character?

No. I didn't start reading mysteries actually until I was a senior in college. An English professor of mine gave me some Rex Stout books, and I became sort of a habitual reader of them. I've written since I was fourteen. I wanted to write fiction, but I didn't want to write that sort of self-indulgent, first, autobiographical novel; so I thought that if I wrote a mystery it would give me some discipline and make it less easy for me to indulge in that kind of ennui or whatever it is that young writers do when they write their first books.

Henry's gayness is treated quite matter-of-factly. Still, every now and then, there are places where you nicely insert a subtle but trenchant point about gay life. In The Little Death, *Henry, who is narrating, says, "The sexual aspect of homosexuality was, in many ways, the least of it. The tough part was being truthful without painting yourself into a corner: I am different, but not as different as you think." Would you like to elaborate on that?*

You mean on the sentiment or on how I do that?

Both.

Well, yeah. I'm a very sort of literal-minded writer. I don't have theories about how my life should be. All I have is my experience of living as a gay man, and whatever lessons I've learned about that are organic. There are places in the books where Rios comes up against the bias and the hatred and the bigotry, and he responds with these commentaries. Because we're gay not only internally, but we're gay in the world. A person like Rios, who interacts with the world all the time, because of his calling, has more occasion to see how the culture thinks about homosexuality and how people treat it. So he has this acute consciousness of self, and he has this internal dialogue about it.

How do you go about plotting the Rios novels? Does the plotting follow a certain formula? Do you make an outline?

The plotting has, in many ways, become the easiest part of it. In the first two books I made elaborate outlines, really chapter-by-chapter outlines. As I've gotten better at it, I find that that's much less necessary. I have a general idea of where I'm going to go with the book. I don't need to fill in the spaces as much as I used to. It's just become easier to do that, because I can hold it all in my mind now instead of having to see it on paper.

Are there any ways in which the plotting aspect of the books becomes old hat? Are there ways in which you can keep surprising yourself?

Well, you know, there are certain mechanical requirements of writing a mystery: you have to produce a dead body at some point, and you have to produce suspects, and then you have to produce the killer. That doesn't change. Those are the givens. What I try to do with my plots is to integrate them more fully into the story I really want to tell, which is usually not about the whodunit aspect.

I'm interested in your style, which is so economical and clean. Is that something that you learned through writing poetry? Is it something you learned through the Ross MacDonald and Dashiell Hammett school? Where does that spare, clean, economical style come from?

Well, it does come from the years I spent writing poetry, because in poetry every word has to do a lot of work, because you don't get that many words to express what it is you're trying to say; so each one has to resonate. Oddly enough, it also comes from my legal training, where the same thing is true. Contrary to what people think about lawyers, you really do try to strive to write well. It's just that few lawyers can do it, just as few people can do it. I am always looking for the precise word I need.

[Poetry] taught me that there *is* the right word for something. I work very hard to find the right word. I rewrite my books, from start to finish, five or six times.

One thing that I've noticed as I've read the Henry Rios books is this theme of the outsider. There are many people in your novels who sense themselves as outsiders, or are social outsiders of one sort or another.

Well, yeah. It's one reason I was attracted to the mystery genre, because it is really the novel of the outsider. The protagonist, the detective, is someone who stands at the margins of society. In the old books—in the Chandler books, for instance—he was someone who held himself out at the margins of society, and who, in a particular way, embodies the virtues that the society purports to hold in esteem but actually seldom practices. It's a natural form for someone like me, and for other gay and lesbian writers, for women writers, who, in fact, are outsiders, and I think we've brought a fresh vitality to the form.

There are quite a few gay and lesbian mystery writers practicing now. In fact, the Lambda Literary Awards even have categories for gay and lesbian mysteries. Why do you think gay and lesbian mysteries are so popular?

It's partly for that reason, because it's the outsider form. I think it's also true that mysteries in general have undergone an intense revival of popularity in the last decade, heralded largely by women writers—Sarah Karetsky and Sue Grafton—this new wave of feminist detectives. Most readers are women, I think, so now that these books are being written specifically from a woman's point of view, I think that's really increased the popularity of the genre.

Generally, gay male writers have attracted a male audience, and lesbian writers have attracted a female audience. You seem to have crossed over and caught the interest of both male and female readers.

Yeah. And when I do signings in, you know, regular bookstores as opposed to gay bookstores, I'm always surprised by how many women fans I have—heterosexual women, not always lesbian women. I think for them Rios represents something that they want in men.

And that is . . . ?

He has this strength, but he also has this vulnerability. I think that women respond to that. I'm also very conscious when I'm writing these books to accurately mirror my world and the role women play in it. For instance, I work for a female judge, and all of my professional life as a lawyer, I've had women colleagues and women supervisors; so when I'm writing the books, I put a lot of women in positions of power and authority, because that's been my experience.

Joseph Hansen once told me that if he had to rely on his gay readership alone, his mysteries would never sell very well. He was referring to the tremendous crossover audience he'd achieved. How about you? Is that the case also?

Yeah, it's becoming increasingly the case. It's because mystery readers tend to be more open-minded about what they'll read, because they're really interested in the form. If you write a book that satisfies the expectations, then they're willing to accept a lot of the commentary that goes with it. At least that's been my experience.

What's your relationship to your readers like? After all, you're playing a sophisticated game with your readers, handing them clues and dragging red herrings across their path. Do you, as a mystery writer, get pleasure from throwing your readers off track?

I wouldn't say I get pleasure from it. It's a lot of work, trying to stay one step ahead of them. There's some sort of mechanical satisfaction when I can pull it off, but I think people have come to see my books as not being so much about those mechanical aspects, but really the mystery is, How do these other seemingly unconnected elements of story and plot and character relate to the mystery?

In the first Henry Rios novel, The Little Death, *which you published in 1986, Henry is a heavy drinker. But over the course of the next three or four novels, he acknowledges his alcoholism and gets himself into AA. Why was it necessary to work these details of his life into the novels?*

Well, now we get to that part where life and art merge.

Is this the "self-indulgence" part you were referring to earlier?

Not exactly self-indulgence. I mean, all any writer has is the experience of his or her own life, and my own life took this particular turn about five-and-a-half years ago. So I ascribed it to Rios, because it was something that was happening to me. It was also something that was very interesting and something that changed my life. Also, having stopped drinking myself, it would have been very hard for me to continue writing about a detective who was a heavy drinker.

Are there things that you would still like to speak and write about that you can't do through the genre of mystery?

Yes, there are. I have been thinking for three or four years that one of the things that I really want to do is to write a memoir of my childhood. I don't know up to what point: part of the problem is I don't know where I'd stop. These essays I wrote for John Preston have really given me the opportunity to think seriously about doing that. I said a moment ago that I wasn't a teacher in the conventional sense. I don't have the patience to deal with people who don't know as much as I do. It's a kind of arrogance. So I recognize it and there it is. I try not to act on it. But because of the response I get from the Rios books, it's clear that I'm a teacher of another kind—just sort of a moral example for people who struggle through some of the same things I've struggled through. And I want to set it down without the veneer of fiction: what it was like, what happened, and what it's like now. I need to do that to heal myself as well.

As you know from reading my books, there's very little distance between who I am and what I write. Frequently the veil of fiction is gossamer thin. I sometimes wish I were a different kind of writer, a writer who could imagine things that he hadn't experienced, and construct characters from pieces and scraps of his observations, but I'm just not. I'm the kind of writer who writes very close to the bone. That's my strength. It's also my struggle.

Well then, what about this attitude I've been picking up about self-indulgent writing? In many ways, you use the autobiographical material so beautifully and so successfully that it seems unnecessary to be that critical about that kind of self-indulgence.

What I meant by "self-indulgence"—and what I guard against in my own writing—is to draw conclusions about my experience: to draw sentimental conclusions or unnecessarily punitive conclusions. What I've tried to do as a writer, especially when I write about my own life, is simply to set things out as they were, and to let the reader draw his or her own conclusions, and not to editorialize. And that's what I mean by self-indulgence—the editorializing about one's own experience.

Is that also something that comes about through your legal work?

I hadn't thought about that. I suppose it is, but in the law you really are making arguments, you're marshaling your facts and your research to a particular end. I guess I am, too, as a writer, but I try to do it more invisibly.

In The Little Death, *Henry says, "'If I believed that people are basically good, I would have gone into plastics. People are basically screwed-up and often the best you can do for them is listen, hear the worst and then tell them it's not so bad.'" Henry is, of course, modeled, in part, on the hard-boiled detectives that populate the mystery genre. But to what extent do you believe that "people are basically screwed-up"?*

I don't believe that anymore. I wrote those words a long time ago. I'm thirty-eight. I finished that book when I was twenty-nine, so it's been almost ten years. I don't feel that way anymore. I wouldn't write that now.

Is it difficult for you to hear old words read back to you?

No, not really. These are artifacts of my past. They don't really have any power over me anymore.

There seems to be a growing trend among writers and people who think they know about writing to adhere to certain politically correct ways to portray characters—gay characters, for instance—in fiction.

What I've decided is that I'll write what I need to write. I really can't worry about whether it's going to offend someone, because we live in an age when sensibilities are so fucking refined that you're going to offend someone. In *The Hidden Law,* I was nervous about some of the AIDS stuff I was writing because Rios—he's older than I am—is not of the generation or persuasion of ACT UP or Queer Nation. There's something about it he doesn't understand. The stories come from his perspective. I write something and think, Oh, this is going to piss some people, but it's how he feels about things.

We're going through a hard time because all of us gay and lesbian writers are aware of the vicious stereotypes which have been perpetrated against us in literature since the novel was created. And with that in mind, it's very hard not to be sensitive about what you are writing.

When you created Henry Rios, did you make deliberate decisions about how you would portray his character?

No, I really didn't, and if I'd been concerned about that I probably would have invented a straight detective. I did make a decision about the sexual content of my books, which was that I would not write about sex explicitly. I mean, there are occasional passages about sex and, especially in the later books, Henry's relationship with his lover Josh when it seems appropriate to me to use them to give the reader some idea of the full dimension of their relationship, that they're not just friends, not just roommates, that they're lovers and this is what it means. But for the most part I really avoid writing about sex because it goes to my problems with homosexuality as a cultural artifact.

For me, being gay is about politics and culture. It's not about my sexuality. I mean, I know what my sexuality is, and it's just not an issue for me. For me, the more interesting part is how the world responds to me. And that's what I write about. I don't write about sexual desire per se.

Do you have any interest in writing about that at all? Was that a decision that brought you some disappointment or regret? Do you feel as if you've cut off a certain amount of experience that is fair game to write about?

I think I would write about it if it were in a context where it had some meaning other than to either titillate the reader or play to some sort of expectations that especially gay readers have about gay books. So, I haven't cut it off for good.

The other thing about sexual desire is that I really don't understand it, Phil. I mean, I know when I feel it! But I don't really understand its components. See, if I could write about sexual desire, as distinct from sexual activity, I might be more inclined to do it, but what one ends up writing about is sexual activity. It's very hard to make that interesting, I think.

A few years ago, you were criticized in Lambda Book Report *for your less than flattering portraits of some female characters.*[4] *What's your response to that kind of criticism?*

Well, one has to walk a very delicate line here. The fact is that gays and lesbians have been depicted so badly in American fiction, and especially in the mystery novel, where we were cannon fodder, that I do feel some responsibility not to reinforce those stereotypes, not so much for political reasons, but because they're not accurate in my experience.

On the other hand, it's not possible for me to write someone else's book. I can only write my books. The criticism I got about some of the women in *Howton,* I thought that in that case the writer of that article had formed her conclusion before she read the books and when she read the books she was simply looking for evidence that would support her conclusion. It annoyed me, because I thought it was intellectually dishonest, but I didn't feel compelled to do anything about it when I wrote my next book.

What considerations went through your mind in making Henry's lover, Josh Mandel, HIV-positive?

It was a way of dealing with the epidemic. I created this character before I knew anyone who was HIV-positive. But then I met a man who was very much like Josh, actually, and it sort of informed the character in the third book. He died this summer. I've heard many gay writers say, "You can't be a gay writer and not write about this subject." And so this was the way I approached it.

---

4. Victoria Brownworth, "Someone Has to Say No," *Lambda Book Report* 2, no. 7 (October/November 1990):6–8, 42.

It does seem to me that any gay writer cannot avoid the issue of AIDS, because it's such an overwhelming fact in our world. So I needed to write about it, and this is the way I did. I created the character of Josh in *Goldenboy,* and then I met a young man who is very much like him, with whom I had a brief romantic relationship but a much longer friendship. It was a funny thing: sometimes I write things and then they happen. Chris died last year, and when he died, that was a signal to me that it was time to bring this story of Josh and Henry to a close.

I'd like to ask a technical question. Your latest book in the Henry Rios series, The Last Days, *switches to third-person narration. All the other Henry Rios books have been in first person with Henry as the narrator. Why did you choose to do that?*

There were a couple of things that went into that decision. In order to continue to write these books, I have to create challenges for myself as a writer or I'll become bored and I'll write books that I wouldn't be proud of or, more likely, I wouldn't write them at all. I had learned as much as I could about writing by writing in the first person. I needed to do something else that would teach me new things about writing, and so I switched to third, which was a formidable challenge for me. The other thing is I wanted to open these books up, I wanted to be able to follow the lives of other characters and I can't do that through Rios' eyes because his perspective is by necessity limited to what he knows or what he can intuit or what he can infer. And that's just not enough.

Was there a way in which it was also easier to write about AIDS and Josh's death in third-person point of view? Did it give you some distance or some perspective?

I actually started out writing this book in first person. The passage I read last night [about Henry bringing Josh's ashes home] I did write in first person. They're very close to each other. But there are some things I can say in third person about their relationship which are easier to do. It would be awkward for Rios to be thinking some of the things that I say about the relationship.

You were raised Catholic, as was your main character Henry Rios. Henry's got a lot of anger toward the Church. In The Hidden Law *he says, "As far as I was concerned, the Catholic Church was just another totalitarian political entity, like the Communist Party or IBM." What's your own personal attitude toward the Church?*

I guess I do see it as a great force for evil in the world, at one level—and I'm really talking about the leadership of the Church, and especially this Pope from the fourteenth century—but, on another level, I have good friends who are wonderful people and who are practicing Catholics. I figure if they can reconcile their faith to their personal beliefs, then it's really none of my business to judge that.[5]

Does Josh's death precipitate new thinking on Henry's part about religious or spiritual questions?

Yes, in the passage I read last night, which was the full chapter of Josh's death, Henry remarks that death brings out the God in everyone. In *The Last Days*, I write about spiritual experience, because it is a dimension of my own life that is of critical importance to me, and since it's important to me, of course, it necessarily is of importance to Rios. In the book, he struggles not so much with what he believes as with what seems clear to him. At the end of the book, he has this mantra, which is that all change is ultimately for the better. That's something you can't believe unless you believe there is some spiritual purpose to your own life. I certainly believe that. I mean, I believe the reason I'm here, instead of dead from drinking or dead. . . . When I was fourteen I tried to kill myself when I realized I was gay. I didn't succeed; I didn't manage to kill myself from drinking. You know, I think about it, because those were serious attempts. It wasn't my agency that kept me alive in those cases.

To what extent to you think of yourself as a Latino writer?

More and more. This has been a very hard thing for me to figure out. I left my family, I left that community, because there was nothing there for me. I burned the bridges of my ethnicity. I never felt much sympathy with the Mexican Chicano groups in college and law school because they were very conservative socially. My experience of it was that it was very family-oriented, as Mexican American culture tends to be. I didn't have anything

---

5. In the 1992 interview, Nava had elaborated: "I was raised Catholic, but Mexican Catholicism is very primitive; it's not intellectual, it's not theological. And a good deal of that has probably remained. I mean, I believe in God, for instance, which is kind of unfashionable, I guess, among gay intellectuals. I pray, and I believe in an afterlife, although not in a Catholic afterlife. So all of that remains a part of me, but I believe, with Bertrand Russell, that organized religion is the enemy of spirituality."

to do with it, because I really didn't accept that. Not to mention that it's also pretty homophobic.

But I had a revelation, which is that simply because I am Latino and I write about those things, that qualifies me to be a Latino writer. I thought I had to be someone else, and now I see, Well, no. Maybe just by being myself I'm lengthening the spectrum. So I accept that identity, which is not to say that it's accepted by other Latinos. I don't know if my works are read in that community and, if they are, I don't know what they make of them.

I write about my experience as a Mexican American man. It's not experience that many Latinos want to hear about, but that's not my problem; that's theirs.

Are there particular Latino writers whom you admire or have been influenced by?

No, there aren't. I mean, there's Sandra Cisneros, who's a wonderful writer. I think she's very exciting. But I haven't read very much. There isn't much to read, and I haven't read very much of it.

You sent the manuscript of your first novel, The Little Death, *to thirteen publishers before it was accepted by Alyson. What made you persist?*

At that point it was a lark, really. I'd finished writing this book, and I'd been encouraged by a writing teacher I'd studied with to send it out. It was no sweat off my back because I had a full-time job as a prosecutor, which was very satisfying to me, and I was in a relationship, and so I just sent it out to see what would happen. Since it wasn't my life, the rejections weren't as painful as they would have been had I been staking my future on the acceptance of this manuscript for publication.

Do you suspect there was a common reason behind those thirteen rejections?

Yeah, this was 1985 when I was sending the book out, which was just before this wave of interest in gay and lesbian writers on which we're all surfing at the moment. Most of the rejections said, "This is a very nice book, but we can't sell it," including rejections from people I know now are gay editors.

After Goldenboy, *the second of the Rios books, which was also published by Alyson, you moved to HarperCollins, who published your next two Rios novels, and are now with Putnam. What did it mean to you to go from a small, alternative press to a big mainstream house?*

It meant respectability, in a way. We live in a culture that takes some things seriously but not other things. It was very difficult for me to get serious review attention publishing with Alyson, not that Alyson's books don't deserve it, but the way the world works is that small-press books get ignored. That's also true with distribution. I want to make a living at this and I wanted to reach as many readers as I can, and in order to do that it was necessary for me to jump from someplace where I was very happy to someplace where I was much less happy.

You have won four Lambda Literary Awards. What do you think about the gay literary community setting up a series of literary awards for itself?

I think it's a useful marketing tool, and I really do think it exists primarily for the publishing industry. I mean, it's gratifying to win awards, but it doesn't really make the work any less difficult, and it doesn't really have much effect on the way I work. But I think that within the publishing industry it really does help to distinguish certain books from the great mass of titles of gay and lesbian books that are now being published.

In addition to writing mysteries, you have just completed a book about gay civil rights with the historian Robert Dawidoff called Created Equal: Why Gay Rights Matter to America. *Can you say a little about that book?*

It's a book I became interested in writing in 1991 after the governor of California vetoed an antidiscrimination bill he said he would sign. Robert and I got together and decided that, first of all, we needed to present all the arguments against gay and lesbian rights and then to make cogent arguments in defense of them. That's what this book is—it's really a primer for people to start thinking about why the gay and lesbian civil rights movement exists, what it means in terms of the American democratic process, and why the arguments against it are ultimately not only irrational but profoundly antidemocratic.

Who's your audience for that book?

We hope every gay and lesbian in American will buy it and give it to their best straight friend.

Are you hopeful about the future?

The Right is not going to go away. There will be this struggle, always. Racism didn't disappear because Congress passed the Civil Rights Act of

1966; homophobia won't go away because people can serve in the military or be protected from being fired. So in that sense, I'm not hopeful, because people seem to have this need to dislike each other.

On another level, on a legal level, I am hopeful. I really think if Clinton is elected, there will be a federal civil rights bill that will protect gays, and that he will issue that executive order prohibiting discrimination in the military. And in doing those things, he'll really change the tone of the argument. Because that's what civil rights legislation does. It makes it not all right to say "nigger" anymore. At least in public discourse. And I think he will make it not all right to say "queer" or "faggot."

I live in Los Angeles, which is a very progressive community. Yeah, I don't think it's happening in places like Nebraska and Alabama. It's a very interesting time to be alive. It's not very often that one sees the choices so clearly.

What advice would you give to aspiring gay writers today?

Yikes! I would say that writing is work, like everything else. It's wonderful work. It's deeply satisfying work, but if you're waiting for the muse to descend from the heavens, you're going to wait for a very, very long time.

Would the advice be any different to aspiring Latino writers?

No.

Michael Cunningham

Michael Cunningham's novel, *A Home at the End of the World* (1991), is the story of two boyhood friends, Jonathan Glover and Bobby Morrow, who, during their teenage years in Cleveland, fall into a homosexual relationship, then go their separate ways after high school, only to reunite several years later in New York where they form, with Jonathan's sometime girlfriend Clare, a family constellation of sorts. It is a novel that explores both the sadness and the satisfaction born from, to quote the novel, "the gap between what we can imagine and what we in fact create."

Critics and readers alike have been especially enthusiastic about the beauty of Cunningham's prose. Writing in the *Wall Street Journal*, Amy Gamerman noted how Cunningham manages to "fuse the taut, distilled imagery of a poem with the immediacy of a snapshot."[1] Joyce Reiser Kornblatt, in the *New York Times*, wrote that "the author's voice . . . informs every page, reaching at times that lyrical beauty in which even the grimmest events suggest their potential for grace."[2] *A Home at the End of the World* was a finalist for the American Library Association's Gay, Lesbian, and Bisexual Book Award in fiction and was shortlisted for the *Irish Times*/Aer Lingus International Fiction Prize.

Cunningham was born in 1952. He studied at Stanford University, graduating in 1975 with a degree in English, and at the University of Iowa Writers' Workshop (M.F.A., 1980), after which he was awarded a one-year fellowship at Provincetown's Fine Arts Work Center. He published his first novel, *Golden States,* in 1984. A third novel, *Flesh and Blood,* came out in 1995 and won the Whiting Writers Award.

The following interview was taped in the studios of WOMR in Provincetown, Massachusetts, on 4 September 1993.

---

1. Amy Gamerman, "Struggles of a New Age Family," *Wall Street Journal,* 28 December 1990, 5.

2. Joyce Reiser Kornblatt, "Such Good Friends," *New York Times Book Review,* 11 November 1990, 12.

You published your first novel, Golden States, *in 1984, and then not another novel until* A Home at the End of the World, *which came out in 1990. You've alluded to that six-year period between your two novels as a period of "hard times." What was going on for you as a writer during that time?*

I was having hard times not so much in the Dickensian sense as in the— I don't know; what's the opposite?—the Sylvia Plath sense. I had my head in the oven, on and off, during those six years—not literally. You know, it's hard to want to do something, like write a novel. The world doesn't want it; no one has asked you to do it. No one is waiting for you to finish it. I probably have a little less self-confidence than a lot of writers.

To write a book worth reading, you [need] a certain precarious combination of hubris and self-abnegation. On one hand, it's this incredible act of egotism to be grabbing somebody by the collar and saying, "Don't read something else, don't learn French, don't sleep with your lover; *read this now!*" And you have to have that kind of bravado, that kind of wild belief in the notion that you have something to say that people ought to hear. And, at the same time, you can't just be an advertisement for your fabulousness. If you're too caught up in your talent, then you're just John Irving. Oops!

It's a balancing act. I think I spent more than my rightful share of those six years sort of off balance, mired in a sense of—I don't know—a kind of embarrassment at the whole notion of having a presumption to write a book.

I'm also struck by the fact that A Home at the End of the World *represented a quantum leap for you in terms of subject matter, that suddenly you were tackling gay subject matter, gay characters, gay themes in a way that wasn't so prevalent in the first novel.*

Well, the first novel is a gay book, though it's about a boy who is right on the brink of understanding his sexuality. I don't feel like I was backing away from *gay* or any other issues in that book. I have other problems with that book, but not that one. I think *A Home at the End of the World* represents, if anything, a big step for me in terms of scale. It's just about more lives. It's a bigger picture. And the new novel—the one I'm working on now—is another step forward along those lines.[3] It's even bigger. At this rate, by my fifth novel, I'll be writing about whole populations.

---

3. The novel, *Flesh and Blood*, was published in 1995.

Has that been a conscious decision, with each book to increase the scope?

You know, I think it's an unconscious decision that I came to conscious possession of. I can't really imagine sitting down and saying to yourself, I'm now going to write a particular kind of book, and coming up with anything that's worth anything.

A lot of novelists say that they work from outlines, that they somehow have the entire thing in their heads or on paper before they start.

God bless 'em! No, no. I need to get the characters rolling and on their feet. I need to zap them with ten thousand lightening volts before they start to come to some kind of unsteady, jerking life. And then I need to see what they do. For my purposes anyway, if there were an outline, if I knew too clearly what was going to happen, I would end up just pushing and prodding these people toward . . . what do they call it? They would move "inexorably towards their shattering conclusion." It can get very false and very forced. I'm trying to tune into the way people help make their fates and the way their fates are made for them. No, I never know what's going to happen next.

One of the things that impresses me so much about A Home at the End of the World *is how you manage to create four distinct voices, four points of view. You're able to get into the skin of each of them, through successive chapters, and give each his or her fair shake.*

Well, people are only interesting to me if they're worthy adversaries. I can't imagine writing—wanting to write—a character who is just a pushover, or who is just evil, or just good. My life, everybody's life, is more complicated than that. I find in writing that my sense of the book keeps shifting. This is true of the new book, too, though it's not written in different voices. Whoever I'm writing about is the main character at that point. In *A Home at the End of the World*, when I'm writing in Alice's voice, it's about Alice. If there's a reason to write fiction beyond the raw desire for fame and fortune and the admiration of your peers, it's to try to get under the skin of other people. It's the thing fiction can do that no other media can. Other media are better at showing you things, at positing a moral or philosophical argument. What fiction can do is take you for a walk into the heart and soul of somebody. That's not a place you can go through any other medium I know of.

There's a way in which the characters each speak with a kind of high, poetic intelligence that's larger than their ordinary selves. Bobby, for instance, who's the least sophisticated of the four, speaks these absolutely gorgeous sentences.

That's the thing the book has been most criticized for,[4] that the voices are high-flown and somewhat similar, but, yeah, that was a conscious decision. I had started off writing it more almost in dialect. But it was feeling sort of kitschy. It was getting on my nerves; it wasn't feeling right. I was reading *The Waves*, by Virginia Woolf, in which she essentially gives one incredible voice to this whole gaggle of characters. They're speaking from someplace inchoate and preternaturally articulate that's beyond who they are and what they are and the measuring out of coffee cups. That's why you read great geniuses like Virginia Woolf—to steal things, and to be reminded of what you can do. I realized, Right, you can try to speak from these people's souls, which are more articulate than their fumbling tongues.

This is a novel about a small group of people—Bobby, Jonathan, Clare, Alice, who is Jonathan's mother—but it's also emblematic of a whole generation of people who came of age in the sixties, full of a sense of, as you put it, the "gaudy possibilities" in the world. But those possibilities keep getting thwarted, and sidetracked, and delayed. This is a novel that's full of an awareness of the big and little disappointments in life—it's a book full of quiet sadness—and yet I don't feel that it's in any way a hopeless book. This is a long-winded way of asking, How would you describe the hopefulness in your novel?

I can't quite imagine writing a novel that wasn't both despairing and hopeful at the same time. We don't need fiction to chronicle our happinesses— our good dinners and great sex. Those are pleasures that are better accounted for in our real lives. Go out and have a great dinner, have great sex! Don't count on books for that. But our lives are also all threaded through with mortality and sorrow and loss. We need to write about that and talk about that in ways that our lives don't necessarily do. At the same time, I have hope, I have tremendous stupid optimism. And the way the hope seems to manifest itself in *A Home At The End of the World* is just the fact that whatever hap-

---

4. For example: "The only time the novel jars is when it shifts from the characters' speaking voices to their more meditative narrational ones. This is most glaring with Bobby, who goes from inarticulate sentences studded with 'likes' and 'reallys' to eloquent, even lyrical passages of prose." Gamerman, "Struggles," 5.

pens to these people, whatever happens to any of us, we're present, we're right here. There's hopefulness just implied in being alive.

Another thing I pick up in the novel is that there's a different kind of hopefulness for each character. Clare does go off at the end with the baby and starts, presumably, a very different life from the life that Bobby and Jonathan and Erich have, or Alice has.

Yeah. Everybody has his or her own screwed-up happy ending. Everybody's happy ending is compromised. People get little slices of happiness, odd little fragments of it.

The shadows of the fathers—Jonathan's and Bobby's—both of whom die during the course of the novel, loom over Bobby's and Jonathan's lives. In what ways do you think sons, maybe particularly gay sons, must contend with the expectations their fathers laid upon them?

Oh, it's something all sons deal with. I do think it's a particular issue for a lot of gay boys. A gay psychoanalyst whose work I admire, a man named Richard Isay, says that for gay boys the whole Oedipal cycle is reversed: you're in love with your father.

It's such a powerful moment when Jonathan says to his mother, "'I adored my father.'"

It was powerful for me to write that. It was actually difficult to write, partly because I knew my father was going to be reading this stuff. If you are in love with your father, I think your experience is likely to differ from that of a straight kid in that your father, unless he's a complete moron, is going to pick up on it in some way, probably unconsciously, and be freaked out by it. For me, anyway, there is this tricky combination of admiration and desire for someone who finds your admiration and desire really disquieting, if not outright disgusting. That's a big wrangle for a gay man.

Death figures prominently in this novel—the fathers' deaths, Bobby's brother's death, his mother's suicide, Erich's death. Aside from the plot requiring these deaths, how do you account for the presence of so much death in the novel?

There's so much death in the world. It just happened. The new novel I'm working on has a lot of death in it too. It's just a reflection of, I guess, my own innate sense of mortality, which is revved up by the times we live in. So many of us go from our jobs to a friend in a hospital room back to our apartments. Everything we do is interspersed with visits to people who are sick, who are dying. I feel infected and informed by it in ways that I can't imagine undoing. The world just seems laced with death. That's not an entirely morbid thing. You know: there it is. There's death all the time. It's part of our lives.

Juxtaposed to death, Woodstock keeps surfacing in your novel as a kind of lost paradise of the sixties, an almost mythical place that looms as the "real home" for, well, certainly for Bobby and maybe for the others. By the end of the novel they, in fact, do set up a home there, but it's certainly not the sixties paradise that Bobby had dreamed of. What is your particular attraction—both personally and in terms of the structure of this novel—to Woodstock and the music of the sixties?

I'm forty now, and I was in high school in the sixties. I'm a member of that generation that could have gone to Woodstock but didn't. Which may, in its way, have been more profound and scarring than actually going to Woodstock, than having been there and being done with it. Anybody who lived through and came out the other end of that period had a certain sense that the world was going to profoundly change. I was foolish enough to imagine that we were going to win, that women and gay people and people of color were going to triumph. And, in some sort of disorganized way, that we would actually defeat death itself. When you're a seventeen-year-old on acid in 1968 that doesn't seem wholly out of the question. And obviously that didn't happen and things have changed in ways we never imagined.

It was pretty much an intuitive decision to bring these people—a man with AIDS, people with other afflictions—into a kind of collision with Woodstock and whatever is left of it up there. You know, now it's old hippies and lawyers with country houses from New York.

There's a lot written these days about how gay men and lesbians are forming new models of families, new kinds of constellations. Certainly Bobby, Jonathan, and Clare, at least for a while, form a very different kind of family when they move to Woodstock. Was it your intention to make their experience paradigmatic for this whole generation of gay men and lesbians?

No, that's never my intention. I would never try to say, if a certain kind of person does a certain kind of thing, that this is what will happen.

Flannery O'Connor once loaned a book of stories to one of her neighbors in Georgia. And the woman gave it back and said, "Well, them stories just went and shown how some folks would do!" And I always think of that. You're writing about how "some folks"—these particular— would do. But, no, Bobby and Jonathan and Clare are particular kinds of people, and certain things happen to them, but, no, I don't think I'm setting up a formula for what will happen if people dare to exceed the bounds of old-fashioned, conventional family.

I ardently believe in exceeding the bounds of old-fashioned, conventional family. That's what I do. I have a family that I've assembled on my own and had assembled for me. These are people whom I have seen do for one another what we're always told only families will do for you. I've seen people mop up the vomit and mop up the shit and hold one another as they died. These are the things they told us you need your family for and—guess what?—you don't. You can make a family of your own. My lover and I are planning on having a baby with two women. They want to wait another year, or so. Yeah, I have all kinds of really hopeful feelings of what we can do for one another that aren't necessarily reflected in what happens to Bobby and Jonathan and Clare.

There's a fairy-tale quality to your novel—indeed, there are references to Peter Pan and Snow White. Clare, for instance, refers to Jonathan and Bobby as the "lost boys."

At a point I was thinking of calling the novel The Island of Lost Boys, and then I didn't like that anymore and threw it out.

And even the movement of the plot itself—toward this lost arcadia called "Woodstock"—has fairy-tale elements in it. Were you aware of those elements when you wrote Home?

Well, you know, I grew up on fairy tales. Like most of us do. No, it's not conscious. As I've said, I don't plan very much when I write, but my consciousness is sort of littered with fairy tales. Yeah, I suppose in some respect what I'm setting out to do is write a fairy tale with sex in it. Actually they had sex in them, too.

You keep subtly subverting the happily-ever-after ending of fairy tales without completely trouncing it.

Right. Well, you have to. We know too much.

Writing in Contemporary Gay American Novelists, *Reed Woodhouse, calls you one of a new generation of gay writers who, "while treating the subject of homosexuality, are more determined and able to make it one subject among others, their gay characters subsumed within a larger social group."⁵ Is that something you'd agree with?*

I hope my gay characters are not "subsumed" by anyone or anything. But, yeah, I do find that when I write—or when I walk down the street—I am a gay man, and that profoundly affects my experience. My lover is a gay man and many of our friends are. And then some of our friends are lesbians, and some of our friends are straight women and straight men. And my parents are straight—as far as I know—and I live in a bigger world than just the world that specifically pertains to my sexual orientation. And I don't in any way want to deny the importance or the impact of growing up with that sense of difference, but I don't want to leave fifty-year-old straight women out of it either—or twenty-five-year-old straight guys, whoever—because there they are, and they have a real effect on me.

What does the term "gay novelist" mean to you?

It actually means less and less to me as time goes on. I think there was, and probably to some extent continues to be, a real need for books about lesbians and gay men, because most of us grew up completely absent from everything we read. We needed a body of good books that were specifically about the experiences of gay women and men, and now we have a body of those books. I'm feeling sort of anxious to take it to the next step. In my ideal world, you'll just pick up a book and it will turn out to have all straight characters in it, or it will turn out to have gay characters in it, or some combination of the two. I'm finding the whole notion of "gay literature," as something distinct from other kinds of literature, to be increasingly less interesting or useful.

We're talking in Provincetown, which you first came to when you were a fellow at the Fine Arts Work Center. You also come back periodically to Provincetown.

---

5. Reed Woodhouse, "Michael Cunningham," in *Contemporary Gay American Novelists: A Bio-Bibliographical Critical Sourcebook,* ed. Emmanuel S. Nelson (Westport, Conn.: Greenwood, 1993), 84.

What did this place mean to you when you first came here, and what does it continue to mean to you?

It's come to mean a great deal to me. It's come to feel like my hometown. It's funny, when I first came here, I still remember driving down Commercial Street with some friends—I'd never been in the East before, never mind Provincetown—and putting my head in my hands and saying, "It's just like the set of *The Cabinet of Dr. Caligari!*" All these slightly too-small buildings and none of them were quite at right angles, and there was no horizon on the street. And I thought, Oh God, what's this going to be like?

Back then—this was thirteen years ago—the "A House" closed,[6] everything closed. It was a long, hard winter. It turned out to be like one of those *Twilight Zone* heavens and the punch line at the end of the episode is Ha, ha! It's really hell! The heavenly proposition was that you got eight months to just come and do nothing but write, and that turned out to be the hellish proposition, too. I remember walking down Commercial Street one Saturday night in February. The street was deserted; it had snowed. There wasn't a soul out. I was walking along and a big plop of snow fell on me. And I was standing there, on a Saturday night, with snow on me, thinking, What am I doing with my life? How did I end up here? And I vowed that once the fellowship was up I would go back to what I thought of as the real world and rejoin it.

I did, I went to New York. But it's funny. Something about this place stayed with me. It's almost like the stories you hear of couples who didn't like each other at first, who were kind of—I don't know—too much alike, maybe, to really click. Because I found myself coming back. Very much like you would go on another date with somebody you didn't like: Why am I doing this? And gradually over the years all my resistance has worn down. I really do think of this town and this landscape as my home in some way. If I died tomorrow, this is where I'd want my ashes scattered.

You recently wrote a piece for Mother Jones *magazine about Queer Nation, a radical gay rights organization. In that piece you wrote, "If you're gay and you're not angry, you're just not paying attention." You yourself are a member of ACT*

---

6. The Atlantic House, a gay bar in Provincetown.

UP. You've helped engineer a takeover of the MacNeil/Lehrer News Hour, *you've chained yourself to the White House gates. Why do you feel it's important to work with a group like ACT UP?*

Because I think there is evil in the world, there are bad people doing bad things. The epidemic is being neglected, and people are making a profit off of it and we need to do everything we can to stop those assholes. I find there is a certain gap between what I'm trying to do writing fiction, which, as I said, involves justifying everybody, finding the way people explain themselves to themselves, and my feelings about a drug company like Hoffman-Laroche that delays testing and suppresses drugs and charges outrageous prices. I have no interest in writing about Hoffman-Laroche's side of this. My interest as far as Hoffman-Laroche is concerned is to chain myself to their gates or to do whatever else I need to do to get them to change.

Some people would say that as a writer you'd be more effective continuing to put all your energy into your writing. How do you respond to that?

I just don't think it's true. I have enough energy to do more than one thing. I don't see my writing as separate from my politics by any means. But it's a more generous, muted version of my politics. I feel that my particular gifts as a writer have to do with getting under other people's skins and I think that there's important work to be done that finally has nothing to do with empathy, that has to do with calling people to account and telling them, "Look, you have to do this; you have to stop doing that."

You're working on a new novel right now, but you're also working on a biography of Virginia Woolf for a series of young adult books that Chelsea House will publish. Can you say more about that project?

Oh, yeah. It's great. Martin Duberman is overseeing it, and he has got a group of lesbian and gay writers doing this series of young adult books. There's a lesbian and gay issues series, and then there's another series of biographies of lesbian and gay people from history. Jewelle Gomez is doing Audre Lorde; Terrence McNally is doing Tennessee Williams. He said he didn't want the correlations to be too cozy. He didn't want only black women doing black women and only black men doing black men and women doing women. He's mixing it up a bit. Sarah Schulman is doing

Allen Ginsberg, and I got Virginia Woolf, which I am thrilled about. I've been spending part of the summer reading her.

Is it hard pitching your prose to a young adult audience? Have you had to make some concessions?

I haven't started writing yet, but I imagine when I do that I'm just going to write it the way I feel it. I've never had much luck getting down on my knees and talking to children in a squeaky little voice.

But you're about to have a kid.

[*Laughter*] Whom I will speak to in measured, adult tones. At all times. Yeah, it needs to be accessible to young queer people, but I don't expect to talk down to anybody. I'm going to try to write the book about Virginia Woolf that I wish had been available to me to read when I was fourteen. I didn't read pabulum when I was fourteen. I didn't read stuff that just pandered to my icky little sensibility.

How will you skew it? Will it be primarily about her as a lesbian, or about her career?

I want it to be about her as a lesbian who had this incredible career. If I end up slighting one or the other, I will feel like I've failed, because the two seem inextricably linked to me. She was a lesbian who was a genius, and the two have everything to do with one another.[7]

Last night at the reading, you read a little passage from A Room of One's Own. *I'm curious to know what your own writing habits are like.*

I do have a room of my own, as it happens. My lover and I are moving, but for years we have lived in an apartment in the Village not much bigger than this little [radio] studio we're in right now. There's been no question of me writing there with my twenty square feet of disorganized papers strewn all over the place. So I rented a studio, over on Broadway and Bleecker, and it's been heaven. I get up in the morning and, like any guy in the suburbs, I get dressed, make the coffee, and "Bye, honey!" and I go off and write. And I like that. That seems to appeal to my bourgeois streak. I like getting up and go-

---

7. Cunningham's volume on Virginia Woolf never appeared in the Chelsea House series, but his fourth novel, *The Hours* (1998), is a homage to Woolf.

ing out to the place where I do my work, and finishing my work and coming home to the place where I don't write, where I carry on the other business.

You have an M.F.A. degree from Iowa. In hindsight, how do you feel about the professionalization of fiction writing?

Oh, God! I hate to quote Flannery O'Connor twice in the same interview, but she was asked a similar question. She was asked whether writing programs stifle writers and she said, "They don't stifle enough of them!" Iowa was good for me. I also saw it destroy people. I saw that kind of competitiveness. That kind of emphasis on producing work that will be published really screwed people up. But it was great for me. It kind of saved me. As far as I know, there's not much in the way of a literary community. I'm not sure I'd want to belong to one if there was one, but as it happens I could never find one.

Before I went to Iowa, I had these ideas about being a writer, but I was living next to a shopping mall, and the idea of doing this—of this as something that you could do with your life—just seemed insane to me. My family, my background isn't especially bookish. It seemed sort of like parlaying some sort of kook hobby into a life. It seemed sort of like building a scale model of the Eiffel Tower out of Popsicle sticks. And I couldn't really invest it with the weight that I needed to actually devote myself to it, and, with certain embarrassment, I went away to Iowa—I didn't want to tell people I was going to the graduate program in creative writing! It seemed like one step away from pot holder making. I got there, and there I was, for two years among people—you know, the talent is really various in any program, any group of people who say they're artists—but there were some really gifted people there, people whom I respected and loved. By the end of two years I really came out changed. I really saw that this could be important. This could have something to do with your life. I'm really indebted to them for that.

What do you think is the most important thing you learned in those two years?

During those two years, nobody taught me anything. I had two years in which to figure out how to do it on my own. You know, I didn't have to have a stupid job. Well, I had a stupid job that I just sort of sleepwalked through. And I started to figure out how to do it by *doing* it. By writing one bum, limp sentence after another, until they started to gather a little more of their own strength, until they started to have some kind of bone structure.

One of the questions I've been asking everyone on this program is what kind of advice they would give to young, aspiring gay and lesbian fiction writers.

Hmm. Yeah. Have faith. That's not especially profound, but it's the best thing I know to tell people. Just fasten your seat belt. Any writer, except the very, very, very fortunate few, writes for years without any reason to think that anything is going to happen with this. And I think that kind of obscurity matches and doubles something that young lesbians and gay men feel anyway. So, I guess what I would say to lesbian and gay writers is, have *double* faith. And screw 'em if they can't take a joke.

John Preston

John Preston was the most prolific gay man of letters of his time. At the time of his death on 28 April 1994, he had authored, edited, or coauthored well over thirty books, including novels, short stories, essays and other nonfiction, adventure thrillers, and gay male erotica, which Preston insisted on calling pornography. His subjects ranged from S/M sex to hometown life in New England, from the relationships between gay men and lesbians to safe sex practices, from Provincetown drag queens to living with AIDS.

Preston was born in 1945 and grew up in Medfield, Massachusetts, the town depicted in an essay he wrote for his own anthology, *Hometowns*. He attended Lake Forest College in Illinois, then moved to Minneapolis in 1970, where he founded Gay House, the first gay community center in the United States. While in Minneapolis, he earned a graduate degree in sexual health, which led to his moving to New York to edit a sex education newsletter. In 1975, he moved again, this time to the West Coast to take up the editorship of the *Advocate*, but returned to New York a year later, where he began to write short stories for *Drummer* magazine. In 1979, he moved to Portland, Maine, where he lived for the rest of his life.

Based on a series in *Drummer*, Preston's 1983 novel, *Mr. Benson*, about an S/M master, and the subsequent novels in his Master series, achieved cult status. These novels, which at their core are about "the ungovernable decadence of the urban sexual underground," as Jane Troxell has written,[1] earned Preston an enthusiastic and loyal readership.

Throughout the 1980s, Preston continued publishing novels in the S/M Master series. He also wrote a series of gay adventure novels featuring superhero Alex Kane. At the same time, his commitment to sexual health prompted him to take up several other projects, including the editorship of two anthologies: *Hot Living: Erotic Stories about Safer Sex* and *Personal Dispatches: Writers Confront AIDS*.

---

1. Jane Troxell, "John Preston," in *Contemporary Gay American Novelists: A Bio-Bibliographical Critical Sourcebook*, ed. Emmanuel S. Nelson (Westport, Conn.: Greenwood, 1993), 323.

Most of Preston's work in the last years of his life involved nonfiction. As an editor, he brought into being several important and highly successful anthologies, among them *Hometowns: Gay Men Write about Where They Belong; A Member of the Family: Gay Men Write about Their Families; Sister and Brother: Lesbians and Gay Men Write about Their Lives Together* (coedited with Joan Nestle); *Friends and Lovers: Gay Men Write about the Families They Create*; as well as the *Flesh and the Word* series of gay male erotica. Some of these anthologies won Lambda Literary Awards and went on to become Book-of-the-Month Club selections. For these and other achievements, John Preston was named by *Lambda Book Report* as one of the twenty-five most influential men in gay publishing and writing in the last decade. At the time of his death, he may indeed have been, as one New York editor noted, the "best-known gay writer" in America.

Our interview, part of the WOMR series "The Word Is Out," took place on 25 September 1993. It is probably the last major interview that Preston gave.

It's been a decade since the book edition of Mr. Benson *was first issued by Alternate Publishing in San Francisco. How did you come to write* Mr. Benson?

Mr. Benson began actually as a short story, and the first chapter of the novel was the first fiction I ever wrote in my life. It was pretty much just a laugh I was having when I was living in Manhattan. This was in 1978; the book publication was much later. I sent in the short story [to *Drummer*], thinking I might hear from the magazine in a few months, when in fact I got an immediate phone call with a request to turn it into a novel.

That must have been a heady experience to go from a short story to an invitation to write a novel.

Well, it was very funny. The whole point from *Drummer*'s perspective was to create a serial, and they would publish it as I wrote it. So I did maybe about four chapters before I realized that I didn't have a plot, and that this would be a fairly essential issue for anything that was supposed to become a novel. So I had to, in midstream, create a plot for this novel.

Tell me about Aristotle Benson. What's he like?

I need to start by saying that I think *Mr. Benson* is a very funny book. As I was writing it, I considered it a comedy, which meant that I wasn't at all prepared for the response to the book when it was actually published in the magazine, let alone when it was published as a book, because so many people took it so seriously.

Aristotle Benson is essentially the perfect master: he's rich, handsome, in control, has no personal needs, and decides he wants to create the perfect "bottom." So he finds Jamie in a leather bar on the New York waterfront. Jamie is sort of an uninteresting but interested clone, whom Mr. Benson then shapes into the masochist of his dreams.

What's the master-slave dynamic all about?

Oh, God, who knows? There's no answer for that. There are so many different reasons why so many different people enter into something like S and M. I think many people do it for quite profound explorations of themselves and their personalities. I think other people do it because it feels good. I think other people do it because they have low self-esteem. The list goes on, and to try to reduce it to a single issue is not anything that's really going to work. I think my writing reflects that entire length. *Mr. Benson* is a very fanciful look at what those dynamics are. Then my third book was a collection of short stories, *I Once Had a Master and Other Erotic Tales,* and that was a much more profound exploration of what are the ways and reasons for which people enter into an S and M experience.

You have, many times, protested that you are not your creation, Mr. Benson, and yet your readers continue to equate you with your character, sometimes with humorous results.

Well, people are desperate that I be my character. It was especially true when *Mr. Benson* was first published. People would come on to me, which I thought was a wonderful thing, because I had written this book. In fact, one of the first things I did once I realized this could happen was to have *Drummer* out me to make sure. We had automatically, unthinkingly used a pseudonym. They just assumed that anybody who wrote for a magazine like *Drummer* would want to hide. I gave it no thought. But once it became clear that I could get laid from all this, I wanted to make sure I was getting all my opportunities; so I had them out me—long before there was outing—in an article. But, in fact, people were not looking to have sex with me; they were looking to have sex with Mr. Benson. And that's been an ongoing issue. I wish it produced more sex, but actually it seems to scare off people more than anything else. I've discovered, for instance, that people are very frightened that I'm going to write about them if we have sex, and they can't get past the idea that perhaps I'm taking notes when we're in the bedroom. Many people won't have sex with me because they're convinced that I'm going to do to them what my characters do to one another in my writing. It's always amusing, but it's more frustrating than it should be.

As you've mentioned, Mr. Benson *was the first in a series of novels you've written—other titles include* Entertainment for a Master, Love of a Master, In Search of a Master—*about the S and M scene. But beyond being specifically about S and M, these novels explore what sex itself has meant for many gay men. Do you want to elaborate on that?*

I guess the major way I can respond to that is to point out a very unexpected response to those books. They're now, ten or fewer years later, perceived as major documents of how gay men had sex. That was not my intention—I wasn't conscious of doing it—but I wrote about real places and things that real people did with one another, and/or the fantasies that we gay men had, in a way that no one else was really doing. So I'm quite stunned to find these books perceived as historical documentation of a specific time in our lives. And very pleased. I think that something like *I Once Had a Master* is a very accurate piece of history; it certainly is the most autobiographical of all my books.

The other books really are much more examinations of our fantasies rather than our realities, because they take place, for the most part, in something called The Network, which is a totally fantasy-driven secret society that I created. But again, simply the documentation of the fantasies of gay men has a validity.

Really, I wrote all these books as entertainment, and I'm always pleased that there's some other way in which they can be perceived and used, but I don't want to go too far, because there's very little pretension on my part in writing these books. They are entertainment. In fact, the truth is that I write pornography the way that other people consume it. I simply don't have great literary intent in these books. All I'm doing is turning myself on, fleshing out my fantasies, and having a good time with them.

And yet, there are literary considerations going on, too. You craft a good sentence. You put together an interesting set of characters and a good plot.

I would hope so, but I'm just wanting to be clear and honest that my intention is not, for instance, the intention that David Leavitt or Edmund White have as they approach their work. I think that my skill has matured and sharpened, and therefore I can present my fantasies in a way that can stun some people in terms of twists of character and narration. God knows, if after all the books I've written I can't do dialogue, then I should give up. But they don't have the same literary intent as, say, my essays do. My essays are clearly where I think my career is as a writer.

It's very strange and difficult to hear people talk about planning a literary career. Certainly no one should have begun a literary career with *Mr. Benson*. But what *Mr. Benson* really accomplished for me in my career—and I do consider it the least literary of all my books—what it did was to prove to me and to people watching me that I had an audience and that there was a large group of men, and a surprising number of women, who wanted to take this kind of writing seriously and who therefore took me seriously. So it created that audience and made me very appealing to mainstream publishers and made me take my writing more seriously. When I as a writer have an audience, then I take myself and my writing much more seriously. I'm very much aware of being in a conversation with my readers.

Let's go back and talk a little about your early years. You were born in Medfield, Massachusetts, in 1945, part of the baby boom generation. What was it like coming into young gay manhood in the sixties?

Well, it was walking into a void. It's quite stunning to imagine and to experience the difference in thirty years of gay life. I had an experience of that recently that was very informative. I edited a book called *Hometowns,* in which gay men, including yourself, wrote essays about the places either where they grew up or where they chose to live. It was an attempt to explore the concept of place in our lives. I got a fan letter from a young reader who was then seventeen, who was a senior in a high school near Medfield, and who had discovered the book in Book-of-the-Month Club. The letter was extraordinarily moving, because he was describing to me the same loneliness that I had experienced as a seventeen-year-old, but also the cracks in the loneliness that I had never been able to find. He had found this book. You and I both wrote about towns similar to the one in which he was living. We never found that in our Book-of-the-Month Club mailing. He was going off to college and he knew that there was a gay students group waiting for him and was very terrified of it but was also looking forward to it. He could pick up a magazine and could find out information about what was out there. None of that was available to us. The only things that existed in the town library were psychiatric journals and that kind of thing. Maybe the Kinsey Report in some kind of abstracted form. We just didn't have things that reflected the lives that we might be entering into.

I remember that those psychiatric journals—and certainly any books about homosexuality—were in the lock and key section of my public library.

Ah . . . Medfield wasn't that bad. I was also perceived as a precocious child, so my family and the librarians were very inclined to let me have access to anything I wanted.

You then left Medfield and went to Lake Forest College, outside of Chicago. I was interested to note that your writing career began relatively late, that after college you did some other things that were perhaps tangential to writing but were not directly related to writing.

I never had a concept of being a writer. I was constantly told that I could not be a writer. I was much too working class. I had an extremely thick New England accent at the time. I was told not to become an English major for that reason. And, as often happens with that kind of—I think "oppression" is not an overly dramatic word right now—I bought into it. I accepted that. Even in the face of a lot of evidence that it wasn't true. One of the things that I could only find the irony in now with hindsight is that, while I was quite explicitly frozen out of whatever might have been the writing groups at my college, I earned my spending money by being a newspaper reporter, and covered local government in the town. But of course in that sort of rarefied society that was not considered writing. And I didn't consider it writing.

I then became an activist. I was the founder of the first gay community center in the country, Gay House in Minneapolis, and through that activism did much writing. Also through that activism I worked in sexual health and eventually became the managing editor of publications for SIECUS [Sex Information and Education Council of the United States], the major sex-information organization in the country, which was in New York. And then I became the editor of the *Advocate*, but that was clearly perceived by me and the publisher and the world as my activism again, not as my writing.

That was very early on in the days of the Advocate.

I was the editor [for] almost precisely the [entire] year 1975. I was there, on staff, much earlier, sometime in 1974, but I didn't take over until the first issue of 1975.

What was it like being at the helm of a national gay newspaper?

It was hell. It was the worst year of my life. First of all, the reason I was hired was to take the *Advocate*, which was the largest national gay publication by far, and to transform it from a local Los Angeles paper that happened to have a circulation outside of Southern California into a national publication. That meant that I was automatically much hated by people in Southern California. So my move there to accomplish this was quite torturous. It also meant firing a great deal of staff who had had the appropriate skills for a local paper but couldn't make the transition to a national paper. And then to make my life more difficult, the publisher moved the paper to the San Francisco Bay Area, so I had to oversee a really tumultuous physical, geographic move. Probably the biggest part was that I learned to distrust and dislike the publisher/owner, who was David Goodstein. As time went on, it became more obvious that he was more interested in organizing a group of supporters for himself than in creating a piece of journalism. And that's why I only lasted for a year. It was a nightmare.

After your stint with the Advocate, *you returned to New York, but then, in 1979, moved to Portland, Maine, where you still live. Why that seemingly drastic move, from the urban excitement of Gotham City to the—may I venture to say quieter?—pleasures of a small New England city?*

I was very consciously doing the dance of the big major gay cities. I call those ten years of my life the "great gay tour."

You did Chicago, L.A., San Francisco . . .

Minneapolis, Philadelphia, New York. I was excited by that. I learned from that. It was quite something to be part of the evolution of that gay life, but I was always alienated from the places in which I lived. For a long time, I thought that was simply being homosexual, but then I eventually realized that a lot of it had to do with not being in New England, and that all of the signals of how life is lived, and how people act, and what things should look like and what the ground looks like, and what the ocean looked like are, for me, New England. This is a major part of my identity. So I wanted to come back. At the same time, this was the moment when it appeared that I could have a career as a writer, which was utterly unexpected. It had not been in the cards, as I say. But in order to be a writer, I knew that I needed a quieter place. The big cities had ceased to be a stimulation and had become a distraction, is the way I usually put it—and also I needed a less expensive place. The initial impulse, of course, was to move to Boston, but there seemed to be no reason to leave New York for Boston. The tradeoffs weren't going to help. So I chose Portland. And pretty much I chose Portland feeling it was the smallest city I could live in. And it's been perfect.

We tend to assume that gay men, more than perhaps any other group, invent themselves; that they have much more geographical fluidity, that they have fled small towns and have sought out those large urban areas, that they don't seem as nostalgically attached to hometown or place of origin. And yet what you say and write seems to go in the face of that.

I don't want to impose this on anyone else, but my life really was to become the ultimate gay man. I'm smirking because you skipped a chapter in my life—after I left the *Advocate*, I became a hustler and stayed in San Francisco for another couple of years. That's certainly an example of ultimate urban gay male experience. And it was important to create that whole world; it was important to create the Castro; and I was in San Francisco at the beginning of the Castro. It was important to create Christopher Street; and I lived in New York at the beginning of Christopher Street. And so we were all focused on this creation of our new lives and our new selves. We did that. It was a very eventful, powerful, and important ten years of my life. I helped to create the concept of a national gay publication. I created the first gay community center in the country. I was very much a part of this creation, and yet at the end of it I recognized that I had not ceased being a New Englander.

Now when I began this whole process, which would be 1968, we saw no other option for gay life than creating a separate entity. The experiment, which is my life in the past fourteen years, was to go to Portland to see if, in fact, one could go home as a gay man. And I'm very struck by how important it is for how many people now to go home or to stay home. That gay world does exist, but I'm intrigued by how many people in Maine, for instance, and in other parts of New England, perceive San Francisco not as a lifestyle option, a political act, but rather as an adult theme park. Gay men now treat San Francisco and Greenwich Village the way the rest of society treats Disneyland: not only is it a place to visit as opposed to move to, but they can't even conceive of living there.

Just a playground.

Right.

It was soon after your move to Portland that you wrote what you call your first novel, Franny, Queen of Provincetown, *a series of dramatic monologues by an aging avocado-shaped queen, who manages to be both tough and bighearted. Such a novel from the "dark lord of gay erotica" seems kind of anomalous. What was behind your decision to write* Franny?

I love the fact that you point out that Franny was an avocado-shaped queen. I really learned so much in writing *Franny.* I don't know if you're aware of this, but that is literally the only description of Franny in the book. I was amazed to watch reviewers talk about the "wonderfully realized character" who was an avocado-shaped queen. But there is not another word that physically describes Franny in the whole book. So that was an intriguing lesson about the effect of minimalism.

I did not perceive of myself as a writer—you must always remember that—when I wrote *Franny.* Or I was only beginning to perceive of myself as a writer, and the basic way I had that was this phenomenal audience response from *Mr. Benson* and the other sex writing I had done. And my immediate response to that response was, Oh, I can write anything for these kids, these guys. And it was the response of my editors that I could write anything. I never felt restricted to what I had been writing. I very quickly, for instance, moved to essays, and published essays in *Drummer,* which everyone had thought would be an impossibility.

As most often in my writing, *Franny* was motivated by anger. There was a spate of books then—this was about 1982—where it became almost mandatory for the gay male author to kill the drag queen. The drag queens were the great victims in many gay books. It's almost as though we were trying to kill off the repressed image of what it meant to be a gay man and create the clone. I've never seen that actually explored—and I don't intend to go back and reread all those terrible first novels—but it was certainly my response that these were heroes, not victims. I wanted to prove what heroes they were and to show how they were heroes. So I created Franny and Isadora, his sidekick, who essentially become the mentors of young gay men as they come out.

On this, the eve of the twenty-fifth anniversary of Stonewall, I think it will be emphasized again and again that it was, in fact, drag queens at the Stonewall Inn who started that riot on the night of Judy Garland's funeral.

Yeah, but it will probably be emphasized again and again in ballrooms and in the Grand Hyatt. You know, it's a lot easier to validate the idea of a drag queen as opposed to living with the drag queen.

Let's talk about the Alex Kane novels. There are six such novels, under the heading "The Mission of Alex Kane," which you wrote in the mid-eighties. First of all, who is Alex Kane?

Well, there's background that we should talk about. I wrote and published *Mr. Benson, Franny, the Queen of Provincetown,* and *I Once Had a Master* in a relatively short period of time. They all came out as books within the same twelve months. I'd written these books and had moved to Maine with the purpose of becoming a writer, exploring this new possibility. One of the first things that happened was I realized I was taught quite cruelly, that I was not going to earn a living as a writer of gay material. The money I received for those books was $500 for *Mr. Benson,* and $750 for *Franny.* This was not going to work. I also knew from the experience of one of my great role models, who was Samuel Steward, and also from my understanding of myself, that I was not going to be a writer unless I lived as a writer, that if I so much as attempted to have a part-time job it would just be in my personality that I could not focus on being a writer. So it was very important for me to live as a writer.

I had by then met some people in New York who were in publishing, and I contacted them and essentially cashed in what chips I had, saying to all of them, "I need a writing gig that will earn me a living. What can you do? I need an agent, I need something." And they responded and eventually I ended up with an agent, Peter Ginsberg, and when I first met him, I said, "What am I going to do?" He said, "Well, the hottest thing right now is male action novels." These were a specific genre of paperback originals, not unlike Rambo. In fact, Rambo—what was the name of that book, *First Blood?*—is pretty much an archetype of the genre. Do you remember the "A Team" on television? The "A Team" is actually the perfection of the genre, which is a group of five Vietnam veterans who bond together and fight to save democracy.

I told Peter that this was absurb, that I couldn't possibly write this kind of stuff, that I was a queer who had never been in the military. And he said, "Oh, of course you can write it. Think about it." And so I read a lot of these books and discovered that they were intolerably homoerotic, just incredibly homoerotic. These men don't just bond, they love each other, they cry over each other, they can't stand to be separated from one another. So I decided I would attempt this. Now the other interesting thing is that at that time one of my two brothers had just joined the Marine Corps. He was, in fact, the perfect market for these books. So I figured correctly that I could call him up and get the voice. He was so delighted that I would write something that he could show his friends.

So I spent the next couple of years following him by telephone around the world as his assignments changed. I remember calling him in the Philippines just so he could describe what it felt like to hold a certain kind of weapon, or what the latest slang was, or what the right attitude was. I became the author of the Black Berets, who were my team, my guys.[2] Now, when I did this, all the "gay lit" types watching me were extraordinarily disdainful. You know, this was a "degradation of my skill," this was going to be the "ruination of my career," no one would ever take me seriously again. Sasha Alyson [the publisher of Preston's previous novels] was actually one of the people who did as well. Until Shasha met by chance with the publisher of the Black Berets and got their sales figures, and then he changed his mind and decided I should write a gay version of this genre.

---

2. The Black Berets were a group of characters in Preston's male action novels, which were published in the mid-eighties under the pseudonym Mike McCray.

I was really into it. I mean, I was whipping off these books one a month. I had the formula down pat and truly had a reputation for knowing how to do them. I wrote a couple other series for a couple other publishers as well. So I took "the formula" of the male action novel and created the Mission of Alex Kane [series]. Alex Kane is, as the formula goes, a Vietnam veteran, whose lover had been killed by an American homophobe in Vietnam. One of the vital things for these books is that essentially the character must bottom out; it must become part of the mythology that he wanders the desert. And after the murder of his lover, Alex does that and nearly self-destroys. Very, very similar in a mythological sense to the AA concept of "bottoming out."

So Alex is in the pits. He's been robbed, beaten, abandoned in a flophouse in San Francisco. Then the other element of the formula arrives, which is the force which is to give him the resources to change from self-hatred to an active force. That's his lover's father, who is unaccountably and brilliantly wealthy.

And straight?

And straight. But he decides that it's Alex Kane's goal in life—the mission of Alex Kane—to save the dreams of gay boys everywhere. And so Alex goes out and does that. In the first book he meets up with Danny Fratelli, who is the perfect Italian gymnast in high school, and who becomes his lover and sidekick. The sidekick is a necessary part of this whole thing, too. It was wonderfully therapeutic, because all I have to do—by the way, I don't think I'm finished with those; I think I could continue those in a second, and probably will—but all I have to do is pick up a newspaper and become incensed at something. And of course we're all trained to be such good boys—you know, I'm a good repressed New Englander—so even if I'm going to respond to something, I tend to do it with rational discussion and essays and so forth. But suddenly I had this way to throw them out the window. What Alex always does to a homophobe is to throw him out a skyscraper window. You know, just do it. I love the books! I just love them.

I want to pursue that a little further, because Alex does, indeed, resort to some tactics that one could describe as "lawless."

Oh, yeah. Well, the whole point of any of these books—Black Berets or Alex Kane—is that they're vigilantes, somebody who will not be restricted by the niceties of law. So they're by definition lawless.

Do you justify that by saying that these books are fantasies? What's the intention behind Alex's resorting to such bad-boy practices?

"Intention" is too big a word for entertainments like this. They are fantasies. I don't even know if I want to respond to the concept of my intention. My intention is to write an adventure novel. And adventure novels are outside our experience.

Many in the literary establishment would tend to write you off, or at least these books off, as the author of "pulp" or "genre" novels. What's your response to that?

They are! I mean, that's what they are. I have no problem with their being written off as that, because that's what they are. I'm very clear when I'm writing entertainments, and I have no problem with doing that. It's very, very clear to me that most of my erotica, and certainly the Alex Kane books, are entertainments. Now, if the skill of my writing elevates them in somebody's esteem, great; but there is nothing in an Alex Kane novel where I'm attempting to be a litterateur. I don't think they should dismiss them as pulp. They should recognize them as pulp and then recognize they're also very good pulp.

There are very few writers of your talent and your stature who would put their own names to genre fiction, to entertainments. Why don't you have a problem with that? Or maybe the question is, why do other writers have a problem with that?

That's the better question, and I can't answer why. I write for an audience. To me writing is a communication with an audience, and my base audience has proven that they will follow me anywhere. And they have, thereby, given me an enormous freedom. I have never aspired to be a literary figure. I'm somewhat delightedly, but certainly amusedly, entertained to discover myself having become one. I never set out to be where I am today. And I think there are lots of people who are tearing out what hair they have left [over the fact] that I did it, because they are the people who attempted to become who I have become.

We've been throwing out these terms "erotica" and "pornography." What's the difference?

Packaging. There's no difference other than packaging. It's just a whole lot of social constructs and people being silly. To me, erotica and pornography are both encompassed by the simple statement that they are explicitly sexual writings. People would like to separate them, but really the only separation you can make is in terms of the package they're put in. *Flesh and the Word* and *Flesh and the Word 2*, which are my erotic anthologies, have been published by a division of Penguin. Therefore, suddenly, they are fine erotica. But these are anthologies of previously published material, and when they were previously published they were done on desktop publications, or they were done by sexual publishers for the most part; and in that previous incarnation they were the slimiest pornography. It's simply in the presentation and where they're sold that there's a difference made.

You were talking last night, at the reading you gave at the Fine Arts Work Center, about the inconsistencies in censorship laws that you have encountered when a book is marketed as pornography as opposed to erotica.

It's not a question of marketing. That implies a conscious intent. It's rather in how it's perceived. Very specifically, my small-press books are routinely seized by Canadian customs, no matter what kind of literary intent they might have. Certainly it's not Alyson's intention as a publisher to market *I Once Had a Master* as sleazy porno. He certainly, of all people, would make the argument that it is somehow fine erotica. But it's a small press; it's not a powerful press. It's sold mainly through gay and lesbian stores. And this is an invitation for Canadian customs to deem the material pornographic. Now *Flesh and the Word* and *Flesh and the Word 2*, if anything, are much more explicit and much more hardcore than *I Once Had a Master*. I'm on my way to Vancouver next week to testify at the trial about Canadian customs seizing my small-press books, and on the same trip I'm going to have a launch party for *Flesh and the Word 2* in Vancouver. And there will be no problem getting *Flesh and the Word 2* across the border, because this is a division of Penguin; therefore it cannot be pornographic. That's a very clear example of what I mean by packaging.

How do you respond to criticisms of pornography that it encourages violence or sexual abuse?

I just think that they're ridiculous and I don't respond. The whole point of writing is to create ideas. One of the things I do in my porn, for instance, is I don't consider it to be successful unless there's at least one scene in every book that gives me a stomach ache. That means I haven't really gone to a cutting edge of my exploration of my own fantasies. I haven't scared myself. My sexual writing is an exposure of my sexuality. If it has any power, that's where it comes from. But I don't want to do all of the things I write about.

Are there any subjects that you feel uncomfortable or unwilling to write about?

Probably the only one is man/boy love. My reasons for that are that I was a sexually active child, a very sexually active child, and had a number of experiences of having sex when I was quite young—thirteen, fourteen, fifteen—with adult men; and I have never, ever heard anyone, on either side of that debate, articulate the debate in any way that had anything to do with what I experienced. I think that the North American Man/Boy Love Association is full of it, and I think that the people who attack them are full of it, and so I'm not comfortable entering into the arena at least until I've figured out how I want to pose the subject, which I have not been able to do.

You do indeed unabashedly call yourself a pornographer, you gave a wonderful lecture at Harvard recently called "My Life as a Pornographer," and in that speech, you said, "Being a pornographer has been the most important part of my whole career." What did you mean by that?

Since I was one of the few writers who was taking that audience seriously and that audience was so responsive, I was able to have a career. I was not part of the Violet Quill, the group of gay writers around whom an enormous mythology has been created. I knew all of them when I lived in New York. They were active when I lived in New York. And by the way, I want to be very clear, I think Edmund White's a pal; Andrew Holleran's a good friend, but I never aspired to what they were after. We had different aspirations. What I wanted to do at that point, the early, early point in my career, was to become a writer, and once I proved to people that I had an audience then I could go anywhere. Many of the same editors that the folks at the Violet Quill were dealing with—Bill Whitehead, Michael Denneny, for instance—were utterly fascinated by me, and I never understood why they were, but I was doing what they desperately wanted the other writers to do, which was giving readings in sex clubs and bathhouses and bars, and going out and creating an audience, while all these others were trying to get an established literary audience. I went out and created my own audience.

You were sort of the Bette Midler of gay writing.

I was afraid you were going to say that! But that still carries with me. I mean, there are all these things that I can do that these other writers can't do, because I have an established audience. For instance, I don't think that Dutton, the division of Penguin that published *Flesh and the Word*, would have touched that book if it had been edited by anyone else.

What you're saying reminds me of something you said in an interview you gave recently to the Hartford gay magazine, Metroline. *You said that in the gay movement's "march toward 'respectability,' we sometimes lose sight of what we were trying to win."*

Oh, yeah. The purpose of gay pride isn't to be able to hire lap boys to be lobbyists in Washington. The purpose of gay pride was to let drag queens exist without being hassled, and to let leather men and leather women not feel that they were terrible and to create a form of lust that was so powerful that kids in the closet would have to come out. I'm constantly amazed when people in the gay movement make this now almost stereotypical statement that it has nothing to do with sex. If it doesn't, then why bother?

In 1986, you were diagnosed with HIV. Aside from the obvious emotional impact of that news, how did learning that you were HIV-positive affect you as a writer?

The immediate effect was to murder my writing. I stopped writing for over a year. I simply wasn't able to write, which actually becomes a symbol in my life of how important writing is. It is how I live. What I eventually did was to come back by facing the issue and facing my emotions, and I did it through my own writing and other people's writing, in the creation of *Personal Dispatches,* an anthology of writing about AIDS.

We're conducting this interview on a beautiful September morning in Provincetown, where you yourself have spent a lot of time. What does Provincetown mean to you?

I've come to understand that the power of Provincetown for me is that, even as I was doing that exploration of being a gay man that we discussed, this was the place where being a modern gay man and being a New Englander intersected for me. This is where they both exist. It's one of the great gay capitals of the world, but it's still a New England town. And that combination fits the combination of my being.

You are incredibly prolific. What are your working habits like?

You have to remember that I never do anything else. The end of my career would be if I ever had a lover. I am very structured. I follow the most basic rule of being a writer, which is that I write something every day.

You're putting together yet another anthology, Friends and Lovers: The Families that Gay Men Create. *I was interested to learn that you won't contribute a piece to that anthology.[3] You said that your own story is "much more about becoming a bachelor." What did you mean by that?*

Oh, I've become a bachelor. I've discovered great strength in a long family line of bachelors. I'm just not a person cut out to live with anyone. My writing is one of the most important things in my life, and so I'll do anything to protect my writing. But I've loved going back and talking to my other relatives about my great uncle bachelors.

What advice would you give to young writers? I'm sure you do give advice to young gay writers.

Constantly. Ah . . . write every day. And publish as much as you can. And any place that you can, so that it becomes something very important, seeing that one's words are formed into print, whether that's in a local weekly newspaper or a national magazine or in a book. Publish.

---

3. In fact, Preston did later include one of his own essays, "A Eulogy for George," in the collection.

Andrew Holleran

In the estimation of many, Andrew Holleran is one of the most important gay writers working today. The author of three novels—*Dancer From the Dance, Nights in Aruba,* and *The Beauty of Men*—and a collection of essays, *Ground Zero,* he has received high critical notice in journals across the country including the *New York Times,* the *Boston Globe,* and the *Los Angeles Times.*

Published in 1978, Holleran's first novel, *Dancer From the Dance,* is often cited as one of the first modern gay novels. Urbane, unapologetic, and full of beautiful and candid descriptions of gay sexual behavior, it chronicles the Manhattan gay scene and especially the reign of the "circuit queens" in those years just prior to the AIDS epidemic, that period after Stonewall when, as it was for *Dancer's* Malone, "the baths were a kind of paradise, and life was our youth and our dreams and our crazy hearts, hunting for ecstatic food."

Andrew Holleran (his name is a nom de plume) was born in 1944, attended New Hampton School in New Hampton, New Hampshire (perhaps the inspiration for his quip in *Dancer,* "Homosexuality is like a boarding school in which there are no vacations"), and then went on to Harvard, graduating in the class of 1965. After college, he served in the army in West Germany, began a law degree, and then went on to the University of Iowa Writers' Workshop. In 1971, he moved to New York. Currently he lives in Florida.

Whether he is writing fiction or nonfiction, all of Holleran's work sparkles with intelligence, verve, wit, and striking aperçus. His novels are breathtakingly beautiful, managing to be, at once, full of sadness and effervescence. The delicious dichotomy that faces the novel-writing correspondent in *Dancer*—whether the novel should be written "along the lines of *Auntie Mame,* or *Decline and Fall of the Roman Empire;* it has elements of both"—nicely hints at Holleran's own stunningly original synthesis.

The following interview was recorded in the studios of WOMR on 2 October 1993.

Let's begin with a vocabulary question. What is, or was, a "circuit queen"?

A circuit queen was, and I think still is, a gay man who followed a certain pattern of life in New York, which is where I lived. And it included Fire Island in the summer, it included a certain gay gym in the winter, baths, and certain dance clubs. And it was unrelenting, and it was very definite, and claustrophobic, I think. I remember my roommate in the early eighties stopped going out on the weekends because he would go to the baths and see everyone he had just been lifting weights with at the gym. And that's what a circuit queen was: it was a very claustrophobic—but thrilling! When you were new to it, it was thrilling, it was exactly where you wanted to be because it was where you saw all these attractive people. But after a while, it became very relentless, and debilitating, really.

Malone, the protagonist in Dancer From the Dance, *is of course the consummate "circuit queen." He's the "central beautiful symbol," as the narrator in* Dancer *calls him. Someone else says, "'All the boys I've ever loved in my life are wrapped up in Malone.'" He is both glorious and tragic, which is, I think, one of the most brilliant aspects of that novel. How did you come to create him?*

Ironically, in the last year, three people, old friends of mine, have all kind of revealed to me in conversation that they consider themselves to be the model for Malone. And I never say no, because it would be rude, I guess. And in a sense, it's true, because Malone basically was a composite character. I could tell you whose eyes I was thinking of when I described Malone's eyes; I could tell you whose body I used for Malone. I could go through a bunch of details and say, I took this from this one and this from that one, but in the end, I think, Malone is much more an imaginary character than anybody else in the book.

He has taken on almost mythic proportions in the years since Dancer *was written. I know more people who are constantly describing other people in terms of Malone, or quoting things that Malone said, or in some way wistfully looking back at that whole period.*

Well, you know, it's odd. Last night at the reading someone came up and said to me that he'd read *Dancer* eighteen times, and I was thrilled and touched. On the other hand I felt, What does that *mean*? I suspect, unfortunately, that I put into Malone what I think the people who respond to Malone must be feeling, and frankly it's basically the unattainable, the one who got away, the one you wish you had spoken to or the one you'd liked to have met and you never do. In a way it's just the old saw: the one you love is the one who got away. I think that's probably part of the appeal of Malone: that he is, um . . . "wistful" is a good adjective; there's something wistful about wanting a Malone, which I think is probably true in straight and gay life: the idea of the love that you never found exactly as you dreamt of it.

Malone runs away to New York, leaving his family. This fleeing of the family for the urban gay delights of Manhattan is a motif in so much of your work. What did New York mean for young gay men in the seventies?

Just that it was a place where you could disappear. It was a place where you could just leave everything behind and create yourself anew. And I'm sure that's what it still does for people. I'm living in a small town now, and I realize that the thing that makes gay culture possible in cities is exactly that kind of anonymity and freedom, that detachment from your origins. The few gay men I know in the town I live in are incredibly antisocial in the sense that, though you would expect them to have a closer bond because there are so few of them in the small town, exactly the opposite happens: they're much more standoffish. They won't have anything to do with each other, because in a small town or a community of any intimate size, you're connected to a house, to a family, to a school you went to, to a car you drive. There's an incredible lack of privacy, really. And in the city, you're just a creature on the sidewalk. And you go back to an apartment and you leave the apartment and you're just floating all the time. The difference is staggering, and it's what makes a full gay life possible.

I always resented that, though. Even when I was living in New York, I always thought to myself, Why am I condemned to cities? Because I love the country, I love all the pleasures of being outdoors. And I thought, Why do we have to live in these stinking cities? And my plan really was to meet someone and get out of town. And it hasn't happened that way. I think the cities are still necessary for gay life, in part because of that anonymity and that detachment from your familial origins. It's very hard, still, to integrate gayness with family life.

There's a sense of doom that hangs over Malone's and all the other circuit queens' lives in Dancer *that seems eerily prescient. In the pre-AIDS years, during which you wrote* Dancer, *what was that doom that you felt these characters were fated for? He is called a "doomed circuit queen."*

It's true, it's absolutely true. I guess that refers to a quality of self-destructiveness or despair that was endemic to gay life and gay people before AIDS. It's difficult when you're a writer to ask yourself, Do I see things this way because of homosexuality, or do I see things this way because I'm melancholy and pessimistic to begin with? I can't answer that question, but it seems to me still that the fate of being homosexual or of living a homosexual life entails certain hard facts that cannot be glossed over. We have still not evolved into a way of life which gets around those facts. In other words, I think that everybody really wants in life to make for himself some kind of home, some kind of connection to another human being, some kind of nest, if that's not too corny a word, and gay people, I think, have still not solved that problem.

What are some of those hard facts?

Just *that*, that it's very hard to connect in a long-lasting way and to form a shelter against the world, a home. There's a wonderful line in Hannah Arendt: "The task of man is to make a home for himself on earth." I really think that's true.

Is that harder for gay men to do?

Well, of course it's politically incorrect to say it is, and yet I think it is.

Why?

Well, I'll be brutal and I'll simply say that it comes back to the issue that I came upon reading a biography of Gerard Manley Hopkins a few years ago. I really came to the conclusion after reading this wonderful biography that Hopkins was obsessed with fertility toward the end of his life. He came from a fairly large Victorian family, and he grew up in a culture and at a time when Victorian ideals were about productivity and fertility and making use of your life, and I have a feeling that Hopkins was obsessed with the fact that, even though he had chosen to be a priest, there was a sterility to his life. It's very very moving. It's in the things they call the "Terrible Sonnets."

I think that's true, unfortunately, of gay life. You face the issue of fertility versus sterility. Now, I know that the world is tremendously overpopulated. I think it's our major problem. Gore Vidal is absolutely right to have been ragging that for years now. It's clearly the worst thing we face right now. And it's also very easy to romanticize what one isn't living. And, God knows, I've been exposed to real parents who have said they'd never do it again. I've heard all the despair and disillusionment that comes from that, but I think there is an issue of infertility in gay life that explains the lack of unions. I *know* I'll get flak for this! And this could be totally wrong, but that's basically my honest feeling.

Indeed, other people have noted that, too, and used that same idea to explain, in part, why it is that so many gay men go into the arts or go into creative fields, because that's where the creative instinct travels.

Exactly. And Plato said that, that another kind of children you can leave is works of art.

Malone disappears at the end of the novel, and we're led to believe that maybe he's been killed in the fire at the Everard Baths. But there's always been an ambiguity about his disappearance. I'm sure you've been asked this many times, but in your mind what exactly did happen to Malone?

I think Malone escaped. I think he did swim across the bay, I think he did end up in Southeast Asia or somewhere, where he's spotted in one of the letters. On the other hand, to be statistically accurate, I would have to say that, when people ask me what would Malone be doing if he were alive today, statistically the probability is that he would be dead, since a great many of the people who inhabited that world have died.

There is a strong sense in both your novels that the glory of being gay is so much tied up with youth and beauty, and physical desire, and that by middle age, as the narrator says in Nights in Aruba, *"any life: surgeons or housewives, homosexuals or cops—goes stale for a while and one is a prisoner of habits that no longer bring happiness, or even pleasure." What about middle age and gay men?*

It's true, it's true! One of the things that has struck me in going back through old manuscripts and reading things like this is that I was prematurely middle-aged. I began to go through this gloom and doom stuff much earlier than I had to. But I'll be quite honest, I haven't changed my opinion of that.

I think that one of the fascinating things about gay writing and gay culture is that for the first time we get to see a whole gay life lived to its conclusion, and it's just obvious that gay writers are going to start writing about these things because they're going to start experiencing them. Frankly I can't wait to see what happens. I mentioned a book last night by Christopher Isherwood called *A Single Man*, which is the only book I know which really deals with that kind of bleakness and that kind of feeling that you're on the shelf and that kind of alienation from you own tribe, which is really what happens. And I'm starting to write about it, too.[1] It's another thing that's got to be faced and it's got to be, not solved, but at least absorbed and dealt with.

One of my best friends in New York always used to say that had AIDS not occurred and everybody had lived, people would have just gotten better and better and we would have all had these really wonderful friends—and you can see in retrospect how wonderful some of these people we've lost were—and that we would have just gone, you know, from house to house visiting each other on the weekends and it would have been wonderful. Perhaps he's right. The other part of me thinks that you would have gone the other way, that we would all have faced the difficulty of isolation and of aging and of having to reshape your identity, really. I got up this morning and I said to myself, You're going to get a look and learn how to live the next two decades. You really have to retool yourself. You have to come to terms with yourself. You almost have to create a new identity. You've *got* to find new habits, because the old ones don't work. I couldn't last night go out cruising on Commercial Street or go to the bars. I just didn't feel comfortable. And that's because of age, I think. It's external and it's internal. The two reflect each other.

On the other hand, I know many gay men who are older than I am, who are leading very sexual lives and are completely busy in that regard.

---

1. Three years after this interview, Holleran published his third novel, *The Beauty of Men*, which focuses on the despair of a middle-aged gay man whose life centers on taking care of his dying mother and cruising public parks in rural Florida.

So it's an individual thing, and there are many routes to take, but there certainly are changes and it's foolish for us to be silent on the subject, because sooner or later everybody who's now in their thirties is going to come to this pass, and they should know about it.

On the other hand, it's a cliché. This is so gloom and doom. It's stupid to frighten people. There's nothing scary about it, because everyone ages. There's nothing horrible about it, and straight people go through the same thing.

Although I wonder if a straight person would say, "I've got to retool myself for the next two decades."

I couldn't agree with you more! I couldn't agree with you more! I was thinking, in fact, last night of a friend of my sister's, a divorced woman I used to go to a gym with when I was living in Pittsburgh. And she used to say to me, "After fifty, women should be taken out and shot." This is because she was divorced and she was really feeling down on her chances of getting another husband, and she was kind of a narcissistic person anyway. And I laughed at her and said, "Oh stop that." And she went on to get another husband and she's married again. But last night, as I was thinking to myself, Why can't you just get up and go down and hawk your wares on Commercial Street? I thought of that line.

You've now touched on all the crises of gay middle age. What about the possibility of a successful homosexual marriage? The narrator in Nights in Aruba *briefly has a kind of marriage with a man named Sal but it doesn't work out; and the suggestion is that the possibility of long-term gay coupling is certainly not for him and may be difficult for most gay men.*

My conclusion, having wondered about this, is that it's simply a gift, that some gay men have that gift. I've noticed that of all the people I've known the ones who have lovers tend to be serially married: they'll always have a lover. They may have five or six over the course of their lifetime, but they will probably always have a lover, even though there are periods in between those lovers. But I would say that statistically the majority of gay men will have one or two lovers and that's it, and they'll spend more of their time without a lover than with one. So, you can't say it's genetic, you can't say it's cultural, but it's an individual thing. Then you have to ask yourself, Well, is it better to have a lover necessarily? If the people who have the lovers have them and the people who don't don't, aren't we just saying that the people who want the lovers have them and those who don't don't? Maybe that is it. In the end, the people who don't have lovers fundamentally at some level don't want one. And so don't bitch about it.

A hard thing for some people to admit, perhaps.

A friend of mine told me that a psychiatrist in New York once told him that whenever anybody walked into his office and said, "Oh, I want a lover and I can't find a lover," he'd say, "Oh, stop it. If you wanted a lover, you'd have a lover."

Let's talk a little about your early life. Like the narrator in Nights in Aruba, *you went to prep school, an all-boys boarding school in New Hampshire. Did your interest in writing develop there? Were you at all encouraged as a writer by your early teachers?*

No, there was no such thing as a creative writing course then. My first remembrance of enjoying writing was before that, was in seventh or eighth grade when we would be asked to do reports on states. You'd have to come in and give a report on Alaska or New Hampshire—the main products, the climate, the population, the principle cities; and I would always doll them up with these incredibly long-winded descriptive passages. The class kind of grew to expect this. That's my first memory of wanting to write for the sake of writing.

I didn't write until my last year in college, when I was looking around for a course to fill my schedule, and a writer named Peter Taylor, who's a short story writer, was visiting, and he gave a writing course. It was the last semester of senior year, and because of Peter Taylor, really, three or four of us went on to the Writers' Workshop in Iowa City. And from then on I've always written.

You've written a wonderful essay, which you delivered to the gay and lesbian student organization at Harvard, about your years there. Your years at Harvard, the mid-sixties, were long before the days of gay and lesbian student organizations. What was Harvard like for you as a young gay man?

Well, it was all very suppressed, because I myself hadn't come to terms with it. But I was very conscious of sitting in the library and looking at people and thinking, My God, how beautiful he is! I can still remember exactly the figures I used to track around campus. I was conscious, too, of a tutor in my dormitory who was obviously a very epicene aesthete, who ran a weight-lifting club in the basement and had all these particular friends who went with him in the dining room. It's staggering to me that we all have these cognitive dissonances where we can lead two-track lives, where you're absorbing all the information but you refuse to process it. You absolutely *refuse* to make the conclusions that are screaming to be made, because you just will not do that. It's willful avoidance. That's what I was doing there. On the other hand, I made very good friends. Our bond was obviously based on those kinds of appreciations: of physical beauty, of faces. That kind of glamour.

I'm not saying the whole case. I also went to a psychiatrist there because I was dating a woman at Wellesley. After our dates we would go back to her dorm and I would never kiss her, while all the other dates were standing around in Tower Court smooching each other to death. And I felt so sorry for her, I thought, Why am I doing this to this woman? She must think something's wrong with her. So I went to student health and told the woman who interviewed me before the psychiatrist that I thought I was homosexual, and she was so sympathetic. And then I went to see the shrink, and he said, "Well, next time go kiss her!" That was the end of the appointment.

That would solve everything.

Oh, it was so irresponsible and so awful!

After Harvard, and again like the narrator in Aruba, *you were in the army, stationed in West Germany. It's in the army that the friends in* Nights in Aruba *begin to have a homosexual life. I think it's Vittorio in that novel who says, "'Funny, isn't it. It was the army that freed me from a life in which I was trying to be the perfect son. The army, which I thought was depriving me of freedom. It was in Viet Nam that I melted, so to speak, in the wrong way.'"*

That's a phrase from a friend's letter.

What was your experience like in the Army?

I was lucky: I didn't go to Vietnam; I went to Germany. I was brought ought by a friend whom I'm going to see in Boston tomorrow, who was working in personnel. He used to waylay gay people and have them assigned to the office in Heidelberg. One night I got very, very drunk at an awful party with our sergeant, having to listen to dirty jokes and stuff, and I guess I was pushed to the breaking point. He pushed me into a cab and took me down to the Whiskey-A-Go-Go. That was where I met my first man and went home with someone. But it really took that extreme an environment—away from home, away from everything else I'd ever been doing with my life—and the irony was that the institution that I thought had deprived me of freedom really gave it to me.

I'm also struck by that phrase in which Vittorio talks about trying to be the perfect son. I think about your experience at prep school and at Harvard. Someone, again in Aruba, says that "'love was an escape from the pressure to be successful.'" Has that been a part of your experience?

Yeah. There's a John Reed book that's been around for a long time, *The Best Little Boy in the World,* which I think almost answers your question. Why do gay people feel they must be the best little boy in the world? Is it because they're compensating for a kind of guilt that they already have in them about something they already know to be wrong or feel to be wrong? It can't just be coincidental. There is something going on there. I was tremendously interested in pleasing my family. Anybody is, I think, of a certain kind of upbringing. And homosexuality was, of course, such a violation of that picture that it was a great pressure in itself to deny it or to compensate for it in some way.

And then there's also the element of rebellion. There's a tremendous sense of rebellion among people who think that they are conforming. They're just furious at the whole value system. That's very common in the middle class.

In the late sixties, early seventies, you studied writing at the University of Iowa, which has the reputation for being one of the best graduate programs in creative writing in the country. Why did you go to Iowa?

I didn't want to go to law school! That's it. I had to make a choice. I was accepted to law school that fall and I thought, I can't spend another three years in Cambridge, just reading and writing and sitting in libraries and wearing trench coats and walking through the rain. It was just awful, the thought. So I went to Iowa.

I loved Iowa City. In those days, Iowa had a bad rep. I'm sure it still does to a degree. There were critics who thought there was a kind of Iowa novel, which was a way of saying a kind of mediocre, academic, not-very-good, writers'-workshop novel. Since then I think the Workshop has gotten a little more esteemed, because it's produced a lot of good people. But at the time, it was by no means a universally admired place to go. What they did—it was the Virginia Woolf thing—they gave you a place of your own. You were out there and you could just write, and they put you in contact with other people who were crazy enough to want to just write, which was a wonderful thing. That's where I met Robert Ferro and Michael Grumley. And they put you in contact with writers. I had Kurt Vonnegut and Nelson Algren that year.

On the other hand, when I think of what it would be like to teach other people writing, I almost think it would be like selling heroin to them, that it's an immoral thing to do and nobody should be encouraged to do this. I think it's remarkable that places like Iowa can get writers to come and do that.

Did you try out gay material while you were out there?

Never, never, never.

That all came later?

That was my whole problem. Counting the Writers' Workshop, I was writing for ten years, desperate to be a writer, unable to find any material or theme that mattered. I wrote two books one winter, one which ended up actually being a novel about the Workshop—that's how desperate I was for material!—and the other was the novel that became *Dancer From the Dance*. It wasn't until I turned to my own life and what really mattered to me that I became a writer.

How did you persist for those ten years?

Oh, the usual things. I was a waiter, I was a bartender, I worked as a clerk-typist.

By this time you were in New York?

Yes, in New York and Philadelphia. I dropped out of law school, and I went to work in an insurance company, typing up letters refusing people's claims. I did all the things writers do just to stay alive. Which is depressing, because if it doesn't have the payoff at the end—of getting published—then you've really wasted a great deal of your time.

There's been a tremendous proliferation of writing programs in the last twenty years. Some people have said there are too many programs and that, as you said, fiction is becoming the homogenized, professionalized product of these schools. How do you feel about that?

I met a poet at the Miami Book Fair a couple of years ago—we were in a cab—a British poet, and we were talking about the difficulty of writing, and I said it was more and more difficult now because of TV and the news and all the other competing forms. All the material that used to be in a Dickens novel has been siphoned off into so many other mediums. And he turned to me and he said, "You know, I don't think that's right. I think it was just as hard to write a good novel in Jane Austen's time as it is now."

I think he has a point. It's probably just as hard to write something that's really good—any excellent work of art now—as it was in the eighteenth century. That hasn't changed. It's just that we're in a product culture now. Everything is produced in such incredible, staggering quantities! I just read an article coming up on the plane in which someone said that there were no books from major novelists to speak of this past year. And I thought, What an odd assumption that is, that every year there has to be a new crop, a new set of products to review, that the pipeline just demands it.

So we're in this product culture in which people are just churning out books, and it's staggering to me that there are bookstores and chains opening still, because the other feeling you get about our culture is that writing and reading is becoming something like lace making or blowing glass, that it's a very eccentric occupation, practiced by very few people relative to the society at large. I'm grateful that there are readers and people who still love books. It's just touching to do a reading like last night and realize that there are people who love books, too.

I wonder if—once Hollywood latches on to lots of gay themes—even this proliferation of gay books will start to dry up, because everybody goes to the movies nowadays.

I agree with you totally. I went down a river in Florida this spring with two young gay men—we went on inner tubes down this beautiful river—and at the end of the day, when we got off the river about four hours later, I thought to myself, Wasn't that odd: our whole conversation was references to TV shows and movies. We *never* referred to books. All our common jokes and our references were to video things. Now, that may have just been them, but it's also true of what you just said, that it's a video culture.

Because the seventies are fashionable again, I've been getting nibbles from young gay men in New York who are filmmakers and want to make a movie of *Dancer from the Dance*. One part of me is thrilled and flattered—you know, that a younger generation wants to do this, and the part of me that does love movies would love to see that dialogue spoken on screen—but the other part of me has got his heels set against it. Movies just suck it all up and somehow—not trivialize it—but they seem to make the book less potent.

In both your novels, the theme of the "double life" that gay men lead is a prominent one. It would be tempting and obvious to say that the characters in your two novels, which were published in 1978 and 1983, are merely part of that generation of gay men who still felt embarrassed or guilty about coming out to their families. But, in rereading your novels, I get the feeling that the double life of these men stems from more than that, that you think every gay man experiences himself as having one foot in one family and one in another, and that the two worlds can't be reconciled. Do you want to say something about that?

It's an immense subject. As you spoke, I was thinking of Robert Ferro, who made an absolute point of integrating his gay life with his family's. I visited his family's house many times on the [New] Jersey shore with Robert and his lover, Michael Grumley. Robert was adamant about having Michael included in absolutely every facet of that family's life, and I just admired him enormously for it, but I also recognized the fact that I could never have done that. I think that Robert is probably in the minority as this goes. A part of me wants to believe that every gay generation is "an improved generation" and is further along and is more evolved and is more at ease with their homosexuality; and another part of me thinks that nothing changes, that it's just as difficult for a gay man of nineteen now as it was twenty years ago. I mean, I know it's not just as difficult in certain ways, but I still think that there's a fundamental schism there.

I just went to visit the grave of a friend in Florida who died a few months ago. His stone is right next to his parents' stone. I was standing there, looking down at these stones, and I was thinking how ironic it is that in the end my friend Bobby is buried with his parents—that this is still the family unit—and I thought to myself, Is this just a consequence of his being homosexual? The way we escape our families is to found a family of our own. If you don't found a family of your own, your family is still the one that produced you. And because of that fact, you do have a kind of different take on life.

I wonder if Robert Ferro's comfortableness with his family stems at all from his Italian American heritage.

I think it was. Let's deal in clichés if we can: I've understood that in Italy, for example, until recently—I don't know if it's changed—there's no equivalent to the circuit in America, that gay men in Italy don't leave their families and live quite the same way we do as homosexuals, because family is much more central. And if that's true, then it was reflected in Robert.

What's your own relationship to your family like?

Well, I came out, finally, unavoidably, to my sister, and I'm very glad I did. She's been wonderful about it. Never came out to my father, and she and I both agree that it would have been difficult for him to take. Have come out subliminally, probably, to my mother, because she's too shrewd and too perceptive a person.

And mothers always know.

And mothers always know! And yet I've never come out explicitly to her, which is a failing on my part. There's an irony in all this. I was talking about this with a friend of mine, who just buried his parents (and one of his brothers is gay), and we were talking about the fact that your siblings can accept you, and they can say that it doesn't matter to them, but in the end, if it matters to you, you're the one who has to forgive yourself in the end—if "forgive" is the correct word—*you're* the one who has to come out to yourself. You can come out to every member of your family and still, on some level not accept it. That's really the problem in the end.

I think there are several stages of coming out, and that deep, deep self-acceptance is probably the last and maybe hardest stage.

Yes, I agree with you. And yet there are some people for whom it is not an issue at all. It's just remarkable. And I peer at those people and try to see, Is this real, is this genuine? And in some of them I have to conclude that it is.

I met a young man in Provincetown who said that it was his parents who told him he was gay.

Yes, I love those stories! One of my favorite stories is about a friend of mine, who finally got the nerve to tell his parents and they leaned forward and they said, "Oh, thank God. We were afraid you'd never know." I love that.

We were talking earlier about prep schools. There are several prep schools in New England—and, in fact, several high schools across the country—that now have gay and lesbian student organizations.

But my question is, Is it just as difficult though—for the person who wants to be the best little boy in the world—to go to those meetings? Is it or isn't it? That's what I really wonder about. Are there still young men, or young women, who will deny it and fight it until they can no longer? I don't know.

You lead a fairly private and somewhat reclusive life. You rarely give interviews, didn't want your photograph on the posters we printed advertising your reading, and perhaps most significantly, you've left New York and the orbit of the circuit queens. In fact, for the past ten years, you've lived in rural Florida. Why these choices?

Well, the first choice is just the writer part of me. I hate being a writer, in a sense, because you never know . . . Writing is an incredible communicative act of intimacy. When you're writing to someone you'll never see reading your book—you must sense this—you can be so confessional, so intimate. You're speaking just to yourself. It's just the most intimate form of communication there is. And if you're a good writer . . . Well, this gets down to the issue of being an autobiographical writer versus a writer who doesn't draw on his own life. I think if you're the first kind, and you draw on your own life, then what you're doing is very confessional, and you put everything into your writing. So there's two issues when you meet a reader: first, you're slightly—not embarrassed—but you feel odd; and secondly, you've put everything into the book and there's nothing else that you have to add. And you don't really know what you can give them. It sounds a little pompous: it's not as if you have to give them something, like a quart of blood or a way to live life, but there's an odd cognitive dissonance about it. So I love being anonymous. And I also think that's the best writing: just to be a little fly on the wall, to go around and just let yourself absorb stuff. So the anonymity part I've always loved.

And the move to rural Florida was basically for family reasons—the family that you can't exchange for another. A family illness brought me down there, and that's still why I'm there. It's almost more isolation than I would like, but that's that.

Do you live with your family?

I'm living mostly in an empty house by myself. It's a very bizarre experience. It's not something to be taken lightly. All the clichés are true. It does alter you. There are pleasures of solitude that I can see, but there are also liabilities to it. You become a little nuts, I think.

When you published Dancer from the Dance, *you adopted a pseudonym, a nom de plume.*

Because of that small town. I said to my editor at the last minute—I wasn't going to do it—but I said to my editor one day in conversation that I didn't care who knew I was gay, but I was kind of afraid if certain people in the town my parents lived in found out that they would hold it over them in some way. And I didn't want to put them under any pressure whatsoever. I said to her one day, "I just don't want the wrong people to get this book." And she called me up a few hours later and said, "Well, you know, the wrong people are always the first ones to get the book, so why don't you?" And so [I] did.

Do you ever wish that you could crawl out of Andrew Holleran's name?

No, no, I don't. I love the fact that there's the little envelope of anonymity and a little envelope of distance. And I also wonder if it doesn't allow me to be more honest than I would be. There's something very embarrassing about writing. After the reading last night, I went home and I thought to myself, It's like being an ax murderer, and you wake up the next morning and you see blood all over the room and you say to yourself, who did I kill last night? What did I just *do*? Did I really read that stuff? It's kind of a striptease, writing is, especially when you read in public. So the pseudonym really just gives you an excuse to be more honest perhaps.

Catholicism figures prominently in both your novels. What's your own relationship to Catholicism?

I was very religious at a certain point in my life. You never get rid of that, on some level. But I am no longer a practicing Catholic, I guess because of a kind of agnosticism that has affected a lot of people in this very secular age. Belief in the divinity of Jesus and the belief in all that follows from that I don't have. I've often thought that the aesthetic element of homosexuality is just a transference of the religious impulse: I mean, instead of adoring Jesus, you're adoring the man in bed with you. There's a great element of adoration in sex, and you come to conclude that God is in human beings, and the only thing you're going to know of God is in the vessel of another human being.

I'm reminded of something [the character] Mr. Friel says in Nights in Aruba. *He's both promiscuously gay and a practicing Catholic of sorts, and he says that while the Church considers homosexual acts a sin, he believes "'homosexual acts saved my life.'"*

Does he say that?

He does say that.

Well, I absolutely believe that. I absolutely believe that! I cannot imagine never having gone this way. I cannot imagine what life would have been like without it, without that contact with another human being on that level. I know that the Church still believes in celibacy, and I know that people can lead productive and valuable lives as celibates, but I think celibacy is probably a "gift," too, as they call it. You either can do it or you can't; and if you can't you shouldn't try to. Yeah, the Church's position is one of those wonderful oxymorons: the acts themselves are sinful but homosexuality itself is not. [The position is] just crazed.

At the risk of reducing your novels and your ideas to simple sentences, I want to quote yet another passage, again from Aruba. *"At the age of twenty-three," the narrator says, "I felt that the only rational use of life was not to go to Heaven, in which I no longer believed, or to avoid Hell, which was the motivation of so many of my actions as a child, but simply to achieve happiness." How does that sound to you today?*

Well, I think that's still the only rational approach to life. There's a line of [George] Santayana, I think, that there's nothing to do with the interval between birth and death but enjoy it. It's absolutely true. I can't see anything else that is rational as an answer to the problem of what to do with life. Of course, the problem is that people take those kinds of sentiments and lines and immediately translate it into hedonism. And, of course, the joke is, as the serial killer in that Flannery O'Connor story, "A Good Man is Hard to Find," says after he slaughters the family, and each time he shoots somebody, he turns and says, "'Ain't no pleasure in it.'"

You know, the thing about our society that is so meretricious and outrageous is that we keep selling people this bill of goods, that if you just have the right gel in your hair, and you just have the right body, and if you just go hang gliding or to Bermuda, you're going to be happy, and that is *such* bullshit. It takes a long time to figure out what makes you, an individual, happy, and it may be the exact *opposite* of all these hedonistic things. And the horror of life is that you can live it so long in ignorance of those things and of yourself.

I would like to say that I know what I should be doing with my time and what makes me happy, but I'm still stumbling along. I've always envied people that I've met along the way, even back in college and when I was in my twenties, who I could tell knew what they wanted to be doing with themselves and what they valued and what they didn't value; and they made their choices and they were pursuing those things. God, I envied them! Knowing yourself, as the Greeks said—it comes down to that.

What's been the effect of the AIDS epidemic on your life and work? You haven't published a novel in ten years now.

It's just been awful. Tom Steele, an editor at *Christopher Street*, years ago said it so well on the street one day; he said, "You know, it's been like a shark attack." And it *was* like a shark attack at first. It was something so violent and unsuspected and inexplicable that people were just disappearing under the water. It took a long time to absorb the fact. I still think the problem of gay writing today is this: A, you can't write about AIDS; B, you can't *not* write about AIDS. It comes down to that.

Now, a friend of mine pointed out in a letter recently that this hasn't stopped a lot of people from writing during this time. And it is true that some wonderful books have come out: Paul Monette, in particular, *Borrowed Time,* and his poems, *Love Alone.* And Larry Kramer has written on AIDS very well. But for some gay writers it has been an incredible dilemma. It's just shut them up. It's just presented them with a problem they couldn't solve. And I think that's in part what happened to me.

It didn't shut you up in the nonfiction mode. You published a wonderful book of essays, Ground Zero.

But that's an aspect of AIDS. AIDS was the thing that presented a writer with this dilemma: that there's nothing you can make up that matches what you heard that day on the telephone. What has happened in real life to people is so staggering and, while there is something universal about all the experiences, there's also something totally individual about every one of them. So in a way, you can't write a story that stands for them all— in fiction, that is. There's no need to, there's no need to make up, at least not yet. The holocaust analogy actually holds true here, I think. It would be like writing short stories about a concentration camp while people were being put in the boxcars. I mean, would you do that? What would be the point? Art obviously has a tremendous role in everything in life, and I just haven't found the fictive mode to be useful right now, and so I've been venting everything I've felt in these essays.

It's an oft-repeated precept in writing classes that an author needs to get distance from his material in order to work with it effectively.

I think it's one way or the other: you either need the distance or you need some kind of being right in the cauldron itself, which is what *Borrowed Time* came out of. That's just right out of the experience of having cared for his lover. In between doesn't work. There's nothing genteel or writers'-workshop about AIDS, nothing at all.

I want to jump back to your early days as a writer and ask about the writers club, called the Violet Quill, that you were part of. Can you say a little about the Violet Quill?

In looking back to how it started, I think it was a spinoff of the Workshop, because Robert [Ferro] and I had gone to the Workshop for two years, and I think Robert started it. We just followed the Workshop format: we would meet, somebody would read a story, and then everybody else would critique it. I don't think we did it for more than seven or eight times. Really, the fun of it was to see everybody's apartment and what you would get to eat afterwards. George Whitmore was living in a wonderful apartment on Washington Square at the time, a big yellow room—it was just beautiful—and Felice had a wonderful apartment, and the Ferro-Grumleys had a great place. I don't know if we went to Ed's or not. It fell apart, I think, because we had a feud. George and Robert had a falling out, or something, or it fell apart of its own weight. But in retrospect, I realize that everybody was working on books that ended up becoming fairly well-known. Robert was working on *The Family of Max Desir*; Ed was working on, I think, *A Boy's Own Story*; I was working on *Nights in Aruba*; et cetera. So, with the passage of time, I guess, and also the rise in gay studies and gay everything, it's become a kind of subject, and now St. Martin's [Press] is going to bring out the *VQ Reader*.

How did you all first meet?

Well, I knew Robert and Michael from the Workshop, even though when we moved to New York we went our separate ways. Totally, I didn't speak to them for years. They lived on the Upper West Side, and they were not on the same circuit that I was. And then I published *Dancer*. I think that sparked it. We started getting in touch with one another. Robert went through the same thing I did: His first book was a kind of Isak Dinesen-like allegory called *The Others*, and he didn't come into his stride until he started using gay life and his own material. So Robert contacted me, and Ed had just published *Nocturnes for the King of Naples*, and somehow we all connected.

You asked me last night if I asked all the writers I'm interviewing in this series the same questions, and I said no, but there is, in fact, one question I ask all of you.

What do we do in bed?

No.

What's our favorite color?

No! What advice do you have for young gay writers today?

Referring to what I said earlier about how teaching writing is like teaching people to shoot up, I think you're a writer—and this has been said too many times over the years—only in the end because you have to be.

There are many ways to be a writer. I think the most civilized way would be to be something else and to write also. I wish I could be a Chekhov, be a doctor, and to have writing as a mistress, as he said. But that's not the case with a lot of us: we want to be writers more than we want to be anything else, and we think of ourselves as writers, and there is a kind of writer's life and personality, I guess, that you're stuck with in the end.

It's a very isolating life in many ways: you don't get to go to conventions, you don't go into the office and ride up and down in elevators with people, you don't have a lot of human interaction in a way. It's you in that room, feeding off yourself.

There's not a single sentence you can say about writing that cannot be contradicted by a writer. There is *no* way you can generalize about *any* aspect of writing or writers. So if you want to do it, do it! That's really all you can say: if you want to do it, do it because it pleases you.

Randall Kenan

Randall Kenan's first novel, *A Visitation of Spirits* (1989), was a strong debut for the then twenty-six-year-old writer. It is the story of Horace Thomas Cross. Dubbed by his friends "The Great Black Hope," Horace is a precocious sixteen-year-old who buries himself in books and hopes to become a famous physicist one day, but whose attraction to other men has "frightened him beyond reason." When all of Horace's attempts to rid himself of the demon of his desires fail, he turns his bedroom into "the secluded and mysterious lair of an apprentice sorcerer," where, surrounded by the talismans of a magical liberation, he attempts "to escape from that sin he would surely commit if he remained human."

Kenan's vision in that novel is a somber and anguished one. The world—for blacks, for gay people, for those who try to have faith in a secular age, for all who try to avoid possession of their souls by any kind of power—is "peopled with new and hateful monsters." It is a nostalgic and lyric vision, too, for the land, the rhythms of rural life, and the love available in families.

Kenan's second book, a collection of stories entitled *Let The Dead Bury Their Dead* (1992), was a finalist for the *Los Angeles Times* Book Prize, was nominated for the National Book Critics Circle Award in Fiction, and was named a Notable Book of the Year by the *New York Times Book Review*. His work has been likened to that of Alice Walker and Gabriel García Márquez.

Our interview, the final one in the WOMR series, took place on 16 October 1993.

I was surprised to learn that you began college as a physics major. When did you begin to think of yourself as a writer?

It's a strange transformation, because I'd always written. I wrote two execrable novels in high school, and my dream, the paradigm, was to do something like Arthur C. Clarke and Isaac Asimov—be a scientist and write science fiction on the side. Somewhere around my sophomore year I encountered Max Steele, who was then the head of the writing department at [the University of North Carolina at] Chapel Hill, and he challenged me quite aggressively to think about fiction more seriously. Somewhere between my sopho-more and junior years, I really caught the bug, and science started to fall by the wayside. Much to the chagrin of my parents.

You studied for a summer at Oxford before you graduated from the University of North Carolina.

Yes. I studied drama criticism, the literature of Oxford, and Shakespeare.

One thing that has struck me about both your books is your fluency with so many different voices and so many different styles of speaking and writing—the high-brow, the lowbrow, the rural, the academic. I can't help but think that that sum-mer at Oxford must have been one more contribution to this cornucopia of voices that you juggle so beautifully.

I don't know if it affected the voice per se. I know it certainly affected my vi-sion—you know, the old cliché of the writer having to leave where they're from in order to see it more clearly. That helped me to create a firmer vision of America and of our problems and our situations. That crystallized a lot of my thinking, the sheer distance.

In fact, after you graduated college, you did leave North Carolina and moved to New York.

First bus out!

And you took a job at Random House?

Yes, I was very lucky. Two weeks into New York, and I started as an office-boy-in-waiting, as the chairman of the board laughingly referred to it. I was an in-house temp, and then I became a receptionist at Knopf, and then moved on to become an assistant, and then became an assistant editor.

How long were you at Random House?

From 1984 to 1989.

What kinds of things did you do as an editor there?

In many ways, I like to think of it as my graduate school. I got to work with the likes of García Márquez and Toni Morrison, distantly. And eventually to acquire books. I published a book by a Chinese dissident astrophysicist and a novel by a North Carolina writer. So it really was a learning process.

And during that learning process, you were pursuing your own writing?

Yes.

In 1989, you published A Visitation of Spirits. *What was it like trying to negotiate a career as an editor and at the same time try to write a novel?*

It was heady stuff. Here this country boy from Chinquapin, North Carolina, had the audacity to come to New York, get a job at a tony New York publisher, and on top of that decide I'm going to write a book. I was feeling my oats in an intellectual way, and the very dare—all the odds that I imagined, and some weren't so imagined, that I had stacked up against me—really fueled me. I put in hundred-hour work weeks at the job and then would work on the subway and on the weekend. I practically destroyed my social life on many occasions. But I was so wrapped up in the idea of doing it, as well as the book. The book possessed me at some point. I won't say it wrote itself, but it forced itself.

Let's talk about that first novel. How did you come to write it? How did the subject matter grab you?

I'd certainly been interested in the tensions that obviously acted upon me growing up in that part of rural southeast North Carolina. When I grew up in the late seventies and eighties, it was almost a time warp. Many of the old folk, people in their eighties and nineties, were holding on to ways and living their lives as though it were the forties or the thirties. Here I was, very interested in things like *Star Trek* and comic books and obviously science, but living among this society that I felt hadn't caught up. And the disparity, especially when you bring in things like sexuality and interracial relationships and that whole gamut of issues, the collision that occurs! Even though I wasn't thinking of it in that abstract a term—I was thinking about it in a more visceral way—I wanted to try to play with that, come up with something that would document in a sense how that world was grappling with video games and cable television and at the same time dealing with their religion. The supernatural aspect of the novel to me is a logical outgrowth of believing in this man who was crucified and rose three days thereafter. It all makes perfect sense to me.

I want to get back to the religious aspects of your work, but before we do that . . . Tims Creek, North Carolina, a town that figures in both the published books, has already been favorably compared to that other fictional Southern place, Faulkner's Yoknapatawpha County. What's the attraction for you in visiting and revisiting the same place in several works of fiction?

I will never dare to compare myself to Faulkner. I think it was Flannery O'Connor who said, "Who wants to be on the tracks when the Dixie Special comes?" But just the idea—there is an attraction to a place that you find virtually inexhaustible. I don't think this is exclusive to Southern writers. I think anybody who is firmly rooted, or has been firmly rooted, to a place would realize that there is an inexhaustible supply of stories. You will never live enough. And once you really get into a place and put your stamp on it, it's hard to leave. It becomes irresistible to you. You brush up against stories as you're telling one, and you say, Ah, I have to come back to that. It's like a drug in a way.

Tell us a little about Tims Creek.

Tims Creek, North Carolina. "Down East," as they say. What we would refer to laughingly as a one-horse town. When the front bumper is at one end of the town, the other bumper is at the other end. Largely agrarian. Poor black folk and poor white folk. Everybody knows each other. A lot of folk are kin to each other, black to white as well. What I hope to try to do is create not only a landscape but a dreamscape in which the people's ordinary, banal existence [is] coupled with those unconscious, subconscious, and supernatural day-to-day things, which in truth, not only in the South but all over the world, really make up who we are.

A Visitation of Spirits, *your first book, is a recognizably gay novel, that is, the central character is gay and the issues the book deals with largely stem from the character's homosexuality. But in your second book,* Let the Dead Bury Their Dead, *only a few of the stories actually bring homosexuality to the foreground. Was that a deliberate decision, to downplay the gay element?*

No, I don't think it was deliberate in any calculated political sense. It's the way my life is; it's the way I view the world. I don't think any type of sexuality, any type of love or romance, makes sense if it's taken out of a context. Even with the first novel, there are two other sections which deal with his family history and with these two powerful people who have influence over his life. I think in many ways it enriches any discussion about love or sexuality to place it in a broader world in which you can see the forces acting upon a person and the tensions around any type of romance.

You, like a few other writers in this [radio] series, bring together experiences from several different worlds, not only the experience of being homosexual in the straight world, but, in your case, the experience of being black and religious. What is it like to be a writer pulling together the strings of so many different kinds of experiences?

In one way—and I don't mean to imply that black writers have an easier go at it—but just from the sheer experience that one has at one's fingertips, one has a broader tapestry to work with. Not just black or African American writers, but any minority group in this country knows more about the majority culture than the majority culture will know about them. So already they have two cultures to work with. And if their sexuality happens to be different, if they come from another geography, or a very specific or remote geography, again that just multiplies the dimensions they can bring to their work and allow it to become more complex. Again, I don't want to cut off any majority writer. As [Marcus Aurelius] said, "I am a human being; anything that is human cannot be alien to me." So I don't think that people are necessarily denied that access, but I think that by a circumstance, by accident of birth, certain people do inherit another vision.

When I first read A Visitation of Spirits, *I remember being surprised that a modern gay writer would opt to have his gay protagonist commit suicide. On the surface it seemed like such an outmoded—almost clichéd—gesture. Of course, Horace's suicide is, in fact, an integral and carefully prepared-for moment in that novel, but I still wonder what kinds of decisions you as a writer—and specifically a gay writer—had to make before you could let your character point that gun on himself.*

Yeah, I caught a lot of flak for having done that, but I stick by—no pun intended—my guns. The choice was, on one hand, very personal and aesthetic. I am a fan of tragedy. I think that tragedy is one of the most profound art forms. Thinking about my influences, suicides figure heavily into it. I didn't necessarily think of it as a cliché, but as a form with which I was working and trying to plumb another depth, if I can say that without sounding self-aggrandizing.

The other one was political. I don't like to call my choices political choices, but in this case it was, because I did definitely want to bring a tension to circumstances in this country in which, unlike places like Provincetown, or the West Village of New York, or San Francisco, or certain parts of Chicago, et cetera—where folk who happen to be minority, who happen to be middle-class are running around saying, "Everything is wonderful! Come out, join the party!"—I wanted to point out that in other parts of the world 'tweren't that way; and not so long ago, in fact a year or two ago, these tensions were very real and that they could, and do, still cause this. The highest rate of suicide is among black teenagers right now. Which is something you don't hear a lot about on CNN and I felt needed to be addressed.

Very few gay writers today take as much interest in religious experience as you do. Indeed, one could say that A Visitation of Spirits *is as much a religious novel as a gay novel. And certainly many of the plots and themes in* Let the Dead Bury Their Dead *frequently turn on questions of religious faith. Robert McRuer, writing about you in* Contemporary Gay American Novelists, *makes a distinction between "faith" and "religiosity" in your work.*[1] *What's that distinction mean to you?*

Ah, well. How you live your life and what you truly believe, to boil it down to its essence. In African American culture in particular—and I think that's where I play with religion and religiosity and faith the most—there is a constant tension between the legalism of Protestant faith, Protestant religion—Baptist, Methodist, what have you—and the codes and rituals and forms that one has to adhere to, and the bedrock, when you call on religion when you need it most. Not only the blues, but you're in debt, your wife has left you, and your youngest child is sick—*that* is faith, where you go to in those moments. How the two can often be contradictory, and how they can—"warp" is a harsh word—but transform a soul in ways, and affect it.

Fact and fantasy, history and mythology, the real and the supernatural coexist beautifully in your fiction. I'm thinking in particular of the long title story in your collection Let The Dead Bury Their Dead, *which purports to be the record of a conversation between two elderly residents of Tims Creek, Ezekial Thomas Cross and Ruth David Cross, the great-uncle and great-aunt of Reverend James Malachai Greene, who, marvelously enough, was the other main character in*

---

1. Robert McRuer, "Randall Kenan," in *Contemporary Gay American Novelists: A Bio-Bibliographical Critical Sourcebook,* ed. Emmanuel S. Nelson (Westport, Conn.: Greenwood, 1993), 235.

your first novel. In that story—or rather the fictional monograph, which supposedly is published in the year 2000—you create a fictional editor, Reginald Kain who, I can't help but notice, has the same initials as you do and who, in his scholarly footnotes to the transcript of that conversation, makes reference to both actual works of history and fictional stories, including a book of stories by one Randall Kenan, Go Curse Your God, Boy, and Die, *published—I was tickled to see this—in 1996. So my question is, What's going on here!?*

What is going on indeed! I use two women to defend me, one who is quoted in that story, Zora Neale Hurston—"You are now about to hear lies beyond suspicion"—and the other, Eudora Welty, who in her essay, "Place in Fiction," says—I'm paraphrasing here—"fiction is a lie in its outside dress but it is to tell the truth." Yeah, I figured, Why not have some rollicking fun with this?

It's all about myth in the end. The best stories always resonate—I was trying for that—on the level when fact collides with fiction and you get this wonderful frisson from the action. That story brings together everything—*everything!*—that I ever wanted to do in fiction, from dead people rising and gay botanists and wealthy widowers dealing with runaway slaves and these two wonderful people who are bickering at each other between the lines. It was just a wonderful delight to work on, and I hope I can convey that to the reader.

You bring a wonderfully lyric quality to your descriptions of rural southeast North Carolina. What is it about that place that you love so much?

Well, it is the place I first knew, and so love the most deeply. Of all the places—I've had the great privilege to have traveled a lot over North America, and there are some breathtaking spots—it's the only place I can't separate people from the land. I can't go into a field without thinking of an incident. I just love that connection. The land is populated with ghosts for me. Of all the places I've been, I've heard other people talking about it, and the way I've understood that connection is to think about home. That's something I'll never be able to exorcise, and don't think necessarily want to.

You are still living in New York. Do you plan on returning to the South to live?

Well, I go back a lot. I go home several times a year, sometimes for long stretches. So I think of myself as a bifurcator—New Yorker/Southerner. As to whether I'll actually take up the sink and the bed and move back, I can't say yet.

What's the gay scene like in the South? Maybe that's too general a question. I'm sure the gay scene in Atlanta is very different from the gay scene in rural southeastern North Carolina.

Well, in North Carolina itself, I think it's unique from Virginia or South Carolina—which are north and south—or to Tennessee, which is to the west. Because of its history, because North Carolina never had a major seaport, the real epicenter of the state is in the center, in the Research Triangle part, and that's extraordinarily different from "Down East" or even north, along the Outer Banks. As one could imagine, attitudes there are very repressive and noninclusive, whereas in the Research Triangle part, it can be wild, wonderful, and progressive. So in the place like Chinquapin, where I grew up, people don't know what the word "gay" means, let alone envision tolerating it. Whereas in Chapel Hill or Durham or Raleigh, people are quite open and quite happy.

I want to get back to Tims Creek. In that long, final story in the collection, you give Tims Creek a history. It was, you say, a "maroon" society. Tell us about that.

I had the great privilege and delight to study under a woman named Sonya Stone, who died a few years ago, at Chapel Hill, and she engendered in me this fascination with these facts of history that hadn't been written about much. I think I cite in that story everything that I could find about maroon societies. They are places, remote places, in the nineteenth century, to which African Americans, and sometimes Native Americans, escaped and set up towns and lived away from slave owners and developed. The phenomenon was much more successful in Latin America. The capital of Brazil was founded as a maroon society. And in the Caribbean, on certain islands. In this country, because it wasn't quite as dense and quite as wild, only, I think, in Florida, were such places really allowed to or able to really flourish.

So I wanted to play with that, because I was also playing with the idea of African America self-empowerment and trying to make some connection between some of the lamentable things as I see it, in terms of African American leadership, that are going on now with some of the things that had happened during Reconstruction and during slavery. To sort of reawaken a folk hero, this "bad man," the man who goes into the swamps and liberates his people, because I don't see that character very much, and we all need him very badly.

I wonder if there is a paradigm or analogy that can be drawn between those his-
torical African American maroon societies and communities, ghettos—whatever
term you want to use—that gay men and women have created for themselves,
leaving to a certain extent the mainstream culture and creating places like the
West Village, or even here, in Provincetown. Is that a comparison that can be
made, or are the historical dimensions too different?

On some level the analogy can be made. I don't know how far it can be taken,
because it would break down in terms of cultural lines and color lines. And
class. Whereas this huge separation forced people in that way. But, yeah, politically speaking, I could see that as an analogy.

You create two families in Let the Dead Bury Their Dead, *the two Cross fam-*
ilies. One is black and one is white. And there's been some intermingling there
as well. Rebecca Sarah Cross is the matriarch of the plantation Canaan, in a
town near Tims Creek, Crosstown. She keeps a diary through the antebellum pe-
riod and the Civil War and well into her old age, which also becomes one more
document in that story. I can't help but think that you are now greatly commit-
ted to the Cross family and their whole saga, and that we'll be seeing more of
them in your later fiction.

Well, as I said earlier, it's irresistible. You brush up against a story and it's yours.
You won it. Again, of all the American stories that haven't been told, that's one
of them that I'm very, very eager to tell and to explore. It won't be done in one
story. Obviously, this is just a little bit of it, but the relationship between slave
owner and slave that goes beyond the chattel relationship, and especially over
time. When it goes so far as the name, and sharing the land and all of those
tensions, in many ways it is the history of race relations in this country. But
there is a particular intimate relationship that I don't think has been touched.
It's very dangerous. People get really nervous when you start talking about that
sort of thing. And that excites me. That really excites me.

There's a wonderful moment in that story when the youngest son, Phineas Owen
Cross, comes across the mythical leader of that maroon society. He's variously
known as Menes or Pharaoh, an escaped black slave. Despite the fact the Crosses
are, in many ways, the archenemies of that maroon society, Phineas is not. Un-
like his brothers, unlike his mother and father, he has not shown any ill will to-
ward the blacks. It turns out, in fact, that Phineas is a botanist. Is anything to
be made of that? Does his own outsider status give him a special empathy with
other outsiders?

To be sure, we can never overlook the fact that in the face of slavery being this horrible experience in this country, there were all these good—capital G, underlined—white folk who worked very hard. The Underground Railroad was a very real thing, and people even within the environs of South Carolina, Georgia, Mississippi, Alabama were doing things to alleviate the horror. So I am interested in that complicity, because Phineas didn't go out and do anything. In many ways he was ineffectual in his relationship with his father. But what does make a person who comes from that background, who has a brother who is a stereotypical, whip-wielding SOB, become different? I'm interested in that dynamic. Yeah, I do mean to imply and to explore those elements that make a person liberal in a very faithful way as opposed to a formal, religious way.

There are stories in your collection told in a female voice, and your stories are populated with a variety of interesting female characters. Is it difficult?

Is it difficult? No! My women characters come to me much more readily. I think it was because I was surrounded by women of a certain age. I was brought up by my great aunt. She had this cadre of friends who were responsible for raising me along with her. So that is the most real to me—growing up, surrounded by women talking about hot flashes and the sort of problems that women of a certain age . . . I can't get enough of that. Right now a great many of my women friends are women of a certain age. Maybe sometimes I forget that I'm not.

So as a boy you were sort of eavesdropping on this world of women?

Oh, yes. Oh, yes.

You are younger than most of the other writers we've had on this series. You turned thirty this year. Do you think there are particular issues or problems that young gay writers face that the older generation of gay writers didn't have to confront?

Ah, well, the most looming thing would obviously be AIDS, and how they're dealing with it both physically and psychologically and culturally. I teach writing and for some strange reason a lot of young gay men gravitate toward my class. I don't know why, but they're writing these interesting stories in which being gay is not necessarily the crux to the issue. They're out. I mean, they have these amazing conversations with their mothers, and so I think we're going to see a very interesting take on it—the next step, I should hope. Which we're ready for.

What I was also thinking of is the enormous body of gay and lesbian literature that has surfaced in the last twenty years and whether young gay writers experience that as a crushing burden or as an inspiration.

I'm uncomfortable making this analogy. I don't think the burden—and I don't mean to take away from what's gone before in gay literature, and lesbian literature—but I don't think it's the same crushing burden as an African American writer would have, because no one has established this huge tradition which is freighted with cultural significance. You're getting a lot of gay writers who are Asian, a lot of gay writers who are Native American, a lot of gay writers who are Italian, and their particular takes on their culture, combined with their sexuality, make for interesting musical riffs and potential. So in many ways they are seeing ways in which they can revivify two canons at the same time and are delighting in that. And again, because of the circumstances that make up their lives, they see themselves as in many ways very different, thanks to the work done by a lot of writers in the sixties, seventies, and eighties in particular. They can go on to other things; some of the things that were important to gay writers are in some ways less important to them.

You've mentioned Toni Morrison and Gabriel García Márquez as writers who have been important to you. Who else has influenced you as a writer?

Oh, God, the list is frightening. I'd go with Katharine Anne Porter, obviously, whom I quote at the beginning of the stories. Yukio Mishima, oddly enough, a gay Japanese writer, is very important to me.

Why?

The way he writes women, strangely enough. He's one of the few male writers I've read [about whom] I've said, Damn it, he knows what he's talking about. Combine that with his style and just his understanding and his comically morbid take on the world. He has a lot of suicides in the books. And he does it very deftly. And, not to commit a pun, but he did it very deftly, quite literally.

Isaac Bashevis Singer. I think I love his demons and dybbuks. And also the religion, that very Orthodox. I understood him—not to say explicitly—but implicitly, because I don't know that much about Orthodox Judaism in

Poland at the turn of the century. But certainly that relation to that religion I found fascinating. And his stories were a liberation, because I said, Ah, you can do this sort of thing and get away from it. And be taken seriously! Yeah, that was a great liberation.

What is your own stance toward organized religion?

I think it's fine. What is it that someone in Israel said when they were asked what they thought of Christianity? "Yes, I think it's a good idea. Call me when it happens." Yeah, I think it can be a wonderful force. The thing that I militate against, and I think people don't realize that I'm criticizing, is not Christendom itself or any sort of formal religion, it's the mendacity and the hypocrisy that can be so blatant and demonic. That's what really gets me up in arms.

There are so many categories one could place you in: gay writer, Afro-American writer, Southern writer, postmodern writer. Do you find those categories interesting, helpful, limiting?

I listen to them with a great deal of interest, but at the end of the day, I don't really say, Ah, I am a black, gay, Southern postmodern! It can't be done. I don't really think of myself in any category but as a human person who happens to have access to all these wonderful, sometimes unfortunate, but often liberating experiences.

You mentioned your teaching. You teach at Sarah Lawrence.

Yes, and Columbia.

What kinds of courses do you teach?

Writing. I once taught a literature course at Vassar, and actually found it much more interesting than teaching writing.

What's your approach?

A lot of reading actually. That's the one way you do it, to understand how stories are constructed. And really the way to understand how stories are constructed is to experience the story. It's important to steep yourself in a lot of Welty and O'Connor and Faulkner and Morrison and on and on and on, and then to go for it. And don't be afraid to take chances. A lot of it is trying to release people from their inhibitions, to play on the page.

In fact, I was going to ask you what advice you'd give to young gay writers?

Have a good time. And I don't mean that in a flippant way. I think if you are enjoying—and I don't mean to limit it to humor or what have you—but if you are really interested in what you are writing and are not doing it to get some grand abstract message across, but if you really are invested in the people's lives, in the story that you are telling, on a personal level, then that will come through. Readers are not dumb folk. People who sit down with a book tend not to be fools as easily as we think we are. They can tell if you really mean what you are about. So my advice is to mean it when you do it.

What are you working on now?

I'm working on a nonfiction book, oddly enough. It's a book about African America. I have been traveling for the last three years—it's getting on three years—around North America, including Canada, talking to black folk about their lives, looking at histories in parts of the country that haven't really found their way into the broader conversation about African American culture, and trying to find in that a new way to think about not only what it means to be an African American but what it means to be an American, because in many ways African American experience has been the emblem of the American experience: the rise and fall, the assimilation into the land, the embodiment of the frontier. All those things find expression in the black experience.[2]

---

2. Kenan's book, *Walking on Water: Black American Lives at the Turn of the Twenty-First Century,* was published in 1999.

Later
Interviews

(1994-1998)

Edmund White, New York, New York, 1985

Scott Heim, Brooklyn, New York, 1998

Bernard Cooper, Los Angeles, California, 1989

Michael Lowenthal, Amagansett, New York, 1998

David Plante

Best known as the author of the Francoeur Trilogy, about a young Franco-American gay Catholic from Providence, Rhode Island, David Plante has published over a dozen novels, including *The Family*, which was nominated for the National Book Award; *The Catholic*; *The Accident*; and *Annunciation*.

Among gay novelists, Plante is noteworthy not only for his clean, spare, elegant prose (a style highly praised by many, including poet Alfred Corn, who called him "the most hypnotic novelist of his generation") but also for the way he usually understates his homosexual material. As Thomas Dukes has written, Plante "uses homosexuality—among other things—to examine the protagonist's relationship to the larger culture."[1]

Born in 1940 (the same year as Edmund White), Plante attended Catholic schools in Providence before matriculating to Boston College, a Jesuit university, where he majored in French. Also like White, he spent some time in Rome. He taught there briefly before returning to the United States to take a job as a researcher. Moving to London, where he still lives, Plante published his first novel, *The Ghost of Henry James*, in 1970. The first of the Francoeur novels, *The Family*, was published in 1978.

Plante has served as a visiting writer at various universities in Britain, the United States, and Canada, and has lectured at the Gorky Institute of Literature in Moscow. In addition to a Guggenheim Fellowship, he has been the recipient of awards from the British Arts Council Bursary and the American Academy and Institute of Arts and Letters.

On tour to promote *Annunciation*, Plante came to Boston in May 1994, and agreed to tape an interview with me over coffee in Boston's

---

1. Thomas Dukes, "David Plante," in *Contemporary Gay American Novelists: A Bio-Bibliographical Critical Sourcebook*, ed. Emmanuel S. Nelson (Westport, Conn.: Greenwood, 1993), 312.

Hotel Meridien. The interview first appeared in *Frontiers,* in the issue for 9 September 1994.

Is Ticknor and Fields (the publisher of Annunciation*) an American publisher or a British publisher?*

Ticknor and Fields used to be—and, alas, I have to use the past tense—one of the most prestigious and perhaps oldest publishing houses in America. They published Nathaniel Hawthorne. They were bought up by Houghton Mifflin and in February [1994] they ceased to exist. I'm one of the last to be published by Ticknor and Fields.

How sad that the publisher of Hawthorne should cease to exist.

Absolutely. Listen, the world of publishing is just so uncertain and so neurotic-making that actually it gets me into a panic when I think about it, and I try not to think about it. I was saying to somebody the other day that when writers get together now that's all they talk about: the future of publishing.

And the future of reading, I suppose. You said a wonderful thing in the first story you read last night. You described one of the characters as someone who "wants reading to be like looking."

That's it. That's what I want: I want reading to be like looking. That's what I strive for. I try to make it as acutely visual as possible.

And it's there.

Well, it's there by the grace of God, I suppose. But at least I make an attempt. Not that I believe in God.

We'll talk about the grace of God a little later, but let's begin by talking about how you began as a writer.

I think I started writing when I was thirteen, around puberty; and I've often wondered what the connection between writing and puberty might have been. I suppose I find writing sort of sexual. Where it comes from, I have no idea. There was literacy in my family—a small, Franco, working-class parish in Providence, Rhode Island. My grandmother couldn't speak English; my grandmother was illiterate. When she sent her children out for shopping, she'd draw pictograms. She was a half-breed Indian; she was a half-Blackfoot Indian.

And my father was uneducated. My mother was a bit more educated and read novels, only novels I brought back from the library. She wouldn't have done it on her own. So where it comes from I have no idea. That I should, at the age of thirteen, start writing—short stories, plays, poems, everything, anything!

What was the subject matter?

Everything. But mostly, I think, attempts to get down, as accurately as possible, scenes from the neighborhood. I remember distinctly writing about flowering forsythia and a cement driveway and a dog lying on the cement, and the shadow of the forsythia and the shadow of the dog. And just those things—going to the grocery shop to get melons, walking to mass early on winter mornings, and the snow in the branches that would fall from time to time with a soft thud into the snow, that sense of calm. So mostly what I think I tried to do was get down my impressions. Of course, I had grandiose ideas of writing about the universe.

You said that your early writing may have been sexual. In what sense?

Well, in the sense that it offered me possibility. It sort of got me out of this little parish in which I lived. As I grew I certainly wrote a lot about sex. I used writing as a way of indulging my sexuality. It was the only way I could, except for masturbation, I suppose. I mean I created my own fantasies, which would then lead to masturbation. And so it was a great recourse for me.

And those fantasies were homoerotic?

No, not entirely. I mean, some of them may have been written from the point of view of women, some from the point of view of men. I remember—I must have been about fourteen—writing a poem. I remember the line, written from the point of view of a woman: "He was as heavy as earth on me." I thought that was *terrific!* But there was something deeper than just the sex of it all; there was a sense of humanity.

You know, one of the things that influenced me so much, and this is going back a long, long way: my mother bought me a book called *The Family of Man*, which was a photograph book. It had just come out, and I was very excited. I wanted to have this book. We went downtown and she bought it for me. And it filled me with a sense of humanity and the sufferings and joys of humanity. And so I saw sex, birth, death—all of this—in terms of this romantic, Whitmanesque sense of humanity. It's a sensibility which is over I think for the newer generations, but it still survives for me.

It's a Catholic sensibility, too, I think.

It probably is, it probably is. So all this sexuality had a greater meaning than mere indulgence. It had a context.

You went to parochial schools?

I went to parochial schools. I went to a French Canadian school in Providence, Rhode Island, taught by Les Mères de Jésus-Marie. We had French in the morning, English in the afternoon. Then I went on to a Christian Brothers school called La Salle Academy; then I went on to the Jesuits [at Boston College]. I did my junior year abroad at Catholic University of Louvain. So all my education has been entirely Catholic.

And when did you start writing for publication?

Oh, I'd always had a fantasy of doing that. I think, perhaps, after college when I went to Rome—and I went to Rome with the idea of becoming a writer—but it didn't happen. Then I came back to New York, with the idea of becoming a writer in New York, and it didn't happen. I came to Boston, with the idea of being a writer in Boston, and it didn't happen. But it happened in England. I had a short story published in a magazine called the *Transatlantic Review,* and at that time publishers actually read little magazines and were looking for interesting writers. I got two or three letters from publishers asking was I writing a novel. And that's how it began, with the one short story written for the *Transatlantic Review.*

What was the name of that story?

"The Buried City"—an adolescent story, about a young man who goes up into the attic and opens boxes and gets dressed in his mother's wedding gown. You know, a bit clichéd, really. But that's how it began.

You're a self-taught writer. You've never done an M.F.A. or any other writing degree.

No, never. There was a writer-in-residence when I was at Boston College—I can't remember his name—and I never went to him because frankly I was embarrassed. I thought I'd never get in. So I'm completely self-taught. Even in journalism. I'm writing nonfiction for the *New Yorker:* I don't know how to do it! I really don't know how to do it. So I do what I think is going to be interesting. And of course Tina Brown or my editor, Dan Menaker, will have suggestions, and I say, "Yes, okay," and I go home and do what they tell me to do.

You do mainly profiles for them?

I'm doing profiles for them now, yeah.

What are you working on now?

I'm working on a profile of a woman named Doris Lockhart-Saatchi, an American, who married a man named Charles Saatchi, who with his brother founded what became the largest advertising agency in the world, Saatchi and Saatchi. Doris and Charles put together one of the most important collections of twentieth-century art in the world, and actually opened their own museum for it in London.

Was this Tina Brown's idea or yours?

It was my idea. I proposed it; she said she liked it. I'm doing a profile of Glenn Close for them, which will come out in the autumn when Glenn Close goes to New York with *Sunset Boulevard.*[2] I went to California to see her in February.

Was that fun?

Oh, it was marvelous. She's terrific, she's marvelous!

Had you ever met her before?

No. You know, I went to her dressing room—she said to come around to her dressing room after the performance—and there she was in her terry cloth robe and that little skull cap that they wear for wigs, and she was taking off her makeup. She just turned to me and I went and put my arms around her. I mean it was that kind of immediacy. We got on very well. She was very generous. She gave me a whole day, and she'll give me, I'm

---

2. Neither the profile on Doris Lockhart-Saatchi nor the one on Glenn Close has been published by the *New Yorker*.

sure, more time. I have various other ideas for profiles. I hope I'll get some fiction in there from time to time, too. I haven't given them any fiction. As I said to my editor, I'm terrified that they'll turn my fiction down!

Your first novel, The Ghost of Henry James, *was published in 1970.*

That's right. It was nine years after I had graduated from college. It was published in England, and then it was published here by Gambit, a small publishing house based in Boston. And then I continued to publish in England books which were never published in America.

Is that why in your latest novel, on the page that lists your previous work, only your last eight novels are listed?

That was my idea, because I feel I've written too many novels. I got embarrassed.

What does that mean? Do you think you're too prolific?

I think I've published too much. I think I've published too much, too thoughtlessly.

Are you disavowing those earlier novels?

No, I'm not disavowing them. One can't, because there they are. But I would like to think of what I consider my "important novels"—keep those—and let the others drift away a bit. Again, I think I wrote too many, too quickly, without considering carefully enough what I was doing. But then again, I wrote with enthusiasm, so that's what I did and that's what I had to do. Nevertheless, I certainly don't apologize for that.

You are now in your mid-fifties and have published thirteen novels. What are you able to say now that you weren't able to say when you first started out as a writer?

Well, because I didn't have any education in writing novels, I never knew quite what a novel was, except what I read and read and read. So my first novels were very fragmented. They consisted of nothing but paragraphs, completely disconnected paragraphs, one from another. Well, that wasn't so much a device as a necessity, because I didn't know how to do it otherwise. You see, I focused on these impressions, which I suppose I had been doing in my youth from age thirteen. I hoped that these impressions would be strong enough that they would create a sense of something larger in which all the moments would participate and form, as it were, an hour or a day.

What I'm able to do more and more is, I think, work more and more with a greater understanding of the novel: cause and effect, plot, story, characterization. Curiously, all those conventional things which it's taken me a long, long time to be able to deal with.

Of course, the other is sex. In the seventies I couldn't have written as frankly as I do now. I think I've written as frankly as anyone possibly could in *The Catholic*.

Also, just getting older and more mature. I find myself wanting less and less to write about myself. As a matter of fact, as I grow older, I believe more and more that writers don't write about themselves. Even Philip Roth doesn't write about himself; he writes about something greater than himself. I'm trying to pay more attention to that whatever, is greater than oneself.

And yet, more so than almost any writer I know, you've mined your autobiography for stories.

Yeah, I do. And I keep a diary.

I read somewhere that you've kept that diary since 1959 and that, at last count, it tallied up at over four million words.

About four and a half million now. I don't "mine" it so much, yet, so much as look at it for ideas. No, that's not true. I've used it, I've used it a lot in my [Francouer] Family books.

What's going to happen to it?

I don't know. I can't imagine it will ever be published. It's too long. If it's published it will have to be condensed, vastly condensed. I just keep doing it. It's the thing I most enjoy. I love writing in my diary. Because I'm not thinking about *anything* but the sheer pleasure of writing down things.

You travel with it?

I travel with it, oh yeah. I like taking trains or planes. A seven-hour plane trip is terrific because I can have seven hours of writing in my diary.

Is it scandalous?

It just has everything in it. Everything, everything, everything. If I have terrible fights with people, I put those in. If I've done something awful, I put that in.

It seems to me that you're in possession of an extraordinary document.

Well, you see, I've been very, very fortunate, in living in London and meeting so many people. That's not strange in London. You meet everybody. I have met not everybody, but a lot.

Would that be any different if you were living in New York?

Yeah, because New York is compartmentalized, whereas in London all novelists would know one another. Even novelists living in New York don't know one another.

They've put themselves into niches?

Yeah, and that surprises me. So what happens when I'm in London in conversations, I talk about people I know with great ease, but in New York if I talk about them in the same way I'm "name-dropping."

Does that have something to do with the "integration" we were talking about earlier? Is there more of a sense of the integration of all the facets of one's life in Europe than in America? In traveling through Europe and talking to gay people, I've found that their take on America is that we have made gayness something so unique and special and have called attention to it in ways that Europeans don't.

That's true, that's absolutely true. I live with someone. We're invited as freely as we invite. I never think, Oh God, we're all gays tonight, or We're all gays and one straight man. I just never think about it. That's Europe.

You've been living in England for close to thirty years now. What attracts you to living as an expatriate?

It used to be a sense of difference. I wanted things to be as different as possible. It would excite my sense of awareness, to be in Europe, to be excited visually by *details*—traffic signs, window latches, doorknobs, light bulbs—the simple things. I had this terrific sense of distance, difference, and I loved it.

Did it make you see America more acutely?

Oh, yeah. Very much so. And then I was able to look back at America and see it in the same way. Now America is to me much more exciting than Europe. Very exotic. In thirty years it's changed enormously, America. I was saying to somebody earlier that, when I was growing up in America, I had fantasies of the way I wanted America to be. I wanted it to be integrated. I wanted it to be accepting of homosexuality. I wanted a greater appreciation of beauty in America. I wanted Americans to stop smoking. And all of these things have happened.

To a greater or lesser extent.

To a greater or lesser extent. People will say, "Oh, you don't know, you don't know." But look: when I was living in Providence, and going to [the] Christian Brothers high school, I had a great idea for a term paper, which was to go to the NAACP office in Providence and interview the head of it. He was marvelous. I wrote my term paper and said to myself, Well, this is going to be *loved!* I got a C! And I thought, Well, it's probably not good. It only occurred to me recently that that teacher—he was a lay teacher—simply disapproved of my writing about a black man. It had to have been that, because it *was* a good paper. If he wanted originality, if he wanted an expression of someone doing something different, I did it. Well, that's changed, that's changed. That teacher would have been expelled today. I remember his scowl when he gave me the paper back. I didn't understand it. Now I understand. That's changed.

I live openly as a homosexual, totally. I have no secrets—at all. Whereas, if we were still back in the fifties, I'd have secrets. I don't like secrets particularly. I want to be open.

I think Americans do have a greater sense of beauty. My God! Providence, Rhode Island, has become one of the prettiest places in the world! The center of Providence, with the opening of the river, and the quays—it's as beautiful as the Seine. And that little amphitheater, where I presume they'll have little concerts! And also, fewer and fewer Americans smoke.

So your vision has been realized. Let's talk about visions some more. In Annunciation, *one character, Lidia, asks another, Claude, "'You believe there may be, still unknown to us, a vision that will save us?'"; and he answers, "'I have to be-lieve it.'" Is that your own quest—for a "vision that will save"?*

Yeah, sure. I mean, what other reason do I have for writing?

What does that mean?

I don't know. And I hope it occurs to me before I die. And that's one of the reasons why I go on writing. I go on writing for something that will occur. You know, I believe in inspiration. It's a mysterious thing. It makes one aware of what one hadn't been aware of before. And I just hope that somewhere along the line, while I'm writing a sentence, something will occur and I'll think, That's it! That's what keeps me writing.

In the novel, Claire is doing research on a minor Italian Renaissance painter, Pietro Testa. Testa's "vision" is that of the classicist. You write, "He was by his own intention a classicist, but by temperament he was a romantic." Does that describe your sensibilities as well?

I hadn't thought of that. I think it's true. I think that's absolutely true, and that had never occurred to me. I like great clarity, simplicity. I like the forms to be defined, and yet of course I want it to be all mysterious.

I want to talk more about mystery, because it seems to me that mystery is at the heart of your work—this elusive, ineluctable mystery that permeates everything. And that seems to me to be a particularly Catholic sensibility.

Oh, yes. You see, I think that what is most important in one's writing is not what one intends, but what occurs in the spaces one leaves. What it is that occurs, because it's beyond one's intention, because it's beyond one, is mysterious. Talk about revelation, I want to write in such a way that I create spaces enough—deep enough, wide enough—so that something will occur in them; which, because it's beyond my intending, [is mysterious].

What would the deconstructionists do with that answer?

I don't know. I have great respect for all theories of literature, but I don't know what they'd think. Mary Gordon is a close friend of mine, and we talk a lot about this and what we want our writing to do. We're boosting one another. We are both more and more confirmed in our beliefs that writing has to be first and foremost moral and spiritual; and deconstructionists would, I think, wonder about that. I don't think we're interested in a text as such as in a vision. You know, my parents read—whenever they did read—and, if they didn't read, thought of literature as morally and spiritually uplifting. What other reason did one have for reading?

And the Jesuits at [Boston College] certainly taught you that.

I guess they did!

Do you consider yourself a Catholic writer?

Yeah.

What does that mean?

Well, it means I was born a Catholic and, as I said last night, inculcated with longings which are the strongest longings I will ever, ever have; and they are simply a longing to be united with God in eternity. I remember that longing, and as it's the greatest longing I will ever have, however inculcated it was, I've got to write out of it. And that's being a Catholic writer. Now do I believe? No. I don't. But I think this longing is greater than my believing or not.

You are no longer a practicing Catholic—you describe yourself as an atheist— and yet you've said, "My intentions hardly matter." Maybe you've already answered this, but what did you mean by that statement?

Just that as a writer the most I can do is create spaces in which something occurs, which is beyond my intending it.

How do you do that?

How do you do it? You describe. The person who's the great master is Chekhov. You use images that suggest much more than they contain. There are tricks, sometimes. And they've gone out of my mind. You don't give everything. You hold things back. You try not to state the obvious. You don't make comments.

　　I try to leave myself out as much as possible. And *that* actually has a lot to do with Ernest Hemingway. I was once speaking to Raymond Carver, and I asked him, "Well, what do you think of Hemingway?" He said, "Hemingway is our grandfather." It's absolutely true. There is in Hemingway a great sense of something.

He was a Catholic.

There you are. There is a scene in *The Sun Also Rises,* when they're in a car driving towards Pamplona. Hemingway describes it beautifully—the wheat moving in the wind. And one of the men in the car turns to the man in the back and just nods. Now, if Hemingway had put into the mouth of one of them, "Isn't it beautiful," he would have been *draining* the scene of its mystery; he would have been *imposing* beauty on it. Well, it's more than beautiful. There's a sense of maybe something tragic even in it. And to say it's beautiful is to limit it. That's very much in my writing.

You've said that Annunciation *represents "a deepening of my devotion to my native religion." What do you mean by that?*

It means that I'm using my Catholicism more in *Annunciation* than in any other book, though it's not about my life, or my family, I'm using it more. I hope more profoundly.

You're actually one of a number of gay writers who have pursued at least part of their careers abroad. I'm thinking of James Baldwin, Gore Vidal, Ned Rorem. I suppose we could go right back to Henry James, who moved to England midway through his career. Do you think there is anything in the gay experience that makes life abroad particularly appealing, or maybe even necessary?

Used to. Not anymore. That's gone. One of the reasons why I went to Europe was for that liberation from what I thought was American oppression. There was always that oppression in Europe. Because I was a foreigner, I didn't feel I was subject to it. America is much more liberal than Europe now.

I want to write something about the end of my romance with Europe. My romance with Europe is over; my romance with America is beginning, I think. The fact is, Europe is not more cultured than America. Europe is not more liberated than America. All of these things that one went to Europe for . . . now gone.

Do you say that with sadness?

Yeah, I do, because I had great hopes for Europe, coming together and forming a United States of Europe, and these hopes are dashed. I don't believe it's going to happen. And America holds together.

I went to a lecture that Alfred Kazin gave last week. He talked about being in Europe in the fifties and how he had this fierce, passionate desire to learn how to "read Europe."

Yeah, that's right. That's right.

Speaking of Henry James, your first novel, The Ghost of Henry James, *pays homage to the master. What has been James's influence on your work?*

Ooh, I tell you. I've written a piece for the *New Yorker*—I think it's going to come out sometime in June—about *exactly* that, my changing feelings towards Henry James, which are very complicated.[3] I mean, it's so complicated I think I'm going to have to leave that question to that piece. Changing feelings, very changing. He was a fantasy figure for me. He's buried in Cambridge, Massachusetts. I used to visit his grave.

I was at Westminster Abbey for a memorial service when they put [James's] plaque down in Poets Corner. I had contributed five pounds to that, so was invited to the ceremony. I saw a procession which was headed by his great-great grandnephew, or something like that—a beautiful young man carrying a laurel wreath. And as I watched it, I thought, WASP culture is dead. It's gone. That was sort of liberating, and with it Henry James went.

As a younger writer, were you in the thrall of WASP culture?

Yes!

I think every ethnic writer in America is, to a certain extent.

Oh, yeah. Which is terrific. I mean, *yes.* You know, I say this not with regret. I read Emerson, I read Nathaniel Hawthorne, I read Henry James, I read Melville. With a great sense of their meaning something to me. Very powerful. But I also thought that I had to be like them in some way, and then I realized, *no.* It's gone. Who is it—[Louis] Auchincloss—is the last of them, and, my God, if he isn't a sort of bloodless, half-dead writer! WASP culture is over. Needless to say, *the* most powerful culture that took over in literary terms is Jewish.

You mentioned Philip Roth. Has he been a big influence?

---

3. "The Secret of Henry James," *New Yorker,* 28 November 1994, 91–99.

He's been a very, very close *friend*. Very close. I love Philip very, very much. A supporter, in ways. In some ways, he hates my work, because it's too spiritual, arty-farty for him. He'll say, "'Trapezoids of sunlight'! Come on, that's easy." [I'll think,] God, he's right: "Trapezoids of sunlight." What a terrible image. But on the other hand, I think there's something in my work he likes. He's helped me to a large extent in making me see that, however high you go in the eyes of the world as a writer, all your work has to be based in the truth of some kind. He *grounds* me.

What's it like to be a gay writer who has crossed over into mainstream respectability?

Have I? I'm not sure. Have I done that?

You're reviewed by the New York Times, *you're sent on fancy book tours by your publisher.*

I mean, have I as much as Edmund White, say? I don't know. I can't see that. I'd like to be.

Do you think you're put in a niche?

No. As a matter of fact, if anything I have very little identity in the gay world.

Why is that? Because the homosexuality has been so reticent in most of your work?

Well, I wrote a novel called *The Catholic*, which has the longest sex scene in literature, straight or gay. I mean, I couldn't be more outspoken than in that novel. But I called it *The Catholic*, because it's about being a Catholic. I don't know. Perhaps because I haven't addressed the issue of homosexuality in itself. Even in *The Catholic*, it's oblique. It's not as important as [the Catholicism]. And I don't think sex is. I love sex. It's one of the great pleasures in my life, but it's not the most important thing in my life.

What is the most important thing in your life?

Love. Absolutely. Of course. And that can be nonsexual. And when it combines with sex, it makes sex all the better.

Do you mind being labeled a "gay writer"?

In a way I do. Only because life is so much more. What I would like my label to be is: "North American, Franco, Catholic, one-eight Blackfoot Indian writer." Oh, did I put "gay" in there?

You didn't.

"Gay writer." Because, it's all there. It's a part of it, very much a part of it. You know, you can't separate things out. I believe everything does hang together. It's all confused and messy and things interrelate in ways. What I would like to do is write a *big* novel in which all of this came together.

What do you think of the incredible emergence of American gay writing in the last ten to fifteen years?

Wonderful, wonderful. The phenomenon is wonderful. What do I think of particular writers? That's difficult to say. To say one is better than another, or I don't like this one and I like that one, is sort of incidental.

No, I didn't mean to pin you down. I guess this question comes out of what you were just saying about wanting to write a novel in which everything is incorporated. Do you see ways in which some gay writing limits itself to only one aspect of living?

It depends. Could one say that Philip Roth's novels are limited because they have so much to do with his Jewishness? No. I think it has to do with, again, the depth of one's moral and spiritual vision. God knows, Jane Austen was limited, but she's not limited. One day I would like to write a more overtly homosexual novel, that is that might be called *The Homosexual* or something—bring it right up to the surface—but the success or failure of the novel would depend on what I bring to it.

Who have been some of the other writers who have influenced your work?

Well, Hemingway. Each of my early novels, not only *The Ghost of Henry James* but the others, had behind them an American writer. The second was Nathaniel Hawthorne. The third, *Relatives*, had Henry Adams—this figure to whom I referred everything in my own mind, a kind of invisible reference point for me.

What other writers? American, really. Not European. Flaubert, yeah, to a degree. I'd like to think the Russians have. Chekhov. Dostoevsky. Dostoevsky, at least in translation, reads often as very, very messy. But, my God, the end of *The Idiot*! I reread it a couple of summers ago, and I was stunned, really stunned for about three days. It's *so* powerful.

You've spent some time in the former Soviet Union, at the Gorky Institute of Literature.

Yeah. I was lecturing there.

Have you ever taught writing?

No.

What was that experience like, to be living in Russia?

Oh, it was *wonderful*. Russia is a holy country. You have to be there to get the sense of it. It's a mess, it's horrible, but it's a holy country. It fills one with a sense of holy grief. You see everything through tears in your eyes. I don't know to what extent that's because of the received ideas that I bring to Russia—you know, the "great sufferings of Russia," the "holiness of Russia." But if they are received ideas, my God, the ideas are fulfilled when I'm there!

Maybe it comes from all those years of praying for the conversion of Russia that I remember as a Catholic youth.

Exactly. You know, I said that to a Russian, and tears dripped down her face and she said, "Well, your prayers have been answered." Well, let's see.

What do you think of Solzhenitsyn's return?

I think, personally, it's a dreadful thing. I think he's a heavy-handed absolutist. No subtlety. I don't like his novels. I've tried to read them. To me they lack real compassion. They're from the head, not the heart. They seem to be written in a very pedestrian way. There's absolutely no mystery in them. I'm frightened of him as an absolutist.

Last night, at the reading, you expressed surprise upon learning that Boston College had an active gay and lesbian student organization. What would it have meant to you to have had such an organization on campus when you were a student there?

Why, *everything*! I would have been able to make love. I think. I hope I would have met somebody with whom I would have fallen in love rather than have to go off to Europe for it.

Would that have changed everything? Would you have been a different writer today?

I don't know if it would have changed everything. It would have changed a lot. I would have certainly made me think twice about going to Europe for sexual freedom, because I would have had it. Would it have satisfied my desire for difference? I don't know. I wanted to be a foreigner, you see. I wanted to be a foreigner.

You were doing in the sixties what Auden and Isherwood and Spender went to Berlin for in the thirties.

In a way, yeah. And I had these fantasies, and indeed I did fall in love, in Spain. With somebody who was born and brought up in Turkey. I was nineteen; he was twenty-one. I fell totally in love. That first experience was *wonderful*! Wonderful, wonderful, wonderful. The fact that it took place in Europe, with a foreigner who had never been to America, who was sort of fascinated by America—he asked me questions about America—made me feel that it was an experience that detached me from the world. Oh, it was wonderful. I remained friendly with him until he died about six years ago from AIDS. In fact, I wrote a short story about it, which is in the David Leavitt anthology.[4] Everything is true about that.

What advice to you have for young gay writers?

God, I don't know if I'm even in a position to give advice. I wish someone would give *me* advice! I would say, just keep at it. The disappointments—gay, straight, however you are—it is an impossible task, writing. And you have to live with the impossibility of it, day by day by day. Sometimes it gets you so down that you want to give it up, and you don't. You just keep at it. It's not so rewarding. It's not. The only time writing is rewarding is when you're actually doing it. And then you're in a state of ecstasy. That's

---

4. "The Princess From Africa," in *The Penguin Book of Gay Short Stories*, ed. David Leavitt and Mark Mitchell (New York: Viking, 1994), 394–414.

rewarding. Everything that comes after—publications, agents—none of that is rewarding. And any expectations you have are always going to fail. [When] I started off, I suppose I had read enough biographies of writers to know that this was the case. But of course I thought it would be different with me. Well, it wasn't different; and it won't be different. If anything, it'll get worse.

What are some of the pleasures and some of the anxieties of entering middle age?

Middle age. The anxiety is that I haven't done what I want to do and that I won't do it. That's a great anxiety. The pleasure is—well, it's both a pleasure and it causes anxiety—I can sort of see now what the rest of my life is going to be. That's it. And that is both reassuring and, at the same time, causes a degree of anxiety because I think, Well, can't there be something else? Maybe not.

I know a ninety-one-year-old man in England who said to me the other day, "Every time I go to a party, even at my advanced age, I think I may meet somebody who'll *completely* change my life." Ah, how wonderful that is! That's wonderful. And he said, "Well, that may not happen, but there's always a possibility." That's what I want to do. I want to still go to a party and think, God, there'll probably be someone here who . . . I'm very happy in my life and relationship—utterly and totally—but there's that sense of possibility, of something happening which is going to be wonderful and, well, the revelation, the revelation.

Alan Hollinghurst

Alan Hollinghurst's debut novel, *The Swimming-Pool Library,* received the 1989 Gay/Lesbian Book Award from the American Library Association and a Lambda Literary Award. The novel was admired not only for its rich language and high aesthetic agenda but also for its complex exploration of the principal theme: that exuberance is better than decorousness, eccentricity better than conformity, passion better than repression. Without offering easy or sentimental resolutions, the novel beautifully captured what it feels like to negotiate that two-edged ideal of sex and romance.

A British writer, Alan Hollinghurst was born in 1954. In various capacities, he has worked for over a decade for the *Times Literary Supplement* (London). In 1993, the British literary journal *Granta* named him one of the best young British novelists of the year. A year later, his second novel, *The Folding Star,* appeared. In 1998, *The Spell,* his third novel, was published.

The Folding Star centers around the obsessive love of an English teacher for one of his teenage pupils. It is a story about the gulf between urgency and indifference, and the doom of one's erotic needs. The winner of a 1995 Lambda Literary Award, the novel received high critical praise from, among other notable journals, the *Times* (London), the *Tatler,* the *Independent,* and the *Sunday Times* (London), which said, "Louche, melancholy, both sexually and intellectually potent, *The Folding Star* has its own distinctive atmosphere compounded of a grand 19th-century *fin de siècle* lusciousness, a seamy 20th-century carnality and a generous pinch of true wit."[1]

In his novels, Hollinghurst's fictive method is to juxtapose the present and the past, the highbrow and the lowbrow, uncovering parallels and letting images play against each other. Sentences of high Georgian elegance collide against ones that sizzle with the salty lingo of urban gay life.

---

1. Lucy Hughes-Hallett, "Some Beddings and a Funeral," *Sunday Times* (London), 22 May 1994, sec. 7, p. 13.

Our interview took place on 26 October 1994, over lunch in a restaurant in Boston's South End, during the author's book promotion tour of the United States. It appeared, in a different form, in the *Washington Blade* (25 November 1994).

Taking on the theme of the obsessive love of an older man for a younger man seems to me to be, in at least two ways, a risky enterprise for a gay writer: it's artistically risky because it's such an archetypal—indeed, almost a clichéd—theme in gay literature; and it's politically risky because the idea of men loving boys, teachers loving boys—even sexually active adolescent boys—can be seen as one of sexual abuse. Why did you tackle this theme? What excited you about it?

Well, I'm probably morally defective in some way, but I was never particularly struck by the political impropriety of it. From the start, the book was about finding that you were getting older and finding that the objects of your desire remained at the same age whilst you would continue to get older. I remember that being the curious thing about teaching when I briefly did it—since year by year you got older and your pupils always remained the same age. I suppose [the novel] is partly a way of dramatizing that fact: of Edward's slight sense of panic about life's brevity. It was quite a common path earlier amongst gay people to have affairs with younger people when you started to feel yourself getting middle-aged. I suppose it's an attempt to recapture, or lay a final claim, to your own youth. As you say, it does have a lot of literary and artistic predecessors, which I hope I shared I was aware of.

What do you want readers to make of those parallels? The obvious one, of course, is Death in Venice.

Yes, well they're there: archetypes or tropes of that kind. *Death in Venice* is one; and in a sort of gender-flipped way *Lolita* is another one. I guess I am quite a bookish writer; I'm fairly self-conscious from a literary point of view. So I actually take a kind of constructive pleasure in redeploying established literary situations. It would have been curiously innocent to have written such a story without [such references].

It is, I suppose, strictly speaking, a form of sexual harassment. Of course, it is actually the boy who seduces Edward, who has, for various complex reasons not managed to do that to the boy.

I was wondering, in fact, if you deliberately set the novel in Belgium, where the age of consent is lower than it is in Britain, in order to get around that problem.

Yes, I did feel as if I cleared that one at the beginning. I have a part very early on where he's in this ghastly nightclub and sees these young boys and thinks they're illegal and then realizes that in a civilized country like Belgium they're all right.

Do you think it's easier for gay men to bring that kind of desire out of the closet than it is for straight men? I found it interesting that you brought up the business of the gender reversal of Lolita. *It seems to me that* Lolita *is so much about the scandal of that kind of love, and your novel is not about the scandal of that.*

Yes, that's right. Edward has an occasional sense of anxiety or embarrassment about it, but really he's too locked into the whole thing to see it [in that way].

I love what he says to his friend Edie: "'It happens, it happens.'"

Exactly. That was really very much the point. I certainly wasn't doing it to be especially provocative. I was doing it just to tell a story of something which very well might happen to somebody. Life and art are profoundly colored by one's sexuality. I wouldn't myself be particularly interested in reading about a thirty-three-year-old man falling in love with a seventeen-year-old girl. Actually, maybe that would seem striking. There are, after all, precedents, going back to antiquity, for the love between older men and younger boys.

Starting, I guess, with Zeus and Ganymede.

Yes. There aren't those precedents for the portrayal of middle-aged men and teenage girls, which somehow seems sort of squalid.

In fact, those relationships were burlesqued in ancient literature.

That's right.

So what's the difference?

The difference is that one seems fascinating to me in a way that the other doesn't. The rules of gay life are different in so many respects. That's one of the refreshing things about it.

Can you say something about the balance you maintain, stylistically and the-matically, between the refined and the elegant on one hand and—to quote one of your own adjectives—the "sluttish" on the other? One of the things I really admire about your two books—and especially about The Folding Star—*is that it rides that fine line between elegant bookishness, in a kind of high Georgian prose, and the sleazy, the sluttish.*

What you've just said makes it sound more formal and deliberate than it really was. There was some attention to join up or integrate things which had been separate before. Particularly in the case of the first book it was a question of bringing sex—because the book is about the life of someone who is living through his sexuality entirely—very much into the contin-uum, of showing that it was an essential element of life, of his life. And thus the different literary registers which tried to do justice to the way that life was actually experienced. To be honest about these experiences, you had somehow to mix the things up together. There was a certain stylistic fun to be had from oscillating between one register and another, quite rapidly and without warning.

It's very characteristic of masses of gay people I know that they are tremendously interested in things like the history of the string quartet and also are into major sleaze.

Did you have a sense that some of the things you were exploring in your novel had not been explored before, that you were bringing things out of the closet that gay writers hadn't wanted to deal with?

Yes, I suppose so. I remember talking to Edmund [White] about this and him saying that he thought we were both always writing about sexual ex-perience just as part of the continuum of everything else, that giving lit-erary place to the description of sex between men was rather a novel thing to be doing. Before it had only happened in designated pornography or was dealt with so archly or metaphorically that you weren't sure what was going on. So, yes, there was a sense of doing something a bit new.

There is a larger question, I think, too, of wanting to write a book in which the homosexuality of the narrator was an absolute given, that no apology or extenuation was made, and that he wrote or thought nat-urally through his sexuality as a heterosexual writer would through his. I didn't want to have to keep clearing my throat and explaining; it was just a given. Which I'm sure other people have done, but that still seemed like something worth doing, really.

Toward the end of The Swimming-Pool Library, *Will, in talking to Lord Nantwich, says that he likes Ronald Firbank's idea of "'seeing adults as children.'" He goes on to say, "'His adults don't have any dignity as adults, they're all like over-indulged children following their own caprices and inclinations.'" Do you think that adulthood is an overrated virtue?*

Very. I certainly don't feel I've attained it myself. Personally I've always had a feeling rather like the one I've ascribed to Edward in the book: of being at the same time both just out of school and also about sixty-five. I think age is an immensely fluid notion, really. There are times when one feels very young and times when one feels much older. I don't conceive of responsibility [that way]. I don't think I'm irresponsible, but, you know, I don't have kids in school and stuff, which I suppose is one way by which children discover that they have turned into adults after all.

Do you think that fluid notion of age and responsibility is more the prerogative of gay men than straight men?

Well, I think there's a strong tendency in all men to, sort of . . .

Wander?

Yeah. I mean all men like being with men quite a lot, don't they? And they like to revert to the sort of preadult thing where they go out, have beers, get together, kick a ball around—that whole thing where they're longing to be children, to cast off their responsibilities. Of course, a lot of straight people long looked with envy at the gay world for its freedom from all these constraints, and protocols, and responsibilities. I guess that's changed in some respects.

And yet Edward doesn't fully claim that freedom for himself. There is something that holds him back. I don't think it's moral scruples. He certainly gives himself permission to fall passionately in love with this boy. Is it simply Luc's indifference that holds it in check?

I think it is, probably. He gives himself permission presumably because he knows at some level that this is something that is never going to work out. He sort of knows, before he goes there even, that this is going to happen—he has the photograph of him—and he's sort of looking for a crisis to happen to him. He's got an instinct for suffering, I suppose. He has a rather melancholic, introspective temperament. There's a distinction in him between his inner, imaginative world, which he inhabits, which is all to do with his fixation on Luc and this striving after something unattainable, and the almost inadvertent sexual relations that he has, the other relationships he gets involved in, without quite noticing what's going on. I suppose the heart and the sex instinct have become rather separate in him. Which I think is something that happens to a lot of gay men.

Who is your ideal reader?

I'm honestly not sure that I have one.

Do you have an audience in mind when you write?

I don't, really. I try deliberately not to think of a particular reader or a particular readership. I have a great desire not to feel under any kind of pressure to meet anybody's expectations apart from my own. When I'm writing, I try to absorb myself in it and do it as well as I can. I'm often quite startled when—because I don't show anything to anybody until I'm finished—when I show it to one or two close friends and get their reactions, and all sorts of things which never struck me at all then come into focus, and I react to their suggestions or not. They're the people for whom I first see myself writing.

It's such a vague and mysterious thing: you write this stuff and send it out there and, if you're lucky, people read it, and occasionally you meet some of them and sign their books. I don't think my books conform to any particular sort of [readership]. I'm aware that there are obviously books that are written by gay writers that very much have some sort of gay community preoccupation—they're often published by gay presses— and I guess read almost exclusively by gay people. Which is fine, but that's not actually what I've ever felt particularly interested in doing. I want to be read by as many people as possible.

What did the success of The Swimming-Pool Library *mean for you?*

Well, I suppose in practical terms its meant all sorts of things, I mean apart from making me a certain amount of money. It enabled me to change my professional life, meet all sorts of people, travel all over the world, buy a flat and a car.

Sounds very nice. But in terms of how you saw yourself as an artist, did that change?

It was tremendously confirming in that sense, I suppose. I did the whole thing rather sort of secretly—when I got home from work, on the weekend, and so on. My closer friends knew I was writing something, but they never saw what it was. The whole thing, of course, could have been a complete flop. And when it wasn't, I was happy that people by and large liked it. It made me feel that the whole thing had been worth it after all. If it had been a flop, would I have carried on? I don't know. But certainly, yes, from a psychological point of view it was very important. Made me believe I was doing the right thing.

You published The Swimming-Pool Library *at an age when many writers have already had two, three, four books out. What kept you from publishing a book earlier?*

Simply never having written one. I mean, I was always writing novels from my teens, but I always grew out of them long before I finished them. *The Swimming-Pool* was the first one that I actually felt I wanted to stick with all the way through. I wrote a large part of a novel a few years before, which I never quite finished, which was a novel with a sort of concealed gay subject set in Venice—rather a Jamesian sort of thing. I haven't been able to bring myself to look at it for the last eight years or so. It may not be as awful as I think. But it clearly wasn't the right thing to be writing. I'm very slow, you see, and it takes me ages quite to discover what I am doing. I write my books very slowly.

I was publishing other stuff. I used to write quite a lot of poetry, which I published sporadically here and there. I thought I was going to be a poet, really, I think. By the time I got to work on *The Swimming-Pool Library,* the poems just stopped coming. The sort of observations and metaphors and things that I would have put into poems I started channeling into the novel instead. And I haven't really written a poem since.

What was it about The Swimming-Pool Library *that made you persevere?*

I suppose I had a deeper sense that it meant something, and was worth doing, and said something which was originally my own rather than being an imitation or nervous pastiche of something else. I suppose it's a question of finding one's voice.

I'm reminded of something Henry James once said, that fiction must "prove nothing but facts." You have written two novels that do not spare the facts, about either romance or lust. And you seem to eschew any easy reconciliation of those two sides of human erotic behavior. Still, I wonder where you personally come down in this human struggle between love and lust. You keep those two strands taut throughout, equally. It's both a celebration of the sluttish, the erotic, the lustful, and clearly a passionate song, or question, about what else is there.

That's right. But it does have a very romantic dimension to it as well. I'm not sure that I ever formulated it, but it did clearly emerge as a theme or major element in the book. Perhaps it does bespeak some kind of, not despair, but skepticism of my own. Both the books are very ambivalent in this way.

That's a deliberate ambivalence?

It 'tis, really, yes. In the first book, the sexual free-for-all seems to be great fun, but I hope people have a sense of a darker undercurrent, that there is some sort of, well, not cost exactly. I'm quite keen to keep the idea of love itself very fluid and multivalent. Some reviewer said, "Well, how dare Hollinghurst presume to use the word 'love' in these situations?" This second book is more deliberately an analysis of love in its various guises.

You seem keenly aware that bubbling underneath love and romance is always an obsession of some kind.

Yes. The thing about obsession is that it's something which takes over your life and runs your life for you. And you have to surrender yourself, not without feeling anger and regret. But you do sort of thrillingly hand yourself over to this power which is larger than yourself and has its own logic and momentum. I suppose it is a desire to lose oneself or lose one's responsibility for oneself to something more irrational. There's a certain emptiness in all these people, either because the beloved is unattainable or is dead. We're not quite sure why, but in Edward's life things seem to have run down. He needs something to fill this vacuum, and so is peculiarly susceptible to an all-consuming obsession. The emptiness in the novel forms a deliberate counterpart to that hunger to be taken over by something. I suppose that is a very romantic thing, isn't it?

In both your published novels you make use of parallels between the past and the present. In The Swimming-Pool Library, *it's the juxtaposition of Will Beckwith's very modern, very sexual life to the octogenarian Lord Nantwich's life in Africa during the twenties; and in* The Folding Star, *we see the same kind of juxtaposition in your use of Edgard Orst, the fictitious Belgian symbolist painter. Why are you so keen on making these juxtapositions of past and present?*

I think in the first book, it had a more programmatic [intention], I hope not in too dogged a way. The book was about revealing certain patterns in gay history, both to do with oppression and persecution, and to do with creativity and the arts, writers and musicians in the past. Which grew out of graduate work I did at Oxford about gay writers like Forster and so on who couldn't write openly about their sexuality. I was very interested in the ways they coped with this problem, through indirection and concealment. A preliminary idea for the book was that it would juxtapose the life of someone who had grown up under such constraints with someone who was living absolutely without them.

The pattern in this second book is much less explicitly one to do with gay history, although it's involved in it. I'm aware that there are great formal similarities, structural similarities, between the two books. They both turn on this relationship between a younger person and a much older one. There's a further refraction in this case, because Edward learns both from Paul and from Luc; so there's a mirroring of the teacher-pupil relationship.

I don't know, it is quite a common thing in novels, I mean novels often turn on the revelation of some secret which stems from the past: *Great Expectations,* or whatever. It's not a mechanism which I shall want to use anymore. I feel as if I've exhausted it now. Both books are about immensely solipsistic individuals who don't appear to be doing anything very much at all. Although they themselves feel actually quite busy following up their own obsessions. This introverted world then runs up against something larger and more structured, something which has a story and a past. I suppose it has to do with coming to terms with what the experience of others means. Because the novel is traditionally about gaining responsibility, understanding of some kind. I always leave it rather ambiguous as to whether these narrators have in fact learned anything from all this. It's very doubtful whether Will has learned anything from all the things he's found out.

I guess that's one reason why I like to do this: the establishing of, well, maybe not exactly eternal verities, but certain recurrent patterns of human experience.

It also establishes that the world and human experience is so much larger than these individual men's lives.

Yes, exactly.

Whether they themselves are personally responsible or not, it's impossible not to see them in this larger context of all sorts of claims—moral claims, historical claims.

Yes. It probably stems from some sort of moral ambivalence of my own. That's one reason that I've been interested in writing in the first person: that one is absolved as a writer from having to reward and blame. And it leaves everything very much more unresolved. It's an interesting way of avoiding moral absolutes.

Both the books—the second one much more so—are tremendously unresolved in a lot of ways and leave all sorts of things hanging in the air. I think I rather dislike the spurious sense of justice and grandness that often comes at the end of novels. In both books there's a lot of plot resolution that comes a bit before the end, and then the final coda of the book throws everything open. I can't quite remember how I came to that point. What was your question?

You brought up Great Expectations, *which is, of course one of the great examples of a first-person novel. Even there, with that famous, original ending, Dickens leaves a lot of things up in the air.*

Yes. Exactly. That's quite true. I'm interested in the very personal nature of the relationship which a reader has with the narrator in a first-person narrative. It's much more like having a relationship with someone in real life whom you don't judge necessarily in absolute terms. The reader is constantly having to make up their own mind and adjust their opinion of the narrator. People have had wildly differing responses to narrators as well, in both cases ranging from loathing to adoration.

Were you deliberately setting out to create a more sympathetic character in Edward than in Will?

I don't think I was actually, no. Edward sort of plots his delinquencies, rather, but one hopes has a certain element of charm and vivacity which will sustain one's interest in him. Will, of course, has a strong element of self-dislike, and is always surprised when people find him attractive or trust him. He's very self-disparaging; he's got on to this slightly masochistic spiral, expecting things to be bad for him. I noticed quite a few unsympathetic reviewers taking him on his own estimation, whereas I hope that something slightly more subtle goes on, where you perceive through his characterization of himself into some larger sense what he might be like. But whether he's really a sympathetic character or not, I don't know. As obsessives are, he's rather an annoying person in some respects.

At one point in The Folding Star, *Paul Echevin says to Edward, "'I'm afraid I'm of the school that rather disapproves of publicizing artists' private lives.'" I wonder how you feel personally about that. Are you willing to talk at all about your own private life?*

I generally don't, if asked to. It's a larger question about the exceptional degree of prominence that mainly the sexual element tends to be given in biography these days. I do think it's become an excessive preoccupation. The sex tends to blot out all sorts of other things that are going on. Similarly, I find with writing a book which has sex in it that people ignore the fact that it's about dozens of other things.

What were you doing before you became a novelist?

I was being a student and a teacher. Not doing anything very much. Hanging out, drinking too much.

Did you ever teach in a small, unnamed Belgian town?

Absolutely not. This book in not in any kind of narrative sense autobiographical. Although obviously it has a lot of me in it. Not just in Edward. There are bits of me in different characters. Paul, too, who I hope is a sympathetic character. I've never thought of writing a book which just told the story of my life. I think the interesting thing is to dramatize yourself, use a bit of yourself, have a dialogue with yourself.

You have been on staff—as a writer and editor—at the Times Literary Supplement *for twelve years. How has that affected you as a writer of fiction?*

Well, it's taught me about all sorts of things, I guess, in that slightly superficial way that you find out about things while your working as an editor. I actually do very little reviewing myself, and very, very rarely review fiction. I rather deliberately don't read much contemporary fiction, especially when I'm writing myself. I go back and read old stuff—read poetry. But I think I have been enriched by it in all sorts of ways which are incalculable.

Can you pinpoint any of those?

Well, finding out a lot more about literature, art, and music. And politics. From commissioning reviews of books and being obliged professionally to take an interest in things which one might not have been otherwise. When I was the deputy editor of the paper for six years, I had to read every word that appeared in it every week. Of course, you forget it with alarming quickness.

Deputy editor is the editor in chief?

The number two. He has to run the paper when the editor isn't there. I think if I had carried on, just pottering along, teaching Tennyson and Virginia Woolf, I would have been more deeply informed about various matters, but I wouldn't have had nearly such wide, shallow knowledge about things as I do.

Your knowledge of the world is larger, then?

I think it probably is, yes.

Where did you teach?

I taught at various colleges at Oxford. I taught first at Magdalen, where I was. And then at Somerville, the women's college; and Corpus Christi College, briefly.

You taught English literature?

Yeah. And then I did just one term at University College, London, after I moved to town, before being offered the job at the *TLS*. This was all rather piecemeal bits of teaching I was doing.

This was in your twenties?

Yeah. I joined the *TLS* in '82, when I was twenty-eight.

Larry Kramer once wrote, "Why has there been no great gay novel? . . . Where's our Dostoyevsky . . ., our Trollope or Tolstoy . . . , our Dickens or Chekhov?"[2] *What's your response to that? Do you agree with that?*

I suppose I do. What is greatness? I don't think there are any great novels of any kind being produced at the moment. My sense of things, which, as I said already, is somewhat imperfect, is that there's all sorts of interesting stuff going on. Our culture, like yours, is a sort of imperium in decline. That's very fascinating, especially British literature, where so much of the interesting stuff is being done by people from previously colonial cultures. It's very vivacious, but I don't actually feel that there are any great writers bestriding the scene.

I mean, what would a great gay novel be? I don't know. Anyone who deliberately set out to write a great gay novel will be mistaken, I think. It's just a question of whether they're a great novelist, really. My feeling is that there aren't [any great gay novelists]. But I'm not sure greatness is the most important criterion which we should be looking for.

I want to ask you a question that was asked of Edmund White in the Paris Review *interviews. He was asked, "When you're writing, do you look more towards innovation or towards tradition?"*[3]

I think that my answer would be that temperamentally I tend to look much towards tradition. Not that I feel quite aware of what tradition I'm in. Readers or critics might have a clearer sense of that than I do. As I've already admitted, my glance tends to be backward. Unlike some writers I adore, like Firbank, for instance, who is very radically an innovative writer, what I write is formally extremely traditional. And I hope a good read.

In The Swimming-Pool Library *somebody says they hate the "Bridesheady" style of writing.*

---

2. Larry Kramer, "Gay Men Writing?" *Advocate,* 22 February 1994, 80.

3. Edmund White, "The Art of Fiction 105," interview by Jordan Elgrably, *Paris Review* 30, no. 108 (Fall 1988): 73.

Yes. That's about the whole question, the whole fatuous cult of the, well, especially of the pre-First World War period but also of the interwar period, which I think has so enfeebled British cinema: everybody's constantly in period costume and there's this whole spurious nostalgia for the Edwardian period. I'm very fed up with all these adaptations of Forster's books, where the treatment is so nostalgic and makes them seem so picturesque. All their point and sharpness gets taken straight out.

What differences do you see between gay fiction in Britain and America?

Well, there's a lot more of it in America, of course. A lot more gays. A lot more gay writers in America.

Because of the larger population?

Yes, but that's not the only reason, I think. From what I'm aware of, AIDS forms a far greater preoccupation in American gay writing than it does in British. That again is partly because the problem is immeasurably greater in America than it is in England. Not that it isn't profoundly serious in England. The scale of the impact here has been quite different.

A lot of gay work happening in Britain at the moment is happening in the theaters. There have been a lot of articles in the London press recently about what someone with supreme tastelessness called "the plague of gay plays in the West End." But there are those moments when British culture seems to be tremendously homosexualized: the whole homosexualization of advertising and all that. But I'm rather straying from the point. Really what I'm saying is that I don't think there is very much really interesting gay writing going on in England. I suspect there's a lot more in the States.

What about the difference between gay readers in the two countries?

They may be more politicized in the States, and then again maybe not. I can only really speak from my own experience.

What do you mean by "more politicized"? Does that mean less literarily subtle?

I think there may be a certain impatience with things which are not so politically explicit. But I may be simpleminded myself in saying that. There are obviously millions of highly intelligent readers in the States. And certainly in England there are of course people who don't understand what fiction or a work of art is. They don't understand the moral complexity of a novel. Certainly some people have reviewed this second book of mine as if what I ought to have written was some kind of safe sex manual combined with an upbeat homily about how to go about a gay lifestyle. Both of which are worthy things to do, but they're not things that I'm very interested in doing myself.

Do you despair of that? More and more it seems that people don't understand what a morally and artistically complex and subtle work of art is all about, and don't even particularly want that.

Yeah. Well, as literacy has in general declined and the media and their messages are getting more blunt and brutal, refinement and intelligence are constantly more under threat.

What does the term "gay writer" mean to you?

Well, it means various things. As I was saying earlier, there are people who are very deliberately gay writers and there are writers who happen to be gay.

How do you identify yourself?

I feel myself more the latter. Actually, I feel myself somewhere between the two. I feel as if it's partly a question of agenda, and I don't feel that I write toward any agenda. I just really write to work out things for myself.

Can you see yourself writing a novel that does not have gay characters at its core?

I honestly don't feel any interest much in that, no. The book I'm planning now will have a bisexual man. Might as well be a gay man! I don't as yet have much interest in that. Perhaps when I'm very old, I might have sense to study the young girl. I never really set out to write a particular thing. It just slowly comes together in my head, and what comes together tends to be things to do with gay men.

What are your writing habits like?

Profoundly irregular. I have long spells of doing nothing at all. And then I have intense bursts when I shut myself off from the world and write very concentratedly for three or four weeks.

What advice would you give to aspiring gay writers?

Really the same advice that I would give to any aspiring writer, which is to be as truthful as possible to their own vision, and to find out as unsparingly of themselves as they can what it is they're really trying to do, and not to try to write to meet anyone else's expectations, but to seek to discover what the unique thing is which they have in them to create themselves, which may be a lonely and perplexing experience, but it's the only way that's worth doing, in my view.

Edmund White

Perhaps more than any other gay writer of the last twenty years, Edmund White, one of the original members of the Violet Quill, has risen to a position of preeminence. Read widely by gay readers and inevitably included among serious discussions of gay literature by scholars and critics, White has also captured the attention of that elusive readership, the "crossover" audience. His work has been praised by writers as diverse as Susan Sontag, Gore Vidal, Vladimir Nabokov, Richard Ford, and Ann Beattie. According to *Time* magazine, White "came as close as anyone to producing the Great American Gay Novel"[1] in his 1982 *A Boy's Own Story.*

Born in Cincinnati in 1940, White attended Cranbrook Academy, a private school in Bloomfield Hills, Michigan, and went on to major in Chinese at the University of Michigan. From 1962 to 1970, he worked for Time-Life Books in New York. A year's sojourn in Rome was followed by brief editorships at the *Saturday Review* and *Horizon.* In 1983, White moved to Paris, where he still maintains residency, though he returns to the United States from time to time to teach.

White's university appointments include teaching stints at Yale, Johns Hopkins, New York University, Columbia, and Brown, where he held a full professorship. He has also served as the executive director of the New York Institute for the Humanities.

Among his many awards and recognitions, White has received a Guggenheim Fellowship, the Award for Literature from the American Academy of Arts and Letters, the National Book Critics Circle Award, and a Lambda Literary Award. In 1993, he was made a Chevalier de l'Ordre des Arts et Lettres.

The following interview is a composite of two conversations I have conducted with White. The first, a brief telephone interview, occurred in the spring of 1988. White had just published *The Beautiful Room is Empty,* his fifth novel and the second in a proposed trilogy (or, as it was then be-

---

1. "Bookends," *Time,* 11 April 1988, 74.

ing reported, quartet) of novels whose overall program is the "unapologetic portrayal of the development of a gay man." The interview ran in *Bay Windows* (5 May 1988).

The second interview followed the publication of White's memoir, *Our Paris*. In sixteen short chapters (engagingly illustrated with drawings by his late lover, Hubert Sorin), White sketches their life in the Châlelet, a neighborhood in the Fourth Arrondissement. "Despite the sometimes catty sound of this book, its name-dropping and archness," White writes in the introduction, "I hope at least a few readers will recognize that its subtext is love."

This later, much more extensive interview took place on 11 November 1995, at Boston's Ritz Carlton Hotel, where White was staying during his Boston appearances to promote the new book. Throughout our conversation, he was soft-spoken and gracious, a reflection, I guessed, of the double heritage of his Midwestern upbringing and his adopted home in Paris. An abbreviated version of the interview was published in *Bay Windows* (22 February 1996).

Toward the end of The Beautiful Room is Empty, *the narrator, who is beginning to write, talks about his fear of being sentimental and self-indulgent. Some of your critics have accused your own work of just that. Do you want to comment?*

The prevailing standards are those of heterosexual men. They're easily embarrassed by too much emotion, and when there is too much they call it sentimentality. They also favor understatement; that is, no direct statements of what you believe about things. There's a hidden agenda, however, in those standards. If you use understatement and control and indirection, and you leave it to the reader to draw his own conclusions, the reader will always draw the same conclusions—that is, the ones he already has. So in order to actually change people's ideas about things you need to be quite explicit, and that's true whether you're a writer on the right or the left, whether you're gay or straight.

I feel that a gay writer who really wants to lead the reader to having new insights needs to be far more explicit than a heterosexual writer who's simply interested in entertaining. But the gay writer who does that will always be criticized by the normal press for overstatement, for sentimentality, for "laying it on too thick"—there's a whole vocabulary there, but it's a vocabulary with a political program.

Still musing on his own emerging writing career, your narrator says, "How could I ask the reader to take seriously love between two men? A plea for tolerance was the best I might have come up with." That seems to suggest that a "plea for tolerance" is the weakest agenda for a gay novel.

There were a lot of books that came out in the 1950s which would often-times end with one or both of the characters committing suicide. There was a feeling of: "See how sick we are?" and "Won't you please forgive us?" And the character's suicide was a kind of expiatory gesture. Interestingly, those books were always addressed to a hypothetical heterosexual reader; they were kind of presented as a lawyer's brief to defend homosexuality. So many of the early books about homosexuality were apologies for it, whether it was a nonfiction work, like Gide's *Corydon*, or a novel.

Once you imagine the reader being a completely open and tolerant heterosexual or, more likely, a completely initiated and sophisticated homosexual, then the burden of the book shifts from being an apology to being an investigation.

The Beautiful Room is fairly programmatic in the sense that it is trying to inevitably lead up to Stonewall.

When the narrator goes off to Europe to recover from a love affair, I was reminded of one of your earlier novels, Nocturnes for the King of Naples. *Is* Nocturnes *an earlier version of what will become volume three of your planned quartet of* Boy's Own Story *novels?*[2]

Yes, you're quite right. Autobiographically, that is exactly the moment I had in mind when I wrote *Nocturnes*. But the difference is that the character in *Nocturnes* is completely different from the character in *A Boy's Own Story* and *The Beautiful Room*. When I was writing *Nocturnes*, I

---

2. With the publication of *The Farewell Symphony* (1997), the third of White's "Boy's Own Story" novels, the series seems to be complete. However, Reed Woodhouse makes a case for considering *Our Paris*, White's memoir, as the missing fourth book of the quartet. See Woodhouse, "Keys to the Kingdom of White," *Harvard Gay and Lesbian Review* 5, no. 1 (Winter 1998): 39–40, 60.

thought it would be fun to explore a character quite unlike myself—someone who is small and blond and passive, not particularly ambitious, a drifter. And while it's true that I handled a lot of the same material that I was to look at in the later books, it's very glamorized, or let's say very mythical, a mythological and transposed version of many things that happened to me.

Are you moving away from that baroque, mythological style that characterizes Nocturnes? *The prose in* A Boy's Own Story *and* The Beautiful Room *seems much clearer and more direct.*

You have to remember that between these books comes *Caracole,* which is probably my most elaborate book of all. So no, I think I have these two different styles. I have an interest in exploring nonrealistic ways of writing, too.

And even in your two more realistic novels, that mythological element is an undercurrent.

Yes. It was Proust who pointed the way to seeing the events of your own life as having a kind of mythical resonance. Once society begins to dissolve and there are no longer large, public conventions and myths that hold true for everyone—religion, for example—then, in trying to find a public language, people are forced to take the events of their own lives and cast a halo over them, in a sense, or blow them up to a larger significance.

Why have you settled in Europe? What does Europe give you?

I think the idea of nationalism is pretty worn out. Today, more than ever, a kind of internationalism is natural and important. Paris, being the crossroads of the world, is the place where a choreographer from Stockholm is going to meet a choreographer from Kyoto. Among my own friends, I know writers from Yugoslavia, Czechoslovakia, Argentina, Germany, and so on. We all speak to each other in French, because it's the only language we have in common. Particularly the Eastern European and South American communities are immense and very powerful in Paris. I find it an extraordinarily exciting place to be, a very cosmopolitan place to be. I believe that Paris belongs first and foremost to the world and only secondly to France.

Some people would say that everything you've just said also describes New York.

It doesn't. Sure, there are lots of ethnic groups in New York. But I feel that many of them are culturally crushed by a kind of triumphant American culture. Foreigners who come to New York are usually more eager to assimilate themselves than to explore their own culture.

Paris is a place where cultures are enormously respected. For instance, one of the first things Mitterand did when he became president was to make Milan Kundera a citizen, and then to make Julio Cortázar a citizen—someone who was a refugee from a regime on the left, and one from a regime on the right.

Do people treat you with less skepticism in Europe than in America?

Yes, I think so. In France I don't think I'm labeled a gay writer. You can read lots of reviews of my books without being aware of what their subject matter is, or without that being treated as if I'm the voice of the ghetto. And in England, I do a tremendous amount of reviewing of books that have nothing to do with my "field." I don't feel as if I'm typecast there, either.

In the opening chapter of Our Paris, *you describe lying in bed with Hubert and hearing a singer outside on the street. When you try to imagine what she is like, you say that you picture her as "someone with a rich, messy life." I wonder if that description isn't, in part, a projection of your own life. Would you say you have a "rich, messy life?"*[3]

Alfred Corn once said that he thought I was like a consumer—a consumer of words, of money, of people, of events; that everything rushes around me. And it is sort of true, I think. One of the reasons, though, that I like relationships is that it gives me an anchor in the midst of this flood.

You have achieved, I think, the position of a kind of éminence grise among the gay literary community.

Someone said "éminence grisette."

What particular pleasures and liabilities come with that status?

Last night my nephew was teasing me about giving so many blurbs to everybody; and I said, "Well, either you start off the way a lot of people

---

3. Here begins the second interview with White.

do and just say you never give them, or, if you are going to give them, then you end up giving them to people you don't know whose work you admire or to people you do know whose work you don't necessarily admire all that much but who are friends." So, I guess, I get a lot of books sent to me and people want me to do something about it.

I read once that Picasso said that an artist couldn't do his best work unless he was famous. I always thought that was such a funny statement. In my own small way, though, I can sort of see what he means. It does give you more of a sense of daring, that you feel that people are going to follow you down almost any crazy path and that you can try new things that you might have been hesitant about before. I think that at the beginning of one's career there's a temptation to just repeat whatever has gained some small success. But later you get restless and want to try new things.

How has that restlessness, that daring, manifested itself in your own work?

Well, you know, doing that biography,[4] which was an enormous project; and not doing a little subjective biography but a very big, objective biography, in which I never use the word "I." I tried to write the most traditional biography I could imagine, with lots of footnotes. When it won the National Book Critics Circle Award, it was cited as being worthy of the prize primarily because of its research, which I thought was exactly what I wanted. It was sort of unexpected of a novelist, although there are plenty of them who have done it, of course. Actually, to my eyes, all my work seems slightly different, from one book to another.

You quote Henry James at one point as saying that only in Europe did one discover America. Why did you move to Paris and what has kept you there so long?

Well, you know, everyone always assumes it was some big thing, but like most big things it's probably just an accident. In my case, I won a Guggenheim, which allowed me to go for a year. I thought I would just stay for a year. And then, once I got over there, I was living with a young American named John Purcell, who's from this area, who just died this last spring, and we were together many years and he was a student at Parsons School of Design over there in Paris, so that was one reason to stay on. And a lot

---

4. Edmund White, *Genet: A Biography* (New York: Knopf, 1993).

of my friends started dying back in America and that seemed sort of depressing to have to go through. And I was tired of being a teacher, and it was fun to be a student again—I mean, to be learning a new language and learning about a new culture, and so on.

French was a new language for you?

Yeah. I couldn't speak it at all when I arrived. The Genet book, which I started in 1987, was probably a way of expressing my love affair with French and France. So, now I don't know. I think if I had a good reason to come back to America, I would. I just can't figure out where I'd go, because most of my friends in America are dead.

I taught at Brown for two years, and I didn't like college very much. After a city like Paris, it's hard to live in Providence. I think it would be easier to live in, you know, Montclair, New Jersey, in a way—either a much smaller town or another big city.

Are there particular problems or challenges that an American writer confronts in Europe?

It's interesting. I was talking to Michael, my friend, about that this morning. I was saying that most American writers who live in Europe either write in a very intensely nostalgic way about their own earlier years in America, which is something I did in *The Beautiful Room is Empty,* or they write about American expatriates in Europe, which is what I did in these stories, *Skinned Alive,* or, in very rare cases—actually the only one I can really think of is Mavis Gallant—she writes about French people in France, and there are no foreigners. They're masterful, though they're not very well liked by the French, or even known. She may just be too talented to draw a lot of attention. I think she's one of the best writers.

Challenges? I think a particular writer like James Jones, for him moving to France was disastrous. He was from a working-class background, he worked very close to the dialogue of other working-class people—soldiers, and his own experiences—and when he got cut off from both his class origins and his national origins, his talent just withered. I don't think it was ever a very conscious thing, his gift; it was very immediate. On the other hand, somebody like Gore Vidal has become a very astute analyst of America, because he lives in Italy. He sees it more clearly.

The same could have been said for Henry James or James Baldwin. In fact, it seems as if so many gay writers and artists—Ned Rorem, David Plante . . .

David Leavitt, Dale Peck. Dale lives in London now.

Is there something particular about gay experience that lends itself to that attraction to being an expatriate?

To travel, I think. If you think of the most classic gay story, like *Death in Venice*, it begins with the desire to travel.

What's the desire to travel all about?

I think it's a feeling that as a tourist, as a foreigner, you'll somehow escape the strictures of conventional society. People won't know you. In your own city, you tend to see people only from your own social and professional background. When you travel, because there's this barrier of the language, and because you don't really fit into society, you can have much more immediate and maybe physical contact with very different kinds of people. And it's exciting.

Remember that idea that a guy [C. A.] Tripp had back in the seventies?

[The book] The Homosexual Matrix?

Right. In that book, his idea was that the big problem in gay life was that gay people were too similar to each other and that they were always trying to reproduce the polarity that exists in straight life by finding people who were either from a very different age group or a very different class background or a different nationality altogether. That might be another reason why travel is appealing.

What differences do you see between gay fiction in France and gay fiction in America?

Well, to start with, the very idea of such a category.

It doesn't exist in France?

No. There's only one gay book shop in all of France, which is in the Marais, called Les Mots à la Bouche—The Words in the Mouth—which is a pun on *l'eau à la bouche*, you know, when your mouth waters.

It's a great paradox, because, on the one hand, France probably has the longest tradition of outspoken, major writers writing about homo-sexual experience, not just from a pornographic but also a very philo-sophic, very social point of view—a classic tradition. In this century, just to name a few, there's Genet, there's Proust, there's Cocteau. There's so many. It's almost [harder] to find the heterosexual writers. So, for in-stance, a novel like *A Boy's Own Story* was treated in a very ho-hummish way by French critics, because there was no need for a coming-out novel in France. I mean, they'd had nothing but that for a hundred years.

Going along with that is the idea that everything is very centrist in French life. They have a horror of the ghetto, whether it be feminist or gay or black or Jewish. So you couldn't find a single person in France who would say, I am a Jewish novelist or a black novelist or a gay novelist. They don't split up that way, neither socially nor artistically. The artistic coher-ence in France is parallel to the social coherence and the horror of any kind of hiving off. They sort of feel, I guess, on a legal level that people should be protected by a rather abstract and inflexible list of the rights of man—human rights—and on an artistic level they feel that there should be a constant dialogue amongst all people.

Americans immediately want to assume that the French are just very closety and be done with it, because they don't conform to the Amer-ican model. But I think that's just too simple, and I think that if you stop to think about literature—forget about politics, or social problems—it certainly should be a goal for all of us that we should communicate with each other. And it's true that writers like Renaud Camus or Hervé Guibert are very widely read and have a big audience, and even if they touch on gay themes from time to time—or in Hervé's case all the time—never-theless they never give up really that claim on the general literary reader's attention.

Do you think that American gay writers have given up that claim?

Well, I think they say they haven't, but I was talking to Dale Peck about this. He's writing a piece for the *London Review of Books* about the gay epic; he's looking at how some people like [Patrick] Gale, Felice Picano, Ethan Mordden—there are a bunch of them—are all writing novels that seem to want to insert gay experience into history. And yet, he feels that the fact that ninety-nine percent of the characters are lesbian or gay (or usually just plain gay), and that there are so many cocks and balls and all that stuff going on, that there's just no way the ordinary reader is going to read that. So there's kind of a confused impulse: on the one hand, the desire to be inscribed into general history, and then a kind of style that addresses so exclusively a gay reader and only a gay reader, that there's kind of a tension at the heart of this. Dale thinks that gay literature is finished. He thinks that it's run its course and it's over.

How do you feel about that?

Well, again, it's too abstract a question for me. I mean, I'm interested in writing about gay experience, which I still feel hasn't really been written about properly. Just from a technical point of view, I feel that there's always an excitement on the page when you start describing something that hasn't been properly described before. Certain areas of gay life, like coming out, have been done to death, but others like the older gay couple who have been together thirty years and who prey on young third people to make their marriage work, that's not a thing that's been dealt with very much, and yet it's almost ubiquitous in life.

Are you working on something like that?

Yeah, a lot of the sinister aspects of gay life that everybody has been too P.C. to deal with.

In the introduction to Our Paris, *you write that you "wanted to—needed to— give a form to my grief that Hubert would have approved of." The book hardly speaks of Hubert's illness. Was that a conscious decision?*

I wrote the introduction two hours after he died, but I wrote the book while he was still alive. He had that kind of French *pudeur* about talking about illness. Plus, I think he wanted it to be light. What Adam Mars-Jones said to me about it when he read the book was that he thought that what was touching about it was that you could see these were two people who wanted to have their pleasures and yet what their pleasures constituted was shrinking more and more and that they really were trying to be very gallant about it all, but really their field of operations was terribly restrained by it.

You were diagnosed as HIV-positive in 1985. How did that knowledge affect your writing career—your subject matter, your style, the kinds of projects you took on, the pace of your work?

One thing, if you ever live in a foreign country, you realize how much slippage there is between the lip and the ear. You have to send out this very simple, unironic, clear signal to another person; and they usually misunderstand you anyway. If you've ever been a teacher, even in your own language, you realize that mostly the students don't get it; they think you mean the opposite of what you've just said. Those two experiences—of being both a teacher and living abroad—made me aware of how little people really understand of what you're ever saying, so that there's constantly a need to send out a very powerful signal. So, that plus the feeling of urgency brought on by AIDS came together in a way to make my writing at least more direct than it ever was before.

You've seen most of the original members of the Violet Quill succumb to AIDS, as have several other notable gay writers. How has that affected you? You mentioned earlier wanting to stay away from America because it was too depressing.

It's partly that. Of course, on the other hand, you cling to the people who are still alive, as I do to Felice or Andrew Holleran. I think there's quite a tendency to memorialize the people who have died. In Brad Gooch's new book, which is called *The Golden Age of Promiscuity,* he has a list of ten people or so [to whose memory] he wants to dedicate the book, and two-thirds of those people are friends of mine, or were before they died. They appear, many of them, as characters in his book under a different name. No matter what solution, technically, one finds to this problem, the problem remains the same: you want to put down all these names.

Those of us who used to laugh at those books in the Bible that are nothing but "begat"—"so-and-so begat so-and-so"—that's what we're doing now. It turns out that we were wrong; that is one of the oldest impulses behind literature, like listing the whole genealogy of a warrior on the battlefield.

In Our Paris, *you write about meeting Diaghilev's last secretary, Boris Kochno. You quote him as saying, "'When one is young, one prizes only intimacy, especially love. But when one is old, one treasures one's circle more than its individ-*

ual members.'" I'd like to ask you to comment a little more on that difference between love and friendship.

My English agent said that what she liked the most about *Skinned Alive* was that it was such a homage to friendship. Also *The Burning Library*, I guess because there were homages to David Kalstone, people like that. Foucault was a friend, and James Merrill was a friend, and Jimmy Schuyler was a friend, and they're all in the book.

I'm wondering if, in some way, we are that people who understand profoundly what friendship is about.

Exactly. I always felt that with my parents their idea of friendship was something very close to hostility. I mean that as a couple you would entertain this other couple and the main intention was to impress them and intimidate them. You felt that dinners were this potluck ceremony where you'd toss valuable things onto the fire. They had so many things that you weren't supposed to discuss with other people. My parents—I mean, they were Southern, and they were rural, and they were much older . . . were in their late thirties when I was born, so they were like other people's grandparents—they were always horrified by the way that my sister and I would tell all our business to our friends. That kind of disclosure really began with our generation; older Americans didn't do that. Now everybody does too much of that.

Except I think there's a particular quality to gay friendship that seems really extraordinary to me and may be one of our contributions . . .

I agree. I think that's absolutely right.

Writing recently in the Advocate, *Larry Kramer asked, "Why has there been no great gay novel? . . . Where's our Dostoyevsky . . . , our Trollope or Tolstoy . . . , our Dickens or Chekhov?"[5] What's your response to that?*

First of all, when you invoke names like that, you'd have a hard time finding that counterpart today among heterosexual writers, partly because the conception of the novel has changed: it's much more intimate, it's shorter, it's closer to the bone of an individual's experience. We have

---

5. Larry Kramer, "Gay Men Writing?" *Advocate*, 22 February 1994, 80.

fewer group pictures of large societies, and the moral issues are less philosophically charged and much more situationalist, I think. So the kind of grandeur of a Dostoevsky novel, which actually makes me giggle—I mean, it seems so irrelevant to me—it's true, we don't have anything like that.

But in terms of just beauty of language and engaging with important ideas and morality in operation, somebody like Holleran or Hollinghurst are as good as anybody writing in English.

What are you writing habits like?

Oh, very chaotic. Well, now I'm trying to finish a novel, so I do tend to work fairly hard, I mean, not really, but . . . I get up every morning, about nine, and I finally get myself together and I stagger off to the café, the Café Beaubourg, and I write in the café longhand in a nicely bound volume. I don't rewrite much. I keep almost everything I write, but then again I don't write very much, so if I rewrote I'd never get anything done. Finally I dictate it all into a tape and then Alex Jeffers, who's a very fine novelist, types it from the tape. He does the same thing for James Lord.

How did he hook up with the two of you?

He was a student of mine at Brown, and I introduced James to him. James is crazy about him. Of course, he's so intelligent and literary that sometimes he'll query things. When you're dictating, just knowing that he's going to be listening to it makes you have a certain embarrassment factor where you just can't bring yourself to say certain things that are superidiotic.

Does the reading aloud also help you to refine the sentences, the prose?

Yes. And also, you can dictate fairly fast, so over the course of, let's say, five days, you can hear a 350-page novel and keep it all in your head. It's sort of like performing the whole thing, and you can discover that you've used that image already before, a hundred pages earlier, or that you've forgotten that character is supposed to be blond, not brunette.

I'd like to talk about the Genet biography a little bit. You said you started it in 1987. What attracted you to Genet? Why did you undertake such an enormous task?

Well, first of all, I didn't think it would be so enormous. I thought I'd be done in three years. I'd never done one before, and I didn't realize that Genet was somebody who hated the idea of biography. If you were to write a biography of a John Updike, or somebody like that, if he was co-operative, you'd find all his papers on file, you'd find articles about him going back thirty years, you'd find reminiscences about him written by other literary people—people who went to Harvard with him and so on. Basically, middle-class literary people become well-known in their late twenties, early thirties, and the rest of their life is led under this constant scrutiny of other people of their kind. Whereas Genet was a foundling, who was brought up by peasants, who was then in reform schools, the army, a vagabond, a prisoner. And those are not milieux where you find people who live very long or who are easily traceable; or if you find them they don't want to speak, and if they do speak you can't believe what they say, and you have to pay them, and all this sort of stuff. You couldn't have found a more complicated modern subject. He'd only been dead a year when I started, but it was really difficult. But it was fun because it was difficult.

You actually traced some of his classmates?

Yes. He never had mentioned his village. Whenever people would ask him the name of his village, he would go blank. He would never say, so nobody knew where he was from, not even his closest friends.

How did you find these people?

There was a little newspaper in Paris called *Le Morvandiau* for people who were from the Morvan who lived in Paris, and after Genet died a man called Joseph Bruley wrote a little article called "My Classmate, Jean Genet." He was from Alligny-en-Morvan. Some friend brought me that article, and because of that I was able to trace the whole thing out.

In the biography, you say that Genet traced every artistic impulse to the bles-sure—*the wound—in each of us. You quote from his essay on Giacometti: "There is no other origin of beauty than the wound, singular, different for each person, hidden or visible, which every man keeps inside him, which he preserves and where he withdraws when he wants to leave the world for a passing but pro-found solitude." What is the* blessure, *the wound, that has precipitated your own artistic impulse?*

When I was young, what got me to write was that I felt such shame about being gay, and yet such a burning desire to communicate it to everybody. It was a funny impulse, because, on the one hand, you'd think if you were ashamed of something, you'd just want to shut up about it, but, on the other hand, at age fourteen I was already writing my first gay novel, *The Tower Window*. So I think I was always trying to express my anguish about—no, not *about* being gay—*around* being gay and trying to make some sense of it. It seemed to me such a crazy thing. I think I was really rather a conventional child otherwise, but it was the one thing that wrested me away from the world I thought I should be inheriting. I think that was sort of the *blessure*.

But I don't really agree with that view of Genet's. In my case, after age thirty I no longer wrote out of those motives, but out of a desire to construct things, to make things. It's funny that he wrote that business about the *blessure* in his essay about Giacometti, who was such a great *faiseur de choses*—he loved to make things with his hands. If there was ever a *homo faber*, it was Giacometti. So, I think it's very true of Genet, but I don't think it's especially true of Giacometti.

Is that impulse to leave an artifact because one is not going to leave children?

No! I think it's just the pleasure of constructing something, whether it would be a chess puzzle or a mathematical solution. I mean, I think art is expressive, but not all that much. The more you work, the more you try to get what you really feel into it all, but you can get a lot of pleasure . . . I mean, in my case, in writing a novel like *Forgetting Elena*—which is certainly parallel to what I was feeling, but not coincident with it—if expression were all, then I think you'd just write letters or you would scream from a rooftop or something. But it seems to me that there's a kind of pleasure in constructing this machine, which is a book that functions well, or at least functions.

I was going to ask you if that impulse that arises out of profound embarrassment and yet a need to look at it and talk about it is, in fact, an experience that lots of gay writers have had.

I think so. I think of somebody like Andrew Holleran, who I find excessively modest in his encounters with other people directly. If you ask him a question, he always asks you a question right back. He'd be my idea of a nightmare interview. He's very unforthcoming about everything in his life, and yet his novels really are wonderfully transparent. I think of, like, *Nights in Aruba*, where he really is able to express his feelings toward parents, toward the tragicomedy of sexuality, and so on. There's a good case of somebody who really isn't very good at communicating with other people, and who blushes easily and flees—he's very rabbity in his dealings with other people—and yet is not at all that way on the page. He's quite forthcoming on the page.

The corollary to that question is, is there something inherently attractive also about that desire simply to make, to construct something that in some way is particularly appealing to gay artists?

On the other hand, though, you don't find many gay counterparts in the postmodernist or metafiction impulse, which sort of passed gays by. In other words, there was always too strong a confessional urge in gay writing to permit gay writers to want to play the elaborate games that people like Cortázar or John Barth or Robert Coover would want to play. I always think they're people who don't have much subject matter or who are kind of bored or are trying to construct chess puzzles or something.

How did you get started as a writer?

I had a teacher in the eighth grade who praised my writing. I think it was really the first time that anybody other than my mother had praised my writing. So that seemed like a good thing. I wanted to do something in the arts. I wanted to be a dancer or a singer or a painter or a musician. I tried all those things. I think music was the art I liked the most, but I didn't have the patience or the discipline or the talent to do it, though I wrote an opera when I was twelve. You know, I scored it and everything. I was ambitious, but not really talented. Maybe writing is the refuge of people who aren't very talented. I mean, in the sense that everyone can write a letter, but not everybody can write a score.

It's the one art form where you really don't need professional training.

That's right. In Europe they're always appalled that there's such a thing in America as creative writing classes.

In a 1977 essay, "Fantasia on the Seventies," you wrote, "The self-acceptance of the seventies might just give us the courage to experiment with new forms of love and camaraderie." In the almost twenty years since you wrote that, has that experiment with "new forms of love and camaraderie" come to pass, do you think?

I think in ways that I didn't expect, and in the ways that I did expect it hasn't come about. What I was talking about then and what I was expecting were friendship circles that would also be erotic. At that point in my life, I was already experimenting with that amongst my own friends. You know, there'd be, like, twelve of us, and we'd all sort of be sleeping with each other without too much possessiveness or jealousy, and a lot of comradeship. And I sort of felt that would go on.

Well, I think AIDS put a stop to that. It killed off a lot of people in their late thirties or early forties, who had been through the whole sixties and seventies and a kind of programming that might have led to that sort of thinking. It left alive the much younger gays, who tend to be more conservative just because of the normal swing in fashions. It encouraged people to couple off and be faithful.

But, on the other hand, the sort of comradeship or love that I couldn't have foreseen was the one that was prompted by illness. I think that there was a remarkable community spirit and community response that was sometimes very gallant and funny and tender and especially unyielding. I mean, I'm just amazed that people can go through so much so many times. Again and again. It's really extraordinary.

In that same essay you wrote, "Suddenly it's OK to be thirty, forty, even fifty. At least we need no longer be relentlessly witty or elegant, nor need we stand around gilded pianos bawling out choruses from Hello, Dolly!, *our slender bodies embalmed in youth, bedecked with signature scarves, and soaked in eau de cologne." I wonder, though, if in the nineties a different de rigueur urban gay style hasn't taken over. What has happened to the liberationist ideal of the gay rights movement? Have we just traded the Miss Thing style for the pumped-up, urban, gym-bunny style?*

There is a kind of body fascism that's very much at work. But I've always felt that that was fairly superficial in some ways. At Fire Island, for instance, even in the seventies, you would see six guys lined up who all looked pretty much the same: they all had big, gym-built bodies; they all had mustaches, if that was what was in then; short hair or whatever; and maybe a tattoo, if that was coming in. But then, you'd talk to them, and they were all entirely different. I mean, one was a lawyer, working on Wall Street, and a Republican; and another one was a social worker who was living with his parents in Brooklyn; and another one had a sixty-five-year-old boyfriend who didn't come out to the Island with him; and so on. And you'd find enormous variety under those superficial similarities.

I think that there's a kind of high school side of gay life. Gay people tend to be isolated in high school, so later, in their twenties and early thirties they make up for that through roaming around in wolf packs and being excessively conformist on one level, because they enjoy that kind of thing. But I don't think that says so much about people, really. That kind of uniformity of look can encompass a tremendous variety in content.

Are you, in fact, hopeful about this emerging generation of gay people?

Yes, I think so. First of all, many of them grew up without any guilt, or very little. It got handled very early on, because they had gay books to read, or they heard gay people discussing the subject on television, or they went to gay clubs or discos fairly young, or they joined a gay student group on campus. All those possibilities normalized their feelings. I think that now maybe we're moving into a period where people are maybe going to be less ghettoized. I'm not sure. I just don't know, because I don't live here. You'd be able to tell me better than I can tell you.

Well, I see a lot of younger gay men preoccupied with the trappings of a kind of elegant, middle-class, bourgeois style, without really having any of the deep cultural underpinnings.

Who was it who said that hypocrisy is the morality of nations? In the same way I think that the pretensions of a group can actually sometimes encourage genuine achievement on the part of at least part of that group. It used to be that the pretensions of gay society was to be cultural—*cultured*—and that people had to have an opinion about Maria Callas or something. And even the lowliest gay ribbon clerk had to have figured out whether he liked Bergman more than Fellini. Now, I think that all that's dropped away. The triumph of the club kid sort of replaced any kind of interest in high culture. My nephew said to me last night—my nephew's thirty-five . . .

And a gay man?

No, but he's writing my biography, so he's very into it all, and I raised him. He says, "You know, your generation is really the last generation that will be interested in high culture."

Does that make you sad?

Well, I just can't quite believe it. When you live in Europe, you don't believe it. For one thing, more people went to museums in America last year than went to all sporting events put together. Now, you say, Well, what does that mean? But still. I was at the Museum [of Fine Arts, Boston] this morning at that impressionism show, and I thought people were trying to look at pictures and make some sense of it. That's all anybody's ever been able to do with paintings.

Maybe we're in a period where we're witnessing the democratization of high culture.

My boyfriend, who's thirty-one, he doesn't like music, my kind of music. He only likes rock music, and I'd say that's a profound difference. On the other hand, he wants to be a writer—he's very serious about it—and he's read everything. We had dinner with his ex-lover, who's his age, and his new friend, the other night in Washington—they're all thirty, thirty-one—and they have this kind of joshing, easygoing, typical, uniform, American young person's manner, but in fact they'd read everything, they knew everything. And they would get kind of insulted if I would say, "Do you know who James Merrill is?" So I think there are still people like that. I think the chance of an individual springing up that way in Topeka maybe is even greater than it was in the past because of the availability of books.

I can remember in the sixties that you and your friends had all read pretty much the same paperbacks. You could go into somebody's apartment and they'd always have about the same books that you had. You know, *The Waning of the Middle Ages,* or something like that. And now you go into somebody's apartment and they never have the same books you do, but they have good books, and you want to read theirs. So it seems to me that there are more and more titles and there's more and more of a diversification of culture. In Europe certainly there's a very pious attitude toward high culture.

David Bergman has said that your initial attraction to Asian thought was your "desire to escape desire." What is the place of desire in your life today?

This is a sort of vulgar thing to say, but I've always been the kind of person who, when he masturbates, doesn't make up new stories but thinks about actual experiences I've actually had. I find myself having sex with the dead a lot these days. In other words, I'm remembering great sex in the past with people who are dead. So it's rather ghoulish. But in a way that's what I'm doing in my writing, too. So a lot of the desire is retrospective, or anthological. But some of it is still directed to people, and also to worldliness. I'm interested in that.

So, have you done a 180-degree turn? What place does that initial attraction to Zen and Asian culture have in your life now?

I have a kind of stoicism and a kind of fatalism that probably comes from that part of my life, but I think that the desire to uproot desire, which is a Buddhist idea and that I embraced when I was young because I was so horrified by the nature of my desires, I no longer have at all. I mean, I find that I want to burn with as much intensity as possible.

What precipitated that shift?

I think self-acceptance as a gay man. When I got into my late twenties, early thirties, partly through therapy with Dr. Charles Silverstein, who was my therapist before he became my coauthor. But even the fact of having chosen finally a gay therapist rather than a straight one meant that I was finally willing to accept myself and my sexuality. That made a big difference.

Did it represent a significant decision on your part to tackle that book, The Joy of Gay Sex? *I mean, here you have this author of Nabokovian sensibilities suddenly writing about techniques of cocksucking.*

Oh, certainly. People were horrified. I remember an editor at Random House laughing in my face when I told her what I was doing. People felt that I was really disgracing myself and selling short my promise. The publisher didn't care whether I signed the book or not, because at that point my name wasn't going to sell one more copy. So he said, "You can sign a pseudonym if you want. I don't care." It was purely optional on my part. But I thought, It's idiotic to write a book urging everybody to be very liberated and then sign a pseudonym, so I decided to sign my own name. And I think that in itself was a great act of liberation and self-defining for me.

Were your parents alive at that point?

Yeah. My mother knew about it. My stepmother tore out all the ads so that my father wouldn't know about it. Although my nephew in his research has discovered that my father did know about it and was appalled, again. But, in any event, I don't care.

You raised your nephew?

His mother, who's my sister, was in a mental hospital after a suicide attempt and all her problems in coming out, which she's now done. She'd been a rather conventional girl who was married and had three children and living in the suburbs—Evanston, Illinois—married the high school principal. Then all of a sudden she discovered that she was in love with the neighbor lady, and it was very traumatizing for her, and involved a lot of heavy drinking, suicide attempts, hospitalization. So my nephew was taken over by his father and his new stepmother. He didn't get along with them at all and was very antisocial, so they put *him* in a mental hospital. So then I got him out of that, brought him to New York. Then his little girlfriend from the mental hospital ran away and joined us, so then I had these two children to raise. It only lasted about two-and-a-half years.

What was your domestic situation at the time?

I was living with a boy named Keith McDermott, who was the boy in *Equus* with Richard Burton. He was this very beautiful kid who looked as young as my nephew even though he was in his mid-twenties at that point. He was very, very boyish looking. So we were sort of like this couple dealing with this child. But Keith wasn't very interested in playing that game, but I was.

What does the term "gay writer" mean to you?

First of all, it's important to recognize that in America there's a large superstructure now to handle that category. That means a lot in terms of the survival, especially, of a literary author who happens to be gay, because there are so few possibilities for selling literary books now in America. To have this particular gig, and this particular audience, and that kind of small but devoted following, is a wonderful thing for a writer. The fact that there are thirty gay book shops in America that keep a back list of all the books on the shelves, the fact that there is *Bay Windows* and the *Harvard Gay and Lesbian Review*, and that there are dozens of other not-quite-so-distinguished but still literary or at least bar rags that are going to review your book—there's a kind of intensity of activity. Fran Liebowitz once said to me that the only two [types of] people who read in America are Jewish women and gay men. So, you know, you've got to write about one or the other. Otherwise, you're not going to sell books. I think something like that's true.

In the Paris Review *interview, you said, "I have always made it a point of honor to write as though I had a million dollars."*[6] *What did you mean by that?*

Well, to try not to have any commercial considerations in my mind. In other words, to write as a form of either artistic expression or self-exploration or public service, but not to get rich or to try to capitalize on what you think the market wants or doesn't want. Mind you, I would also say that that's also the best formula for making money, because I do think that people who try to second-guess the market always fail. The Jacqueline Susanns of this world are people who are writing at the height of their form and they just happen to have a sensibility that strikes a chord with millions of readers, but they don't write to do that. She's fully expressed in that form.

What are you working on now?

The third part of my trilogy. It's called *A Farewell Symphony.* It's named after that Haydn symphony where everybody gets up and leaves the stage, and there's only one person fiddling away. That's sort of the way I feel.

Nocturnes for the King of Naples is also the name of a Haydn composition. Nobody knows that. There was a king of Naples, who was somehow related to the Esterházy family that Haydn was generally attached to.

---

6. Edmund White, "The Art of Fiction 105," interview by Jordan Elgrably, *Paris Review* 30, no. 108 (Fall 1988): 73.

And this king of Naples played a strange instrument which was called a *lira organizzata*, which is sort of like a hurdy-gurdy. He wanted Haydn to write some chamber music for him and a group of strings behind it. It's quite beautiful music.

Is Haydn a favorite composer?

Well, yeah. He's not the most seductive composer in the world, but I think he is one of the most intelligent composers. If you have a good clear head, there's nothing more pleasant than to sit down and really listen to him. It's more rewarding that listening to Mozart, which I think is so seductive but not very intelligent. I mean, that's not true! I'm thinking about chamber music. I don't think Mozart is nearly as great a composer of chamber music as he is of operas or symphonies or piano concertos. I find his chamber music rather boring and like wallpaper.

Would you ever consider tackling a libretto?

I've been asked to by Ned Rorem and other people. It'd be fun, but what would it be? I don't know. An AIDS opera—I keep thinking that has to be done. I don't know.

In that essay I mentioned earlier, David Bergman talks about you as an anthropological or sociological writer.

Yeah, I think that's right. I think I'm interested in psychology, but in a rather primitive way. But I think I have a more refined sociological sense. I oftentimes feel that it tells more about a person to talk about their origins and their formative influences.

It also opens up the world of the story, doesn't it?

Yeah, definitely. Even in my biography, which is peculiar given how strange and almost unique a creature Genet was, nevertheless I still tried to understand him through the environments he passed through.

What advice would you give to aspiring gay and lesbian writers today?

Well, off the top of my head, I'd say you've got to find a gimmick.

Despite what you just said about second-guessing the market?

I think what I mean is that you need to find your turf. It's not because of the market. It's because if you find something that hasn't been written about before and you explore that—I mean, even David Leavitt. He found a kind of middle-class, Jewish suburban scene to write about that, actually, gay writers had ignored before. Not only does that cause certain readers to resonate because they haven't found anything like that before, and that's what they're interested in, but you can feel it on the page, the excitement about writing about something new. I think gay writers tend to write too much like one another. There's a desire to cover the same material over and over again.

Most creative writing classes don't talk about originality of subject matter. It's something that's not much discussed, and yet it plays a tremendous role in the development of a career. For instance, Andrew Holleran found a kind of Fitzgeraldian glamour on Fire Island that he played off against a strong sense of Catholic guilt. That generated the excitement of his work, including the new book.[7] I think that Robert Ferro found his desire to integrate the gay couple back into the rather conservative Italo-American family. That was a project that in real life I would have found pointless. I certainly would never have thought to write about it, but he wrote about it marvelously well. It's very intense. And all of a sudden his writing had a kind of Philip Roth-like rigor to it, and strength, and doggedness.

So how does one go about finding that originality?

Part of it is that you look at your own experience and ask what is new about it. For instance, my boyfriend was living in this sort of funny Anglo community in Pilsen [Czech Republic] among the other English and American—but mostly American—teachers of English there. There was one bisexual boy. He was the one gay one—the rest were all straight—but they were all sleeping with each other, but sexlessly. They're all in the late twenties, early thirties. One gay boy would invite a straight girl to come over and spend the night with him. They'd hug and kiss all night but not have sex. My generation didn't do that, but they do. In other words, there's this kind of playfulness.

---

7. White is referring to Holleran's *The Beauty of Men*, which was published in 1996, the year after our interview took place.

And that's material worth mining?

Absolutely. It seems to me there's this new—well, you wouldn't exactly call it bisexuality—pansexuality that is really worth exploring. There's something very interesting about all that, and new, I think.

Is that subject matter that you would also like to pursue?

Maybe. Yeah. But for me it would be more almost anthropological. It wouldn't be tapping into my own feelings so much as it would be observing other people's.

Brian Keith Jackson

Like his almost exact contemporary, Scott Heim, Brian Keith Jackson is one of a new generation of gay writers who finds his stories outside the urban gay ghetto. Set in Welty County, Mississippi, during the 1950s, *The View From Here*, Jackson's 1997 debut novel, focuses on the family of Anna and Joseph (J. T.) Thomas, a poor black couple, and their five sons. Anna, who is pregnant again, awaits not only the birth of the child but a Fourth of July visit from her girlhood friend, Ida Mae Ramsey, a hard-drinking, hard-playing free spirit who has left Mississippi to pursue her dreams up north. The central action revolves around these two anticipated arrivals and the imminent decision as to whether to turn over the new baby ("'too many mouths to feed,'" grumbles J.T.) to Anna's horrid, childless sister-in-law, Clariece.

Excerpts from the novel were included in *Shade*, a groundbreaking anthology of fiction by gay men of African descent.[1] It is interesting to note, however, that little in Jackson's novel would identify it as a work of gay fiction. There is a mild suggestion that the girlhood friendship between Momma and Ida Mae had lesbian undertones; and Junior, the eldest child, is a sensitive, Bible-reading seventeen-year-old who doesn't seem much interested in young ladies. Apart of these quiet hints, there is not much else in *The View From Here* that could be deemed "gay" content. Nevertheless, Pocket Books chose to pitch the book to a gay readership. This marketing strategy is one of the things I made sure to ask Jackson about when I interviewed him.

The View From Here won the American Library Association's Literary Award for First Fiction from the Black Caucus of America. Jackson has since published a second novel, *Walking Through Mirrors* (1998).

Our conversation took place at the Hotel Lafayette in downtown Boston in the late winter of 1997.

---

1. *Shade: Anthology of Fiction by Gay Men of African Descent*, ed. Bruce Morrow and Charles Rowell New York: (Avon, 1996).

Why don't we start with some biographical information?

I was born in New Orleans, in the summer of 1967, which means it was really hot. My parents were both educators; they were in Alabama for a while and then they settled in Monroe, Louisiana, and that's what I consider to be my hometown. It's a nice place, home of Delta Airlines.

When did your interest in writing begin?

I've been writing for a very long time. I don't know that it was ever an "interest." It was more of a need. I was an only child. I liked to scribble things down. When I was about ten, my father, who was a businessman, would give me a dollar to draft letters. He'd give me the information and say, "Okay, put this together," and I'd sit there clunking it out. That was his way of encouraging me. That's how I first learned to compile information and put it together.

When did you start writing stories?

Right before I moved to New York. I was in Flint, Michigan, working for a newspaper there. I wanted to move to New York to be an actor. I went to drama school but dropped out. For one thing, all my teachers told me I was too laid-back to be an actor; and also most of my roles were very low status, something I was not accustomed to: being in a low-status situation. So I started writing plays, writing the types of things that I wanted to be in as well as the types of things I knew other people wanted to be in. I had two plays produced in the city and was to have a third produced, but I had a bit of a falling-out with the producers. I started writing books so that I could cut out the middle man.

Do you ever want to go back to writing plays?

I'm quite pleased writing fiction. I can't say that I will write plays again; I can't say that I won't. I love the theater. I think it's wonderful. What I do like about books, though, is that it takes a great deal of trust, whereas with the plays I can always watch the audience, I can always change it, we can always have a rehearsal if we think it's not working. With literature, once it's out there, there's nothing you can do; you have to commit to that and hope that the audience responds to it. I like that, I like being able to let it go.

Are there things about your novel that you would change now if it were a play and it were being produced and you were getting audience reaction?

I don't think so. I'm very proud of the book. I don't think that I would change anything in it. There has to be a point where you have to let it go. I think I'm still too near to it to examine it to say what I would change. It's like having a child and you send it out and just hope that you've done the very best possible job that you can and that people are kind to it. Then maybe, you know, ten years from now I'll look back and say, Oh, I made that mistake; and then I'll apologize to the child.

I was interested that in the excerpt you published in Shade, *you took out all the letters that Anna writes to Ida Mae. Why did you make that revision?*

For the excerpt, I wanted to make it a whole piece without having to give the other two hundred pages. By including the letters, it would have made it more difficult to do so. I took a portion that stood on its own. It's like what I'll do at readings: sometimes I'll skip the letters because it's too difficult to understand that three things are going on in the context of a reading.

I was also interested to see that you'd published that excerpt because The View From Here *is not a particularly gay novel, and yet* Shade *is an anthology of literature by gay African Americans. I was wondering what decision went into your contributing to that anthology.*

Well, the editors actually came to me and asked if I would include it, and I said I would. I felt it was important to have the piece in there. I think a lot of gay black men respond to their mothers, respond to the women around them. It's also important because the anthology was fiction by gay black men rather than gay fiction by black men. That's the distinction.

Were your plays gay plays? Did they have gay characters?

Yes.

Why did you make the decision with this first major piece of fiction, your novel, not to turn in that direction?

Anyone who thinks that someone is making a "decision" when they create is, I think, mistaken. I don't. I don't sit down to make a decision. That takes too much intellectual thought. I don't do that. I basically write what comes. And what I wanted to write about was how so many things happen before you're born. I wrote the first line—"White folks always love li'l colored babies"—seven years before I wrote the book. I found it one day on a piece of paper and then the next thing I knew came the novel. And the characters kind of presented themselves. Though it may not be filled with gay content, I think the sensibilities are there. The realm of understanding that we all must have as people making the choice to love someone, and what that means and why we love them, and standing up for what we believe—those are very much not just gay issues but human issues.

I've had people who, after they've read the book, have a different perception of me. It goes back to men—even gay men—not being allowed to really express. The book intimidates a lot of gay men with the fact that I've written this book that's very emotional and very, you know, "Everything's going to be wonderful." Some men are [put off] by that and don't know what to think of me.

You said something very interesting—that black gay men have a particular affinity for their mothers and with women. Do you want to say more about that?

Women, for the most part, are the communicators. They're the ones who happen to deliver the information because the men are out working or not there at all. That's what a lot of black gay men are relating to.

What's your history as a gay writer? When did you first confront gay material, themes?

Probably when I started writing my plays, that was the first time I started incorporating gay characters into my work. It wasn't because they were gay characters; it was just the fact that the kind of work I was doing deals with similarities rather than differences. We're all different—that's a given—but once we can begin to look at one another's similarities we can then bridge the gap between what's going on in each other's community. Some communities, I find, have a tendency to become the very thing they're fighting against. I'm adamantly against that. No community is unanimous in their thinking. That's what makes us special. That's what makes communities communities—the constant idea of debate and exchanging thoughts.

Do you think the "gay community"—if there even is such a thing—has become so ghettoized, become so inward-looking that it doesn't look for commonality with other communities?

To some extent. I mean, we all as human beings and animals look for security. We look for commonality. Some people run away from their hometowns to rid themselves of that commonality only to come to another town and set up the exact same thing. I live in Manhattan. Manhattan is basically just forty small cities. Some people never leave that small city they live in in Manhattan.

That's what makes me a bit different: being a lonely child for so long, I was protean. There was no place I wouldn't go to look for more information. I can understand why people would feel the need to bond to one community and feel safe within that, but some people just hide there and never make any other connection with the other people they're purporting to be like. That's unfortunate. If you are going to segregate yourself, at least make that as powerful as it can be.

As I was reading the book, I kept looking for some sort of gay undercurrent. Were you, for instance, at all exploring the possibility of an erotic attraction between Anna and Ida Mae?

It's really interesting. I think women are always allowed to show affection. I don't know if it was an erotic thing. I traveled around the world this summer. I was in Sri Lanka. It's very appealing how, there, young boys and young men hold hands and they're very affectionate towards one another. It's just a given that it's part of their culture. Whereas here in western civilization that's somewhat taboo. With women, it's somewhat easier. If you see women walking down the street caressing one another, that's acceptable.

I also realize that once I send out the work, everyone brings their own story to it. And I want that. It's not just my story anymore. Anyone who reads the book, they bring what they have to give to it. And they find what they need in it. I applaud that. If that excites you, who knows. Maybe you'll see these characters again.

Another character who intrigues me is Junior. I sensed that maybe there was a gay character emerging in him. He's quiet, he reads his Bible, he's always defending his mother. He doesn't seem to be interested in girls. When I got to the end of the book I thought, Well, here's a character who's ripe for further exploration.

A lot of people feel that. The number one thing a lot of people want to see, they want to know more about Junior. He won't be in the second book. I assure people, it will be a totally new book.

How did you come up with the idea to have the narrator be in utero?

I wanted to parallel the beginning of life, a new beginning. But I wanted to tell the story in a very simple way, to make it accessible. Literature has a way of being alienating. I didn't want that to occur. I'm not one of these people who feel that if you use a six-million-dollar word that makes people think you're intelligent. Anyone can pick up a dictionary, write down a word, and use it that day. But to tell a simple story that can appeal to someone who wants to read it and then appeal to someone who can find intellectual stimulation from it I think is excellent.

When you use something as intricate as an unborn baby as your narrator, I learned in playwriting that if you're going to do a simple text then the set has to be abstract. And so the same thing in the book: if I was going to use something as abstract as having an unborn baby narrate, then I have to make sure that the text is simple.

What I wanted to work on was the idea that the freshest eye sees the clearest. You don't know what's right and wrong; you don't know what's supposed to be. You can only take what is at that moment and have some sense of it. Sometimes being naïve is the best thing in the world, because then you can examine without having foresight or hindsight as to what it's supposed to be.

You've told me that you were born in Louisiana and spent some time in Alabama, and yet you've set your novel in Mississippi. What is it about that place that made it appealing as the stage for the novel?

Mississippi is known as very rural. It's like setting a novel in Kansas—you do it because you see it. You see the landscape; you see the earth. You think of farming, you think of trees. Whereas with Louisiana, that doesn't come to mind for me. I wanted *earth*, Earth Mother. That's what this story is about, this character who is the earth. The child is born in the corn fields. You don't think that in Louisiana; you don't think that in Alabama. But in Mississippi I think you do.

What did you have to do to tap into female voice and female consciousness?

Express. Unfortunately, we live in a society in which only women are allowed to emote. Women are allowed to show their feelings, whereas in men it's considered a soft aspect. Hopefully one day I will be able to write with men characters who are allowed what they really feel. But society makes that very difficult. Showing any sense of sincerity or emotion in a man is still shunned upon. That's the job I tried to make in this book: to have a sense of understanding as to why things are the way they are.

In your novel, Momma writes at one point, "'The space between young and old is as far as Detroit is from Mississippi.'" How do you think that young gay writers such as yourself and older gay writers differ? Do you think there are particular issues or problems that young gay writers face that the older generation of gay writers did not have to confront?

The space is so small, even in my lifetime. The AIDS epidemic made us lose a great many writers; and so you have pre-AIDS, you have during AIDS, and you have what's going on now. We are now getting to a point where some gay writers feel they don't need to write about AIDS.

I celebrate everyone who came before, because ultimately they opened the door for me, whatever they were writing about, whether it was for me or something I liked, just by their being out there. That made me able to publish. A lot of young writers have to realize that there's been a life before us. And people have gone through the same things that we're going through now. So we can just open the door a little more for the next people, because they're coming. It's inevitable. I don't think a lot of my young contemporaries. It's all about them, in the moment. You know, I'm this and I'm that. Whereas with myself, I'm constantly thinking, Well, this person made that possible for you. And you have to recognize that and applaud that and support that.

Who have been some of the gay writers who have most influenced your writing?

I've read, of course, a lot of James Baldwin and Langston Hughes and Countee Cullen. I used to read everything that Randy Shilts wrote, but it was nonfiction. I was into information then. I've read Ed White. And I read my contemporaries: I read Dale Peck, I read Scott Heim. Tim Murphy. And a lot of lesbian writers like Becky Birtha. She was my first experience with gay literature. Gay men really need to take a look at some of the women's books out there, so that we can see again how similar we really are. That division that we're experiencing is not good.

Your novel is set in Welty County, in a town called Eudora. What's your relationship with the great southern writer Eudora Welty?

Well, I'm a big fan. Southern writers are just amazing. Just the way they carry themselves—they're very mannered—they are characters in their own right. Eudora Welty is a big, big character. I've always liked her work. Same with Tennessee Williams and Truman Capote. It's something about being down there—maybe it's the sweat. I don't know what it is. She's the woman I thought a lot about when I was writing the book. I kept thinking, She's going to die soon, she's not going to be around. So the book was kind of my way of thanking her.

Who else?

Zora Neale Hurston, Alice Walker. In all honesty, I read mostly nonfiction. I read a great many letters. I love not only reading people's work, but I like seeing the neurosis of their lives: their insecurities, their wanting love, so many things. That helps me prepare for the day-to-day. Because I realize, Oh, I'm not going through this alone, someone else has done it beforehand. Granted, I want to keep my personal life personal, but if you read someone's journals, their letters, you really get a better sense of them than you do in their work. You get to find out where the work comes from.

What are your writing habits like?

Usually the first thing I write in the morning is what I call my "morning missives." I don't have e-mail. I refuse. I write letters. I can be anywhere in the world and write letters; and people love to receive them. Going to the post box and getting mail that doesn't say Amount Now Owed, I think is just a treat, but it's a dying art. So that's how I start my day, and then I'll do my writing.

I still write longhand, because when I write on the computer I'm too judgmental because you can see it: you can see the way it's going to look when you print it out. Whereas when I'm writing longhand, you can't so easily see what you've already written; you just have to keep going. You can clean it up later. It takes more time, but does it? It's a way of not stifling myself. It shows that I'm human. I like to see the mistakes. So many people worry, Oh, is this right? Did I use the proper grammar? That keeps you from actually creating. All of that can be rectified later.

Have you studied writing formally?

No.

What did you major in?

Journalism.

What did you learn from newspaper writing?

I learned that I didn't have what it took to be a journalist. But I also learned the art of debate when dealing with an editor. The most I probably learned is that once you do have passion about something, that there's nothing like it. The cop-beat reporter had a desk next to mine, and I would hear him asking over the phone, "Any murders?" He would say it as if it were nothing. I was twenty-one years old, out of college. And then I moved to New York—so much of the same!

In the novel, Lisa says, "'There's a need to see colored faces in print, to show we exist.'" Which is more important to you—being an Afro-American writer or a gay writer?

I don't think either has more importance. At the moment, many things incorporate my attention. It's like I have four children and maybe one day one child falls down and needs a Band-Aid. So, okay, let me handle this right now. But I can't separate any of them. They all add to what I have become and what I am. I stand up for what I believe to be right and that's for everything—not just gay and lesbian causes or black causes. Because, again, sometimes I don't even know what community I'm a part of. Not everyone's going to like you in either community. To some black people I may be too black, or not black enough, or bourgeois. To some gay communities I might not be doing this or not be doing that. I can only do what I can do and get up and deal with that in the morning.

Do you feel any pressure from the gay community to make your work more gay?

I don't feel pressure. I'm not hiding the fact that I'm a gay man. I'm definitely out there. I'm visible. I'm driving across the country and doing press. We have to start recognizing and supporting other things and moving to that point where acceptance is based on what it is that you're doing and the quality of that work as opposed to our sexuality. I always thought that that's what we were fighting for.

Growing up an only child in the South made me very aware at a very young age of many things—of difference, of standing up for what you believe in. When I moved to New York, I was the ACT UP poster boy. I needed to do that. Now I'm just redirecting my focus. It doesn't make me any more valid, or less. But my journey is different from anyone else's journey. So no pressure at all. I'm going to do what I can do. But it's evident that ultimately I'll have to include gay characters because that's the way life is going. We are included, whether we want to admit that or not.

You have such a spirit of tolerance and all-embracing compassion. Where does that come from?

I knew my great-grandmother. She was alive during slavery. She always had great compassion. I think what made her have that compassion is when she looked around at her family and all that they had accomplished. I'm very fortunate. I've been provided an outlet. I'm from a middle-class family, I've been provided for, I've never wanted anything. I should be a lawyer! My parents always wanted me to be a lawyer, but I always fought and stood up and said, "I'm not going to be a lawyer!" And now I'm a writer and they love it. But the fact is, I have an outlet; and that gives me compassion. It keeps me from killing. A lot of people don't have outlets and I think that's why we have the problems that we have in society: because no one has a way to express and find a way to understand.

At the end of the novel, you write, "The unknown is afloat within each of us." Can you elaborate on that? What does that mean?

In the context of the book and in life, we just don't know. So many answers are left. You're sitting and you're looking at someone and you realize something must be the reason for his actions. Like, if you're dating someone, there is still so much you don't know about this person, but you have to just trust in your instincts and trust that things will be okay and that in time you'll find out the things you need to know and it's worth it. That's kind of how I feel about life in general: that in time you will find out the information that you need to know, and that from that will come the choice that you have to make as a person. In this process I've been going through of becoming an adult, it took me a long time to realize that parents are people and not just parents.

You use a wonderful expression in your novel—"a recipe for joy." What's your recipe for joy?

Potential makes the best recipe for joy, because you can find anything once you find potential. That's what I look for in people; that's what I look for in everything that I do: the potential that it can be a recipe for more than it is. Love is not always a recipe for joy, unfortunately. I learned very early on that sometimes love isn't enough to make two people be together.

What else does it take?

Mutual growth. You can love someone, but if you're not growing, together, then I think that love becomes stagnant. It's not an easy job.

Do you ever feel the urge to return to your roots in the South?

Definitely. Soon. I've been in New York for seven years now, and I'm ready to see some other places. As I said, I traveled around the world for the summer by myself, just to show myself that I could figure things out. And I did. That gave me the confidence and the know-how to know that I don't *have* to be in New York. That's one thing about New York: you get so caught up in it that you can't leave because you think you're going to miss something. Well, no you're not. You're not going to miss anything. It's still going to be there. She's a hard girl, she's a hard girl. And I love her. She's a hard girl, but she wants to be loved like anyone else. If you're kind to her, she will be kind to you. But she has her days where you just, like anything, leave her alone. Just stay in the house that day. And I'm quite ready to return to civility. That's one of the things I find lacking in New York. Try as I may to be civil, people are just not very civil there. It's a "I'm here to do something; out of my way" place. I don't really care for that at all.

I'm not competitive with other people. I get really shocked by this desire. That's not to say that I'm not aware of my contemporaries. I have an appreciation for them. But I don't really care how much money they make or I don't really care about what they got. I deal with my thoughts the way I deal with them. No one's going to be the more competitive with me than I'm going to be with myself.

Do you have a day job?

No, I don't.

Any advice for young gay writers today?

I didn't write this book thinking, Okay, one day this is going to be a novel. I wrote because I needed a voice at the time. The written word is a very powerful medium. If you're going to write things down, don't judge it before you finish writing it down. We spend too much time in our lives being judged to judge ourselves so harshly. If you put it down, you'll feel better automatically, I assure you, and that's what you should do, and don't let anyone stop you from doing that.

Peter Cameron

Peter Cameron is the author of the highly praised *The Weekend* (1994), which the *New York Times Book Review,* citing its "complexity, precision, lyricism and compassion," likened to the work of Virginia Woolf, E. M. Forster, D. H. Lawrence and F. Scott Fitzgerald.[1] Cameron's work—some of it gay-oriented, some not—has received wide critical acclaim from writers as diverse as Michael Dorris, Francine Prose, Lorrie Moore, and Joseph Olshan. The *New Yorker* has described his writing as "full of observations that ring like porch chimes and flicker like fireflies, evanescent yet indelible."[2]

With *Andorra* (1997), Cameron not only extended his authority as a masterful prose stylist but also ventured into new territory that surprised readers of his previous work. He is also the author of a third novel, *Leap Year,* and three collections of stories. His short stories have been anthologized in three volumes of *Prize Stories: The O. Henry Awards.*

Cameron came to Boston in January 1997 to give readings from *Andorra* at The Living Center and We Think the World of You bookstore. I interviewed him for *Bay Windows* at the Colonnade Hotel, where he was staying in the Author's Suite.

Andorra is so different from your previous novel, The Weekend. *How did you come to write it?*

That's an interesting question. I don't know how well I can answer it. The part of my process that I don't understand is how I conceive books. That's the most mysterious to me.

The Weekend was published in May of 1994; I had finished it sometime that winter, so I had not written in about six months. When I'm not writing a book, I feel like I'm never going to write again. For some reason that summer, shortly after *The Weekend* came out, I started to have this

---

1. Joyce Reiser Kornblatt, "Simple Truths Are Hard to Know," *New York Times Book Review,* 29 May 1994, 16.

2. "Books Briefly Noted," *New Yorker,* 13 June 1994, 107.

idea about a novel that would be sort of experimental. Since *The Weekend* was so compact and formal in a way, I wanted to do something more original and, for me, more challenging formally. So I had this idea for a novel that was going to be a correspondence between a prisoner and a mentor, someone in a prison writing program. And the mentor's lover was going to be dying of AIDS; so you'd get scenes from his life. It was this big hodgepodge that was hopefully going to add up to something.

It came to me very quickly. I wrote a lot of the novel that the prisoner was writing and a lot of the letters back and forth. Very quickly I started to realize that the part that intrigued me was the part that the prisoner was writing and that all this frame around it was not coming alive, and I was really working hard to make these letters interesting. And then the scenes from the mentor's life seemed very flat to me. It was weird because the part of the book that seemed most alive was the part that was farthest removed from life, the most artificial. I decided that was the part that was intriguing me. And I knew that there was this character writing the novel but I didn't want the reader to know that.

Some people had read the early drafts of the novel with the frame and really liked it and thought it was interesting and did not encourage me to jettison the frame, but my editor was really good about thinking I could make the novel work on its own. So I had trouble beginning this book, and a hard time finishing this book.

I wrote probably another whole half of the book that didn't finally make it into *Andorra*, because I didn't know where it was going. I had a lot of dead ends. So there was a lot of down time in writing the book and then it was a matter of looking at all that other stuff I had written and figuring out what really was the story.

To whom do you show your work?

I show my work to a couple of readers. They're invaluable to me. My brother is a great reader. He knows me and what I'm trying to do in my work. He's smart. A great combination of things. And also, because he's my brother, he'll be honest with me. If you're showing your work to people at that early stage, you really need somebody who's going to be critical and honest.

This is the first book actually that I'd sold on the basis of a very small part of it. I worked on it with my editor John Glusman, on the weekend. He's such a fabulous editor; he was very encouraging. There were a lot of points where I kind of lost faith in the book, and the book seemed very inert and dead to me, and he kept telling me that it could work. He was somebody I really counted on while I was writing the book.

And then I have a couple of friends. Edward Swift, who's a writer, is a very generous reader. It's a burden asking somebody to read your manuscript. I can do that with him. He read *The Weekend*, too, but the nature of this book appealed to him, because his work is a little out of the ordinary. He really got into this book and was very encouraging.

Andorra is not the real Andorra, but an imagined place. That got me comparing your book to Borges and Nabokov.

Those are two people I've read and certainly been influenced by. I wanted it to be this world that you started out feeling was artificial and then somehow make the characters real enough that by the end of the book you forget that it's a totally fake place.

Have you ever been to Andorra?

No, no. And I knew I didn't want to go and I knew I wanted it to be this conception of Andorra. I wanted it to be this place that was more informed by the world of books than the world of life. Which was really fun. I love to read, so it was like drawing on all these worlds of books.

The author Rose Macaulay figures in Andorra. The narrator says that reading her Crewe Train prompted him to move to Andorra; she also supplies an epigraph for The Weekend. Why your attraction to Rose Macaulay?

Well, she's a writer I really love. I started out reading a lot of contemporary American writers when I was in college. Ann Beattie was a big influence on me—somebody who got me really excited about contemporary literature. And Margaret Atwood and Margaret Drabble. But in the last five years, I've been reading a lot of British women writers from the thirties and forties. I love their work. For me the novel reached a pinnacle there—these domestic novels written by British women. The sensitivity that they bring to their subject matter is really consummate, and their use of language is really beautiful, too. It's the kind of novel I'm interested in reading and writing. A lot of that influenced *The Weekend*. I wanted *The Weekend* to be this kind of book that was concerned with domestic issues and people's relationships and about the quality of living—what is it like to be alive in a specific place and a specific time?

So, I had read a lot of Rose Macaulay. Actually, there are only a couple of chapters of *Crewe Train* that take place in Andorra. The character leaves Andorra very quickly and moves back to England. But it was the only book I knew at the time that featured Andorra at all. For some reason when I started this book, I knew that I wanted to use Andorra. A lot of people told me that it should be an imaginary country with an imaginary name. But I knew I wanted it to be Andorra; I just didn't want it to be *the* Andorra. So it was fun. I love alluding to the authors I love in my books.

What do you think is behind people's desire to, as you say in the novel, "begin their lives again"?

Alexander Fox [the main character in *Andorra*] intrigues me because he's at this weird point on the moral scale, where he's moral enough and sensitive enough to know that he's not a very good person, but he's not moral enough to actually change his behavior. That's kind of how I feel. When I was younger, I thought that I was going to turn into a better person than I am. I think it's easier to be a better person when you're young, and then, as you get older, your life gets more complicated. It's a scary thing to realize that you're losing your ability to be as kind and as nice a person as you once hoped you would be, or once *were*, perhaps. It's this dilemma that I'm very intrigued by.

Also, narratively, I'm much more interested in characters now who are flawed, who are wrestling with some sort of moral dilemma. Their behavior sometimes bothers them and they're aware of that. Like Mary in *The Weekend*. A lot of people said, "Oh, she's so unsympathetic." For me she was just very real. I wanted to write about somebody who was very real, somebody who was trying to be a good person and was failing as often as they were succeeding.

So I think this idea of starting your life over again is about getting to a point where you feel that you've not done a good job and it's hard because you are enmeshed in all these relationships, these patterns. So the idea of starting again is very seductive, because you think, "Oh, if I start again, I'm going to do it right." Of course you're not.

Why, after The Weekend, *did you decide to write a novel with very little gay content?*

That's something that wasn't deliberate or conscious. The character who came to me was heterosexual, so the world he traveled in was more predominantly heterosexual. It wasn't a conscious decision at all. The characters chose me. I kept thinking that I wanted to make the book gayer than it was. And then I just realized that the characters had to be who they were. He had to have the experiences that he had. I had to have respect for him as a character. I couldn't force the book. It's like a child you're raising: you can't dictate their sexuality.

Then let me ask the corollary question: why the two gay characters?

Why are they there? Just because in life there are gay characters. It's not a gay world or a straight world. In *The Weekend,* I was interested in how those two worlds intersect. In most people's world there are gay characters and straight characters. I wanted the world of my book to be heterogeneous.

Your narrator, Alex Fox, is an inventor—an imaginative inventor of his own life. "We are free to believe nothing," he says, "or everything." What is it about human imagination that appeals to you?

Writing this book was, in a way, an exaggerated experience of writing a book. It made me think a lot about what it is to write a book. I don't write autobiographically. I write from my imagination. It's about creating this other world. It's weird. I feel very much as if I'm living half a life now, because for the last three years, when I was writing this book, I had this whole other life that was *Andorra,* that was these characters. Now when I think about it, it's like a diorama: I can't go back and move things around or change things. But when I was working on the book it was this active, alive part of my life. And now it's frozen. When I was working on *The Weekend,* too, although that book is much more literal in terms of the world, it was like an escape for me into a fantasy world that I lived in.

When I read, too, if it's a good book, you feel that when you're sick with your life there's this other whole world you can feel a part of. I was thinking of all those things, in a conscious or subconscious way, when I wrote *Andorra*, and I wanted the book to be about how you can escape, or try to escape, through your imagination, and how the process of reading is about entering into another world, and how people use that in either good or bad ways. I feel that some of the richest parts of my life have been the parts that I've encountered through reading.

It seemed to me that all your characters were, to a certain extent, inventing things. I never knew whether I was supposed to believe them or not. There was a kind of fluidity to the truth they were telling.

I knew Alexander Fox, I knew what he was doing in Andorra and what his past was. And then these other people that he encounters—for a long time I didn't see them as people who had as problematic a past as he did. But, for some reason, they were all behaving in slightly strange ways, and they felt sort of troubled as people. And then it was sort of interesting to think that maybe Andorra is this place where everybody is escaping from something bad that's happened in one way or another. To think, Well, what happened to the Dents and to Jean Quay, and giving them stories, though I tend to believe them more than him. But, yeah, I wanted it to be this book that asked what does it mean to tell somebody that something happened to you. How do you believe what somebody says to you? What's fiction?

To what extent is Andorra *also a religious book?*

I'm glad you asked that question, because that was something else that I wanted to write about. It doesn't seem to register with a lot of people. I don't know if people aren't used to encountering that in books. Going back to what I was saying about you're not as good of a person as you might want to be, then you think, Well, how do I become a better person? I started thinking about religion: what does it mean to be religious and is that a way to become a better person? A lot of the books that I like are about people struggling with that question.

Rose Macaulay's books are wonderful in that way. For her, the whole problem of faith was a very important thing that she wrestled with her entire life and that she allows her characters to wrestle with. In *The*

Towers of Trebizond, she asks How do you reconcile your faith with your actual physical existence and your sexuality?

So Alexander Fox, in the same way that he aspires to be a better person than he is, also aspires to be religious but he can't make that leap of faith. I think that's sort of tragic, that somebody who can almost see how he could be saved, and sees other people being saved, but for whatever reasons he can't save himself. It's the same as the fact that he can't save himself through his imagination, either—that ultimately fails, too.

To what extent is the imagination our late-twentieth-century substitute for religion?

Right. For me, however you save yourself doesn't matter, if you find a way to save yourself and give yourself something to believe in. Reconciling your faith with your intellect—the older you get and the smarter you get, the harder that is. It's weird because you're cutting yourself off in some way from something that can really sustain you.

In Andorra *you write, "Traveling gives us an opportunity to reinvent ourselves, to take on new personas." Do you like to travel?*

Traveling is hard work. But I like traveling for the same reasons everybody likes traveling: when you travel you're not in your life. Just by physically changing your surroundings, you don't change yourself—I mean, you bring along everything you are—but it gives you some sort of freedom in terms of how you project yourself.

There's a wonderful passage in Andorra *where your narrator says that traveling allows us to feel included in the "magnificence of what we see."*

Right. That's the other thing about traveling: you just look at things differently. As a traveler you look at the world in a different way. When you're going about your ordinary life, you don't look for magnificence because you're inured to it; whereas when you're traveling, things look beautiful to you that would not normally look beautiful to you. It's kind of sad that people are only programmed to look for that when they're traveling.

Is that attraction to taking on new personas something that gay people understand more than straight people?

I don't know. Yeah, I see what you mean. I think that's probably true. As more and more people come out, there won't be a need to do that anymore. I used to work for a place where I wasn't out and it didn't bother me, but now I look back and realize how bothered I should have been by it, because people would talk about their personal lives in a way that I never was able to. It's kind of weird how I accepted that. I pretended to be straight, but I just wasn't being myself.

Now, my job is very much the opposite of that. I'm myself at work in a much fuller, rounder way. And I think that gay people have experienced that—either not being themselves or being somebody else—because that's how you get along in society.

Why do both gay characters in the novel come out to Alex? Is that something that you thought about at all?

Well, Mr. Dent tries to seduce him, so obviously there's this physical attraction there. And Alex is writing this book, so I wanted him to be thinking of himself, presenting himself, as somebody whom everybody finds attractive. And Vere is somebody who's gay and out, kind of, and so his relationship with Alex is through this relationship he had with Alex's brother-in-law; so it's just kind of natural. Their association with Alex allows them to be identified as gay characters; part of what brings them into the book is their sexuality.

What does the term "gay novel" mean to you?

A novel about gay characters.

So in that respect is Andorra *a gay novel?*

I wouldn't call it a gay novel. It's a novel written by a gay man.

Okay, does that matter? Is there a particular sensibility that you, as a gay man, brought to it?

This whole thing I don't understand. Being gay is one aspect of who I am. Growing up where I did obviously influenced me a lot. But there's not this category of novels called "books written by people who grew up in Pompton Plains, New Jersey." There's all these things that I feel contributed to who I am, and at some point my sexuality is important. But this book is not a book that is really concerned with my sexuality or my characters' sexuality. I think it's weird. I don't understand this desire people have to categorize novels according to the sexuality of the authors or the characters.

Would you say that there is no particular sensibility that a gay author imparts to his work?

No. I feel that I'm as different from other gay authors as I am from other straight authors. I feel that gay authors are an incredibly varied subcategory. And gay authors who are writing now are very different from gay authors who were writing twenty years ago. I'm thirty-seven. Gay authors who are twenty are writing in a very different way. Everybody's different. I'm much more interested in looking at what makes people specifically the kind of writer they are.

What do you think of the incredible emergence of American gay writing in the last ten to fifteen years?

I think that's why there is this category, because from a marketing approach it makes a lot of sense. And when I think, too, about what I grew up reading—you grow up reading all these books that are about heterosexuals—it's weird, you just accept that: the world of literature is about straight people. It's very exciting when all of a sudden you start reading stuff about gay people. It's not that I thought those books weren't good or didn't teach me about what it's like to be a human being; I got a proper education from the books I read. But I guess the more closely you identify with the characters, the more you get from the book. If the book is a good book.

Twenty years ago, every gay novel was a coming-out story. And now that's no longer the kind of story people want to read anymore. I think that's really great that that phenomenon of coming out—you know, that very angst-ridden and torturous journey—is a very dated concept now. That's another thing I like about this gay literature now: that young people can read these books now and get to a point where gay characters are an acknowledged part of the world.

I loved the detail about the Necco-colored gowns. I didn't know anyone still remembered Necco wafers! Because of that detail, I'd assumed you had grown up in Boston. Can we talk a little bit about your biography—where you grew up, et cetera?

I was born in New Jersey, in a small town about twenty minutes from New York City. I lived there until I was seven or eight. My father worked in a bank, and was transferred to London, so I lived in London for three years. This was 1968, a great time to be in London. It was a really wild town. The world was a different place then. I took the subway by myself to school every day. I had a lot of freedom. I went from living in this small New Jersey town to London. It was very liberating and exciting.

I'd gone to a public school in New Jersey, and I went to the American School in London, a private school there. It was kind of a weird school where we did a lot of creative writing. We wrote a lot of plays. My mother got a little concerned because I wasn't learning how to spell or to do arithmetic, things that she thought were important. So that's when I actually started writing creatively.

We moved back to the United States. I went to Hamilton College in upstate New York. David Lehmann was teaching poetry there. He was a wonderful poetry teacher. I got very excited about writing poetry, and started thinking that I wanted to be a poet. I was still writing fiction, and I took a fiction workshop and just kind of found this voice.

Right about then was when Ann Beattie was writing and publishing a lot of stories in the *New Yorker*. I started reading her stories and being really moved by them, being excited by them, because they were about a life and characters that seemed not distant from me. Before then I had always thought of short stories as being like John Cheever, and they seemed a generation removed from me, and all of a sudden there was this generation that was not removed from me. She was writing about people I could identify with. So I started writing stories at Hamilton.

It was a small enough school that I got a lot of encouragement and a lot of opportunities there. My senior year there I started sending stories out to the *New Yorker*. They rejected a lot of stories, but they always encouraged me to send them something else right away. So it was sort of this great apprenticeship, where they would reject a story and tell me why it didn't work and then say, "Send us something else soon." And, of course, I would immediately want to write another short story and send it back. I did that for about a year and then I graduated from Hamilton. I knew I didn't want to go to graduate school; I wanted to move to New York and get a job and be an adult.

I moved to New York and got a job working for St. Martin's Press. I worked there for about a year. During that year I sold my first story to the *New Yorker*. About the time I sold that first story, I realized I didn't want a career in publishing. I was no good at it. I worked for the subrights department. I was a terrible salesperson. I hate talking on the telephone, but part of my job was calling people up every day and seeing if they were going to bid—because we were publishing hardcover books and trying to sell the paperback rights. Of course, if people were going to bid they would call you. I just used to dread it.

I also feel that I was learning too much about publishing. I wasn't sure I wanted to learn more about publishing than I knew. It was taking all the romance out of it. And people who work in publishing don't have time to read what you want to read. You have all this stuff you are forced to read. I valued reading too much to get myself in that kind of situation. So then I realized that I just wanted to get a regular office job that I could work at and do my writing. I got a job working for the Trust for Public Land, which was a nonprofit land conservation organization. It was a great job. I worked there for about three or four years. I realized that complement was really good for me: working in an office during the day and then writing.

The stories you were publishing in the New Yorker *were gay stories?*

They were mixed, some with gay characters in them, some with straight characters. They were varied. Again, that is something I didn't do consciously or deliberately. When I got an idea for a story, I got a specific idea about a specific character.

Then I got an opportunity to teach at Oberlin College. So I thought, Well, one thing all writers do is they teach. And you get the summer off. So maybe I should be a teacher. So I went out to Oberlin and taught for a semester. But I was really unhappy living in Oberlin and I missed New York. Teaching was challenging, it was interesting, but I didn't enjoy it enough that I wanted to do it exclusively. So I moved back to New York. Shortly thereafter I got my job at Lambda [Legal Defense and Education Fund]. I've been there for the past six years. It's worked out really well. It's this job that's not about writing at all, so I don't feel that it interferes with my life as a writer.

Writing in The Advocate *a few years ago, Larry Kramer asked, "Why has there been no great gay novel? . . . Where's our Dostoyevsky . . . , our Trollope or Tolstoy . . . , our Dickens or Chekhov?"*[3] *What's your response to that?*

---

3. Larry Kramer, "Gay Men Writing?" *Advocate,* 22 February 1994, 80.

I don't quite get the part A and part B. I don't think there are any great American writers writing on the scale of Dostoyevsky or Tolstoy now, whatever their sexuality is. The world has been around for a long time and will continue to be around for a long time, and great artists come. It's kind of weird how they get bunched up together sometimes. I think art forms evolve. Maybe the novel hit its peak at the end of the nineteenth century. That's a sad thing to think as a person writing novels: that maybe I'm doing something at the end of its arc. But maybe there's another big arc coming up. In a way it's an interesting question, but it's a difficult question because there's nothing anyone can do about it. Are you going to force somebody at gunpoint to go write the great gay novel?

You also write short stories. Are there things you can say in novels that you can't say in short stories, and vice versa?

I haven't written very many stories in the last five or six years, since I started writing *The Weekend*. I wonder about that because I wrote so many stories when I started out as a writer, and I'm not quite sure why I've stopped writing stories. I wish I were writing more stories because I really like writing stories. I think it forces you—gives you the opportunity, I guess—to be pithy and concentrated. And starting out as a poet and liking poetry, I think of the short story as being closer to poetry, although I always try to think of language to the same extent whenever I'm writing. But I like the succinctness that goes with a good short story—boiling your ideas down into something hard and elegant and hopefully beautiful. Whereas in a novel, I think you can be more discursive and therefore more complicated. I guess right now my ideas are not far more complicated. I feel like I'm fumbling more, trying to figure things out, and so a novel's kind of a better canvas to try to work out more complicated ideas.

I would love to be writing a lot of stories right now, but in writing a novel like that you get an idea and then you have it for two years. You don't have to wake up every couple of months and be back at square one. I don't have an idea for a novel now, but it's kind of nice when you're working on a novel. You wake up every day and you know there is this world, there is this book I can work on. I don't have to think of it. For me the hardest part, and the part that's beyond my control, is thinking, getting the idea.

Elegance and beauty very much characterize your prose. Do you ever feel that in aspiring toward elegance and beauty you lose something? Is there something that, because of that gorgeous texture, is lost?

Yeah, I'm sure that there is. Whether it's something that I'm interested in having, I think at this point I'm not, because obviously if I were I'd be doing something different. I'd be writing more immediately, I guess. In my stories the prose is simpler, it's not as lyrical. It's not about language; it's more straightforward. For some reason—I don't know if I got bored with that—but as I started reading more and admiring denser prose, I began wanting to try to do that. But I also feel that you can only go so far in that direction.

In *Andorra* I knew I wanted to write a book where the language called attention to itself in a certain way, and that's a dangerous thing to do because it can call *too* much attention to itself and the reader can recoil. I didn't want that to happen. There's a really fine line between exquisite prose and precious prose. I often feel like I'm treading that line. But to do *Andorra*, I felt I had to create this character who was writing the book. I had to invent a narrator who would make sense that he was writing a certain way. If it was just this regular narrator, I don't think you would buy it. It would be a little hard to take. But because it was somebody who, because of the specifics of his life, was intoxicating himself with the language, I felt it gave me the liberty to go pretty far towards that edge.

I'm curious about where I'm going to go next, because I'm not sure where I'm going to go on that spectrum.

Who's your ideal reader?

I don't have an ideal reader. In the way that I think writers are really varied, I think readers are varied. I like the idea that different people read my book. Like some people read my book and don't pick up on the religious, spiritual struggle at all. It doesn't mean anything to them. Actually, several people have read this book in an incredibly literal way, and thought that he went to Andorra. It just never occurs to them that it's not the real world, that he's making it up. They think he was arrested in France and he's in jail. It's not the book that I think I wrote, but it's the book that they read. If they liked it and it worked, that's fine.

There's this program in New York, *Selected Shorts*, where actors and actresses read short stories on the radio. They read one of my stories. It was very unnerving to hear somebody else read the story, because I thought she read it all wrong. I thought all her inflections were wrong. And then I just realized, Well, every time somebody reads my work, they read it differently, which isn't wrong. I have no control over that. I can't stand over the shoulder of every person reading my book and say, "No."

I want to ask you a question that was asked of Edmund White in the Paris Review *interviews. When you're writing, do you look more towards innovation or towards tradition?*[4]

I think I lean more towards tradition. What I seem to be reading is a lot more secondhand books, old books, rather than new books. I feel like I'm trying to write in this tradition but make it about today and what it's like to be alive at this point in time. I'm very intrigued by the conventions of the novel and by the history of the novel. Originally I thought I wanted to write this experimental novel, but obviously that's *not* what I wanted, or what I was good at doing. I thought that it was going to be ambitious and exciting, and it's not. I just wanted to write this novel. I wasn't interested in innovating.

Do you think that material finds you?

Yeah, because I don't think *I* find *it*. I've realized that when I'm not writing, I'm not writing for a reason and I shouldn't be writing. For a long time when I wasn't writing I thought, Oh, you're a writer; you should be writing every day. It's good discipline. But for me that's not the case. When I'm not writing, then I shouldn't be writing and I have to take it on faith that I will start writing again at some point. This is part of my process, you know. This not-writing part is as much a part of the process as the writing part. Not a very fun part.

When you are writing, what are your writing habits like?

I don't feel that I'm this great disciplined writer. It's because when I'm writing, the actual hours that I sit down writing—that physical activity of

---

4. Edmund White, "The Art of Fiction 105," interview by Jordan Elgrably, *Paris Review* 30, no. 108 (Fall 1988), 73.

writing—is a couple hours a day, because I have my other job. It's also this thing I'm consumed by at some conscious and subconscious level. In the last two years, while *Andorra* was happening in my head, I was there. I was thinking about that fifty percent of the time, I think. So in some ways the writing is always there. For me a lot of the writing process gets worked out in my head. Getting it down on the page is almost like taking dictation. It just has to be in my head before I can write it. I feel like I don't spend a lot of time actually sitting down writing. But in ten years I have written these three novels, so I guess I am finding the time I need to write.

I don't have a lot of patience with people who say, "Oh, I'd love to be a writer but I just don't have the time." I think if you do have something to write and you want to write it, you do find the time, whether that means getting up two hours earlier or not going to bed. There are twenty-four hours in the day and if you want to write a novel you find time to write a novel. Because you're compelled to do it, because that's what you want to be doing.

My job at Lambda, I work twelve to five-thirty every day, so I have my mornings. I write really well in the mornings. That's actually the best time for me to write. I'm not able to write more than a couple of hours. I can't sit there all day and write. There was one year, when I was writing *Leap Year,* serially for a magazine called *Seven Days,* where I was writing a chapter a week. I did have another job—that's all I was doing—and I got really lonely and depressed. And I realized that I didn't want to be a full-time writer. I couldn't occupy myself as a full-time writer. Writing wasn't the only thing I wanted to be doing.

Tell me about your work for the Lambda Legal Defense and Education Fund.

I'm the assistant to Kevin Cathcart, who's the executive director. So it's an administrative job. I've been there six years. I like the job for a lot of reasons. I like the people I work with and what I do there.

I also like—and this is a selfish thing—but sometimes I feel that as a gay man, my writing should be political or socially conscious in a way, but for some reason I'm not interested in making my writing be like that. For a while I went through this crisis where I thought, Oh, your writing is really decadent, that being personal equals being decadent; the last thing the world needs is another personal novel. Then I realized that that wasn't really true, that novels I really liked are novels that are in some way or another novels that are highly personal. And that there's a lot of room for a lot of different kinds of novels, and a lot of different kinds of writers.

I like my job at Lambda, because even though the work I do there isn't really advocacy work, I feel that I'm contributing to something that I believe in that's helping to change the world in a good way. So that's my little bit and lets me indulge myself in my work.

What is it about New York that is so appealing to you, and to writers in general?

When I was a teenager, I got really interested in the theater and loved the theater, and I still love the theater. I grew up in this town, Pompton Plains, where, as far as I knew, there were no gay people. I'm sure there were some, but I didn't know who they were. And I went to New York and there seemed to be some gay people there. And then I went to Hamilton College and it was just a *bad* time to be there. It was a very closeted community there, and so I wasn't able to come out at college. I think I wanted to go someplace where I knew I could come out. I was ready to. When I moved [to New York], I moved there thinking, This is where I want to be now. I wasn't sure I wanted to stay there. But I have really good friends there, I have a job there I like a lot, I like where I live—I find it really stimulating.

I know a lot of people who live in New York as if they're living in a city that doesn't have what New York has to offer, but I'm really interested in taking advantage of what New York has to offer. I go to the ballet a lot. It's weird because my community there is not a community of writers. I'm not part of any publishing social world. That's not why I'm there. It's not what I get out of it. I know that world is there, too, but I'm not really interested in being a part of that world.

What advice would you give to young, aspiring gay and lesbian writers?

The thing that's helped me most as a writer is reading. I've educated myself tremendously with every book I read. I can't read enough. And going back to the question—Are you looking backwards or forwards?—I like that books are objects that stay in the world that you can discover later. Books stay around. I think it's really good to read a lot of books by certain authors, to find an author and get obsessed with them. I feel that you don't find your style until you understand other people's style. I forget who said that bad poets imitate, good poets steal. I do feel that you have to be very brazen. It's not about stealing, but it's about admiring, and being enthusiastic about your admiration and letting that influence you, giving into that.

Who's your big reading passion right now?

Denton Welsh. He is never taught. I don't know how I came across him, really. I think he's a beautiful writer. His writing is so attuned to the physical, sensual world in a way that's just startling. It's just alive in this way that you don't expect from writing of the twenties and thirties. He was an invalid and lived with intolerable pain and died when he was thirty-three; so there are these weird correspondences with young gay men now dying from AIDS. He had this incredible spirit, where he was in pain so much of the time, but he kept on writing and painting and trying to create and trying to live this beautiful life through these awful sicknesses. I've read his journals.

I like getting lost in one author. Like Barbara Pym. She does what she does so perfectly and so wonderfully. It's a very small, parochial little world that she's writing about, but she wrote about it with insight and humor.

Scott Heim

With the 1995 publication of *Mysterious Skin*, Scott Heim emerged as one of his generation's most gifted writers. Critics raved about his debut novel, calling it "as searing and unforgettable as an electric shock";[1] "wrenching . . . poetic . . . powerfully sensuous."[2] "Heim is breathtakingly unafraid to take chances," said the *San Francisco Chronicle*, "and the fact that he doesn't self-destruct in the process is one of the reasons he can rightly be called a promising author."[3]

In 1997, Heim published his second novel, *In Awe*. Like its predecessor, *In Awe* is set in Kansas. It is the story of three outcasts: thirty-two-year-old Sarah, a clerk in a convenience store, who has been branded the town slut; Boris, a gay teenager; and Harriet, the mother of Sarah's best friend, Marshall, a young man who has recently succumbed to AIDS. This motley trio bands together against the brutal bigotry of a group of redneck high school students in their small Kansas town, unleashing a chain of violent events that propels all three characters toward the novel's harrowing and disturbingly beautiful denouement.

Born and raised in a small farming community in central Kansas, Heim studied English at the University of Kansas at Lawrence, and fiction writing at Columbia University. In addition to his two novels, he has published a book of poetry and, at the time of our interview, was working on a third novel and a collection of stories. Heim's work has also appeared in several journals, among them the *Village Voice, Interview,* and the *Advocate.* Currently he lives in New York.

The interview, conducted via the internet, took place on 1 June 1997, shortly before Heim set off on a nine-city book tour to promote *In Awe.*

---

1. Review of Scott Heim's *Mysterious Skin, Kirkus Reviews,* 1 January 1995, n.p.

2. Christopher Lehman-Haupt, "Young Characters Trying to Fill a Gap," *New York Times,* 6 April 1995, C 21.

3. David Weigand, "Two Boys Haunted By Terrible Secrets," *San Francisco Chronicle,* 6 April 1995, E 5.

Were you ever terrorized or gay-bashed in high school the way Boris in your novel is?

Not really. In high school I was sort of the "weirdo" but it was more because I was a punk rocker. The scene with Boris in the library happened to someone else, though—another outcast at my school, a kid I used to ransack houses with. I always knew I had to use that scene of the words written on his body somewhere.

What have you retained from your days in a farming community? What values from that period in your life have stuck with you?

I don't know if any values have stuck with me, but certainly everything I write, or almost everything, comes from that experience. I feel it's always what's going to set me apart from other writers, in a way—the fact that I grew up in Kansas, and know that area geographically and culturally. In some ways I'm embarrassed by my small-town, "white-trash" roots, and in others I'm very happy and satisfied I went through all that. Certain things that happened to me—like the "turtle killing" scene in the first book, for instance, couldn't have happened to me anywhere else.

Do you think embarrassment is key to the formation of a writer? Is writing a way of confronting embarrassment?

You know, I've never thought of it that way, but I think that's a very, very intriguing way of looking at it. In some ways, I write about the things I've always been shocked by, or embarrassed by, things from my past or things that have happened to other people that obsess me and then become exaggerated or warped into my fiction. What I can't necessarily talk about, or admit to, show up somehow in my writing. So yes, I think writing is a way of exorcising demons, or confronting things that embarrass or disturb or rattle me.

You write—in both Boys Like Us *and the novel—about being "slammed" by your discovery of pornography. Is that one of the things that has shocked you into writing?*

Yes. Growing up, I was somewhat shadowed, or oppressed, by both my surroundings—the conservative small towns of the Midwest—and also, admittedly, my parents, who hardly spoke to one another, and never really mentioned sex, et cetera, to my sister and me. Both pornography and things like violent horror films and *True Detective* magazine—things that exhibited a kind of subversive, terrible, sleazy underworld, a dark side of the squeaky-clean, "good" Kansas—were always what attracted me. I'm actually just writing an essay about this now, for an anthology that Houghton [Mifflin] is doing. It's about growing up in the Midwest environment and having this weird longing for something, some kidnapping or murder, to happen—even to the point of longing for it to happen to me, just so I could somehow be the "star" of it all.[4] I'm not sure if this makes sense, really . . . it's sort of a reverse Dennis Cooper in a way—instead of having fantasies of killing some boy, I went through my teenage years half wanting some freak to kidnap and torture me.

What's the difference between someone who turns toward the sleazy underworld, the dark underside, and someone who turns away from it? Why does one person look on that with fascination and another with horror? Do you think that for you growing up in a "squeaky clean" place had something to do with it?

I'm not entirely certain. I think there's an element of fascination in almost everyone when they see a car crash, for instance, or a news report about a serial murderer, or a scene in a horror film. I have people say, "Oh I don't want to see that," or, "I don't want to read about that," and then give the reasoning, "I live in New York already, why would I want to see more horror and violence?" But that seems to me very silly. For me, if there's something disturbing to me, I guess I want to explore it further. I can't rightly explain why. Maybe it does have to do with the way I was brought up.

When did you start to write?

I started writing horror stories, strangely enough, for my friends when I was maybe ten or eleven. I remember the first thing I wrote was this ridiculous story about dolls who come to life and murder a little girl. In high school I discovered the confessional poets and started writing these furious, but quite horrid, poems. But they became more and more narrative and by the time I was in college I started turning to fiction more often.

---

4. Heim's essay, entitled "3 CC CP," appeared in *Personals: Dreams and Nightmares from the Lives of Twenty Young Writers,* ed. Thomas Beller (Boston: Houghton Mifflin, 1998), 190–200.

Who were your early influences?

I think I've always been most attracted to writers who practice a sort of high gothic, often maximalist style—Flannery O'Connor will always be my all-time favorite—and I also really loved D. H. Lawrence when I started. When I was nineteen, I think, I read Dennis Cooper's *Closer,* and Kathy Acker's *Blood And Guts in High School,* and I was never the same again. For the first time I felt like someone was writing for me. This made me want to succeed as a writer and most importantly made me realize it's what I wanted to do.

Desire is a big theme in your novels. I'm wondering about the line that divides passionate desire from violence. Eroticism from pathological desire? Is it a line that's always clear?

Well, to bring up D. H. Lawrence again, I think that's a line he consistently explored. It's almost as if, in many of his works, violence is a means to an end—so much passionate desire inevitably leads to destruction in some way. I think that's the case with *In Awe,* but what I really wanted to ask with that aspect of the book was, If taken far enough, how chaotic and uncontrollable can it get? And if you really desire something strongly enough, so strongly that it completely controls you, how far will you go to have it? That's very much what the end of the book is about. I feel like, so far, with interviews and stuff I've had to, um, *defend* the ending in some cases—and also my agent told me this week that three foreign publishers have turned it down because of the ending itself. It makes me wonder, on one hand, is the ending the right one? But when I wrote it, for me it was the only way I could end it; the entire novel from the beginning was sort of hurtling toward that conclusion. I wanted to see how far I could go, or more accurately how far the characters would go, in this "over the line of desire" situation. Not just with Boris, but with Sarah and Harriet as well.

Is that an aesthetic question you ask yourself as well—How far can I take it (the prose, the language, the themes)—before it gets out of control? One thing I love about your prose is how "risky" it is.

Wow, thanks. For me, I wanted to have the prose in this book mirror the content—like you said, in the way of taking it as far as possible. I hope that the content of the book is "maximalist" in the way that I hope the prose is, as well. Who knows, maybe the next book will be very quiet and understated. But for this one, I wanted to pile it on.

I think I know what you mean by "maximalist," but could you define it anyway?

I see it as a formal, highly descriptive prose style, using the language almost to the point of abuse, using your eyes and ears and nose and tongue to come as close to a synaesthetic prose experience as possible. The opposite of Raymond Carver. For me, it's very much about involving the reader so much that he or she forgets the world around them. It's how I feel when I read Cormac McCarthy or Jayne Anne Phillips.

Two questions: How do you make aesthetic decisions about when "piling it on" is too much? And how has writing poetry affected your prose style?

Poetry has definitely affected my prose. I feel like description is one of my strong points, no matter what the review in *Out* magazine said.[5] Sorry to get snooty there. And about "piling it on," I guess I usually don't have a threshold; so far in my writing I've pretty much consistently gone as far as I can. Maybe some people will see that as a problem rather than a faculty, I don't know. Still, it's the way I write, I guess, something that might set me apart.

Do you think we are leaving the age of the minimalist aesthetic?

I hope we are leaving the minimal behind. I think subtlety and minimalism are two different things, and I'm all for subtlety, and I personally wish there were tons more of that in, say, film or art. But in writing, and I say this from experiences in college writing programs, I think oftentimes minimalism is just an excuse for laziness. I think a lot of people can't, or don't want to, describe things, or get deeply, deeply into a character's head, so they take the easy way out.

Back to violence: To what extent do you see violence lurking underneath everyone's behavior?

I'm not certain *how* to answer it, but I will say that your question is precisely the area I'm most interested when I write fiction. I'm completely

---

5. Heim is referring to a brief review in the June 1997 issue of *Out* magazine, in which the reviewer wrote "Heim doesn't fare so well in the description department." See Michael Klein, review of Scott Heim's *In Awe, Out*, June 1977, 79.

obsessed with, say, the "innocent schoolgirl" who commits a crime, the "bookish librarian" who murders her husband, the nerdy type who then kills a series of young men and sleeps with their corpses and mutilates them. I don't know why people do that, but I want to examine the possible reasons as best as I can.

Christopher Lehmann-Haupt, in the New York Times, *said that you seem to like to inhabit the "mysterious skin of the anti-heroic."[6] What, for you, is heroic? Who, if any, are your heroes?*

This answer sounds almost like something a Miss America contestant would say in hopes of getting extra points from the judges, but I have to say that I find heroism in people who try their hardest to do their best, who are empathetic, who help others as much as possible. These are qualities I'm not so good at myself, so when I see them in others I'm very moved. That sounds so silly, but from living in New York City for six years, it's such a surprise to witness any form of humanity.

In your latest novel, there's this line: "Something like a soul inside Boris breaks free." What's your definition of soul?

This is the hardest question yet! Well, for me, that line sort of echoes a line in *Mysterious Skin*, toward the end, when one of the characters imagines two souls lifting hand-in-hand above the house . . . it's a way of putting something wholly intangible and mysterious into words. I can't envision a soul, and although I'm not really a religious person I think I can be quite spiritual, and maybe this is how it manifests, in lines like these. I think there are moments of extreme beauty or emotion—epiphanies, I guess I'll call them— where we are acutely aware of "something like a soul" inside our bodies. Both those moments from both those books are times where the characters become aware of the "soul" inside them, something unexplainable.

Sarah's epiphany toward the end of the novel is something like a coming-to-terms with the end of her fantasy of being a movie star—the eighties are gone, she says. What did the eighties mean for you?

The eighties for me, looking back anyway, was a time of total freedom. At the time, I'm certain I thought I really had it rough—I was a fucked-up

---

6. Lehman-Haupt, "Young Characters," C 21.

teenager with the best of them—but it was so perfect, just my friends and me, listening to all this great music, driving around in the middle of nowhere in our rattletrap cars, singing along. Days before having to pay off student loans, days before knowing anyone with AIDS, that wonderful time. Sarah, for me, is just as much a part of me as Boris—she's more my age, after all—and I think *In Awe* is possibly even more "her" book than Boris's. She is essentially the one who sets things in motion, after all.

Do you see her epiphany as a spiritual awakening—leaving behind the fantasies? How does one keep invigorating one's life with new fantasy, new sense of mystery and wonder and excitement?

Well, I think it would be unrealistic to think that in this one moment she'll completely come to her senses and leave it all behind, but I think it's through the death of Rex that she can fully assess her silly fantasy life and also the death of Marshall. I suppose she, and anyone really, will always create new fantasies, but Sarah is almost dangerous in hers because at thirty-two she's so strongly enmeshed in them. She's obsessed with horror films and fake blood, but only through real horror and real blood can she come to the truth, so to speak.

What are you working habits like?

They're pretty terrible. When I'm involved in a novel, I try to write every day, although it doesn't always work that way. I have no set time schedule, that's for sure. As I'm coming to a novel's close, however, I get very feverish about it all . . . hours and hours at a time, in front of the computer.

Two of the three major characters in In Awe *are female, and you write from their point of view. Do you find that easy to do?*

Yes and no. I try to take the elements about my own character that are female—my "feminine side," to sound very nineties—and inflate them as much as I can. I'd like to say as a gay man I can perhaps do it better than straight men, but I don't think that's necessarily the case. I like the challenge, however.

Boris refers to Rex as "half hyena, half swan." In what way do you think every love object is half hyena and half swan?

No one is ever as perfect as they seem at first. Everyone I've ever thought as perfect "swan" has then turned out to be weird or clumsy or imperfect in some way. But that's what attracts me most, I guess—I'm always trying to find the weird imperfection that will elevate someone from great to sublime.

Once in the bus station I watched this beautiful, almost perfect boy for like an hour—my friend and I just stared at him—and then he did this incredible thing where he picked a scab off his neck and ate it. My friend was completely mortified but I was totally floored. It was like that moment had elevated him for me. I think that Boris is very much like myself in this—he's looking for the things in Rex that only he will know about, as if this will allow him to "own" the one he loves.

The romantic poets were interested in the distinction between the beautiful and the sublime. How would you make the distinction?

I think my last answer and silly story is sort of an illustration of how I feel about this . . . beautiful is a great thing, but perhaps easily seen or touched—I mean, you can see beautiful any summer day on your walk down to the grocery store—but *sublime* is something set apart from the beautiful, something that's completely idiosyncratic or personalized, something that's made yours through a single gesture or feature. Like a perfect face with a pimple on it, like a missing tooth inside a terrific smile. Something like that.

In your essay about your first sexual experience in Patrick Merla's anthology, Boys Like Us, you recollect a lyric from Adam and the Ants: something about being beautiful, being fearless. Where does fearlessness or courage show up in your life?

I'm not certain really. I think maybe, who knows, this could go back to the stuff I write about. I hope that I'm courageous in what I tackle in my fiction, but I don't know. That's as good an answer as I can make.

You have been named as one of thirty artists under thirty "among the most likely to change culture for the next thirty years." What's it like to live and work with that label?

That was very flattering, but I think it's something that might haunt me. I'm not so certain how a literary writer in this day and age can change the culture, so I guess I've chosen to just ignore it and instead write about whatever interests me.

Do you worry about being labeled a wunderkind?

No, I suppose I like that. In all honesty, it's been a bit difficult with the second novel, though—maybe it's paranoia but I sometimes feel that people are out to get me. I don't want to be one of those people who writes a first novel, and sees a certain amount of success or acknowledgment, and then completely disappears.

Do you think literary writing is valued today, or has even literature just become a commodity? Will a novelist meteor to notoriety for a season and then fade?

It's so sad. I know so many people who are great literary writers who can't land their books. Hardly anyone reads, and when they do they want the instant gratification, the plot-driven [John] Grisham sort of books. That's fine, sure, but I wish a bigger market existed for literary fiction, too. It's sad, but literature is just what you said it is, a kind of commodity.

Do you think there is a way to change that cultural landscape? Will it take an Oprah Winfrey to get people to pay attention to literary fiction?

Yes. I don't want to sound too fatalistic. It's great what Oprah is doing. Now Rosie [O'Donnell] should jump on the bandwagon, and Howard Stern, etc., etc. The New York Yankees should be photographed in their dugouts reading literature. It will be anarchy! But yes, I think there's hope.

I want to ask you a question that Boris wants to ask Rex: What is your greatest wish?

Stardom! But more honestly, happiness and health and financial security. Maybe a little stardom would lead to these things.

Stars actually figure prominently in your novel—real stars, movie stars, and the Kansas state motto. Want to say something about star imagery in the novel?

I haven't thought about that one. I have always wanted to be famous, though . . . maybe it's just something that subconsciously entered. But also as with real stars, the ones in the sky, there's something so mysterious and romantic about them—I love using images that carry this sort of mythical, entrancing meaning and mood. Now I'm starting to ramble.

Your book tour includes a stop in Lawrence, Kansas, where you did graduate work. What will it be like to return to Lawrence?

Great, I hope. I still have a sister and good friends there, and my mentor, a writer named Carolyn Doty, teaches and lives there. They'll throw me a party. I'm excited about that.

Last question: You once had dinner with William Burroughs in Lawrence, Kansas. What was that like?

Somewhat bizarre. He was very friendly and lucid and sweet. But he's such an icon in some ways, so recognizable to so many people . . . and there he was, beside me, eating his striped bass. I have photographs of me beside him on the couch, his arm around me. It was like being hugged by Christ in some ways.

Bernard Cooper

Astonishment is at the heart of Bernard Cooper's work. His first collection of essays, *Maps to Anywhere* (1990); his novel, *A Year of Rhymes* (1993); and his later essay collection, *Truth Serum* (1996), with its more narrative, memoir-like style, are all about astonishment—at the beauty and quirkiness of the world, at the "accident" of sex, at the particularity of oneself and the inscrutable privacy of others.

Cooper is passionately devoted to language. As a child, he says, he fell in love with words, a love affair that he has continually reinvigorated during his writing career. His work has been included in *Prize Stories 1995: The O. Henry Awards* and *The Best American Essays 1995*. *Maps to Anywhere* won a PEN/Hemingway Award.

An instructor of English and American literature at the Otis/Parsons Institute of Art and Design in Los Angeles, Cooper is currently working on a collection of short stories.

Of the twenty-one writers in this collection, Cooper is the only one I have never met. The following conversation, conducted via the internet, took place on 27 December 1997. A few days afterwards, I sent Cooper a transcription so that he could look it over for any changes he wanted to make. "This is the interview I am most proud of!" he wrote back. "I've made a few small changes. What a delight to actually like an interview."

When did you start to write?

Not until I left Cal Arts, Walt Disney's school of avant-garde art. I'd always been an avid reader of poetry, and sometimes composed texts for works of conceptual art, but not until after I graduated with an M.F.A. did I start to write seriously.

Were you first interested in becoming an artist?

First an architect. Then a painter, then a conceptual artist. But this process of steady "dematerialization," if you will, culminated with an interest in poetry and prose. I've always been drawn to the visual arts, and hope my concern with the image, with the visual element of narrative, is evident in my work.

In Maps to Anywhere *you write about the "passion for nomenclature." Was that passion for naming, for getting down the world on paper and in words the primary impetus behind your becoming a writer?*

Yes. First, words seemed like the most immediate and sensuous way to conjure images, events, memories; I was drawn to language as a conceptual artist. Another factor has to do with being raised in a family hushed about its history and emotions; words were an antidote to silence, and the otherwise nameless emotions and sensations that I wanted to identify, to reify, as a child. Experience seems hopelessly amorphous and chaotic to me until it is fixed in words.

You mentioned your long-standing love of poetry. Many of the pieces in Maps *could be called prose poems. The narrative element seems to take a backseat to the sheer love of language and wordplay. Did those pieces grow directly out of your love for poetry? What poets have influenced your work?*

Edward Field was one of the first poets I read whose work was openly queer, accessible, and humorous. The prosaic nature of his work, its narrative drive, appealed to me greatly. Then Anthony Hecht's long narrative poems, Sylvia Plath's intoxicating, musical, urgent language. I love reading C. K. Williams and Billy Collins—two very different poets—these days. Mark Doty, too. Oh, and Kay Ryan.

When did you first try your hand at prose pieces?

My early efforts at prose arose from a frustration with the exigencies of poetry, particularly scansion and free-verse line breaks. Once I wasn't concerned about the shape, the compression—necessary for a poem—the expansive impulse took over and I wanted to reach with prose, so to speak, follow where it led me. In absolute frustration with my future as a writer, I sat down one day and wrote about my mother telling me, I swear, that she swam to America from Russia. When she was two! And so writing about this, in prose, was tantamount to trying to discover, to explain to myself, what might have motivated her to tell me such a preposterous fib. At that point writing, and the discovery of my subject, were commensurate. Prose was an adventure, a trail to follow.

Do you write, as someone said, in order to discover what it is you want to say?

Wasn't it Didion? "I write in order to discover what I think." Or, in the words of Flannery O'Connor, "I'm like the little old lady who doesn't know what she's going to say until she says it." That spontaneity is for me the joy of the work. I'd hate to know too much a priori about a piece of prose I was writing. Of course, this is also a risky way to proceed, since you might discover nothing and—gulp—make a big irreparable mess.

Let's pursue a little longer your idea that experience is hopelessly amorphous and chaotic until you write about it. In A Year of Rhymes, *Burt says that "'the world was a place of shelter or harm, tricks or treats, I wasn't sure which.'" Which is it for you now?*

Always both; shelter and harm, hopelessness and delight go hand in hand. Sometimes I become quite conscious of my trying to temper one tonal extreme with its opposite in my writing. Everything I write seems, on one level, about an attempt to achieve balance. My temperament is very much that way; the trivial sometimes seems to bear a sinister under-current, and tragedy seems laughable after a while.

"'Can anything protect you?'" asks a character in Rhymes; *and the mother echoes by asking, "'Where's a safe place?'" Is writing your safe place?*

Well, in a manner of speaking, writing is a safe place, though I'm fully aware that the safety is an illusion. In other words, writing is a way to make chaos shapely and to momentarily fix the transient. On the page, that is. I bristle at the New-Agey notion of writing in particular or art in general as being "healing." I mean, sure, it feels good to try to make order out of tumult, but there you are when you look up from the page, right back in the big fat uncontrollable world, where art cannot be said to save a life or put a dent in misery. Still, I love art for its sheer uselessness as well as for the hope that it can do some good, can change a few people's per-ceptions. Peter Handke wrote *A Sorrow Beyond Dreams* about his mother's death, and the whole last part—so moving—is about how no amount of prose could alleviate his grief.

Your novel is based on your brother's death from leukemia. I'm not sure what I want to ask about that because the novel is a piece of fiction and I want to re-

spect that, but it's hard not to think of the biographical events that must have informed that novel. Did writing that put a dent in your grief?

Actually, I grew up with three brothers, all of whom died of various diseases. Suffice it to say, that's a heap of grief to put a dent into. In some ways, writing has given me the luxury of finding in the unbearable experience of loss a few images, turns of phrase, dramatic moments that are meaningful to me and possibly to others. There is something that is plain good about being able to salvage from loss something of value—an insight, a group of words that defines the undefinable—but I'll be dealing with the deaths of my brothers, and the deaths of friends from AIDS for the rest of my life. This is not meant to preclude the possibility of joy or love or meaning, but just to say that I'm aware of art's limits as well as its powers of transcendence.

In Maps to Anywhere, *you write, "Around the time of my brother's illness I began to take an interest in art, perhaps in the hope that it could lead to immortality." Is the impetus to write also—in addition to making order out of chaos—an impetus toward some sort of permanence, leaving behind an artifact that will live on, "fixing" our lives like a developer fixes an image on paper?*

Art does hold the promise of immortality, though it may not deliver. I'm sure my having to constantly deal with the fragility of life, as a boy and now, has made me want to thwart death by making something lasting. Let's hope it lasts!

Do you ever, as one character does in a new, as yet unpublished story of yours, feel guilty that you can "mine words from even the worst circumstances"?

Not guilty, exactly. For me, verbal imagination is a refuge, and sometimes I can postpone panic and grief and even boredom with the inner acrobatics of composing sentences. Raymond Carver wrote a hilarious but grim poem about how his dog died and he couldn't wait to get his first wife and kids out of the room so he could write about it. There's something slightly mercenary about being a writer that is necessary for me, some drive to ruthlessly steal from any available experience. On a more dignified note, I suppose one can see it as that salvaging I spoke of earlier. What a pleasure to think that experience, with all its haze and tribulation, can be put to use!

What does it mean to you to be hailed as a "prose stylist"?

All I can say is that the sheer mind-boggling difficulty of writing makes me skeptical when I've been "hailed." But at least all that hard work—rereading a page fifty times, trying dozens of words to find the best one, going to sleep relentlessly reciting a paragraph—is appreciated by a few people. And I do love the alchemy of language, the way it can stretch or refresh the ordinary, which is just the kind of effect I want my work to have. And I'm partial to stylists—Nabokov, [Allan] Gurganus, Dennis Johnson, Deborah Eisenberg—so it is a gratifying brand of praise.

To what extent are you aware that you—and most literary writers—are appreciated by few people? How does it affect what you do?

Wow, that's a difficult issue for me. I mean, I'd like a formidable reputation, a vast audience—who wouldn't?—but on the other hand, I thrive, have always thrived, in a medium of solitude and relative anonymity. I may have romanticized the isolation, but part of me is quite content to do what I do, and let the idea that the work is being read, or discussed, or reviewed, remain somewhat abstract. I've made art constantly since I was little, and I don't mind seeing myself as a nutty inventor secreted away in his garage. I'm often torn between the desire for recognition and the wonderful aloneness that has characterized my most passionate hours as a writer. Most of what has thrilled me, career-wise, has been unexpected, unforeseen, and when I've set out with even moderate expectations for notoriety and praise, I've paid with disappointment.

To what extent do you see yourself involved in a lifetime project, creating, as it were, Le Livre—which you describe in Maps to Anywhere *as "the voluminous book into which all experience settles as beautiful language"?*

It's fitting because in some intuitive way, no matter how my work may change direction, I feel as if I'm trying to tell one boundless story whose content is always unfolding, whose flavor I can only hope to capture, whose parameters I can't clearly see. It's not my story exactly, but rather a singular continuum of human experience, a narrative that is vital because it is singular. I'm afraid that's pretty abstract, but I think what I mean is that what I will have left behind, for better or worse is a single trail, an individual record, and ultimately, however, many books I write will be a single utterance. Yikes, stop me before I get any loftier!

For you, memory is a kind of map. What's it a map to?

The Polish writer Bruno Schulz said, "Memories are filaments around which our sense of the world has crystallized." The resuscitation of memory feels to me like going back to some wellspring of experience. Memory is impure and fallible of course, but when you revisit the past, armed with language, you have the privilege of expressing what was confusing, inexpressible. In the best circumstances you can revive primary experience with exacting language, but also allow it to retain its pull, its mystery, its wonder. In some ways I'd feel successful as an artist if I could offer the reader the world anew, and the way for me to do that has often been to go back to a time when the world *was* new.

What are you writing habits like?

My recipe for success. Morning: massive doses of coffee, stuff grains into mouth, march downstairs. Do not pass go, do not read the cereal box, talk to other Homo sapiens, or make phone calls. A good day: one pretty-cooked page. A great day: two pretty-cooked pages. A typical day: editing several pages for the twentieth time, and two new paragraphs. Night: watch TV so as not to worry about two new paragraphs. Read as much as possible before sleep. Repeat the above till you are middle-aged.

In the acknowledgements at the beginning of A Year of Rhymes, *you mention the "alternate Tuesday nighters." Is that a writing group you belong to? Do you show your work in progress to people?*

I belonged to a group for several years in its many incarnations. I must show work to people; there are just too many words, threads, nuances to keep track of. Now I have a handful of friends I show stuff in progress to. It's trying. I'm often amazed at how much slips past me, how much revision something takes. No matter how hard I bear down on a story or an essay, it could probably be fussed with forever. But I believe most writers cultivate a group of trusted critiques for early drafts.

Wasn't it Oscar Wilde who said a piece of art is never finished, only abandoned?

I think so. An artist named Edward Keinsholz used to deface his work in order to get it out of his own hands and move on.

Do you rely on serendipity—the random firing of synapses (to borrow from your essay "Labyrinthine") to trigger your memories, or do you have specific techniques to access certain memories?

I have no techniques, period. Except, as I mentioned, caffeine and blind faith. In its nascent stages, writing is something that happens *to* me; in other words, I allow associations to take me where they will. Often, of course, I'll try to steer, cut back, nudge here or there. But initially, the process seems to involve an abdication of control, followed by the great rigors of revision.

In A Year of Rhymes, *Marion says, "'It takes years of work and concentration to find a style and make your mark. You've got to steep in the chaos of your thoughts.'" Does "steeping in the the chaos of your thoughts" describe your writing process?*

Why, *exactly*. Sometimes I turn off the computer and blink, mole-like, trying to remember who and where I am. That abandon, paradoxically, takes a kind of practice. But there are sublime moments I feel nearly selfless in the creative act. It's odd, because essays especially are about an authorial voice, about *self*, yet my best seem to spring out of an act in which I'm virtually selfless—not an intruder, but a witness who is all eyes and perception.

In your piece "Make it Good" from Maps, *you write, "The right exaggeration is a wondrous thing." To what extent do you embroider, exaggerate, even lie—as your mother did about swimming the Atlantic—in your memoirs?*

I'm way out of the closet about lying. My students gasp when I recommend it for their nonfiction, as I often and brazenly do. But art is about artifice, and all manner of modification—manipulation—must go on in order to be in service of the truth, in order to convey it as compellingly as possible. Personal essays especially often arise out of subjective experience. There are dangers, of course, and though lying or exaggerating is permissible to get at the truth, one must not be so clumsy or flagrant that a reader will pull back because the spell is broken. One especially must not lie about him-/herself or others in order to be vindictive or make oneself more heroic. But if putting a hat on an uncle who didn't wear hats makes him more stately and avuncular, I say, Go for it. With short stories, of course, I'm lying through my teeth, and part of the thrill, as well as the unease, comes from the fact that I'm making it all up.

Did writing a novel between your two books of memoirs alter the way you conceived of and wrote that second book of memoirs? Truth Serum, *your second book of memoirs, seems more narrative, more storylike to me.*

A Year of Rhymes was like cobbling together a sustained narrative composed of vignettes (the filament Schulz spoke of). So yes, I think I gained a great admiration for the narrative drive. I'm an avid reader of short fiction, and my reading fiction rather than poetry influenced the gradual move toward longer narratives, work based on sequence more than imagery, so to speak. Also, I think it behooves the memoirist to use the fiction writer's devices—dialogue, character, etc.—in order to make what is remembered vivid and convincing. The individual memoirs in *Truth Serum* are more narrative and storylike, though the overall structure is less strictly novelistic, more like significant and scattered points in a chronology which, I hope, resonate in a somewhat unusual and unpredictable way.

In A Year of Rhymes, *the young, nascently gay narrator, Burt, talks about "the thrill, the horror, of being in the body." Is the thrill and horror of being in the body more acute for gay men than others?*

Well, it certainly was for me. First of all, I've never quite understood the rules and restrictions of gender, being an ambiguous little boy and all. So my sense of my maleness, and my difference from females, was never something clearly demarcated in my mind, never something I automatically assumed. Also, I was aware, like most gay men, from a very early age, that nothing could dampen my desire for men. My body had a renegade will of its own, and I was just along for the ride. I can't imagine what it would be like to grow up having the yearnings of your body confirmed by the world. My body was the source of the greatest pleasure and, simultaneously, the greatest betrayal, since its urges were unacceptable and, if known, would seal my fate as a pariah. In part, my hyperawareness of physicality was exacerbated by my brothers' successive illnesses. Not to mention the Jewish art of kvetching about every ache and pain. Oy! I understood the body was joy and anguish, life and the end of life. Boys who seemed at home in their bodies might as well have been another species. I was always questioning the bodily longings that pleased and terrified me, whereas other boys seemed to inhabit their bodies with a blessed certainty.

Truth Serum, your third book, seems the "gayest" to me, in the sense that homosexuality comes to the forefront of the subject matter. Is there a reason why it took you until your third book to directly tackle, in a major way, the gay stuff?

I just think I was ready, that I'd accumulated enough sexual experience, and perspective, to believe I had something to say about it. For a long time, sex just didn't seem like interesting subject matter; I was interested in finding a place in my work for all the objects around me—barber poles, swimming pools, kitchen clocks—like the pop artists, my favorite moment in art history. When I did try to write about sex, with the urging of John Preston, I found it was fascinating, especially awkward sex, that resonated with missed libidinal signals and sad misunderstandings. It suddenly seemed to me, in other words, that there was a way to write about any number of ironies and human frailties *through* sex. Writing about sex as sex usually bores me, like writing about chewing food instead of tasting it. Finally, I came out in my mid-twenties, and it took that long to feel comfortable about it. Now of course, I can't stop. Writing about it, that is.

You mentioned John Preston. And Gurganus and Edward Field. What other gay writers have inspired, influenced you? Especially about writing about sexuality?

Michael Cunningham. David Sedaris is a riot. Your stories in *The Language We Use Up Here*, stories in which sex is so rooted in the characters' lives and wants. I must say, however, that I've learned a lot about writing about sex from writers who are not necessarily queer, or even known as people who deal with sex. Alice Munro, for example, who can write about a single kiss that is ruinous and cruel, more shocking than so much "transgressive" erotic writing.

In writing about your brother's death, were you at all thinking of the untimely death of so many young gay men? Is A Year of Rhymes *in any way a deflected AIDS novel?*

Not deflected exactly, since nothing can deflect Ol' Dr. Death. Oblique perhaps. But one thing that has distinguished my experience of AIDS is that it's part of a continuum of grief I've experienced since elementary school. True, I used my experience of AIDS to inform my novel, but no more than I used my long history of loss to inform it. In an odd way, I think the novel was a way to talk about living with the threat of death, rather than the fact, and that has been my sense of the world for as long as I can remember till now, unfortunately. The book is about a moment in a boy's life when both sex and death are imminent but not quite present.

Michael Lowenthal caused a huge flap this summer when he published a piece in the Boston Phoenix *that essentially said that most gay writing was second-rate and that it only gets published because publishers have created a niche market for it. You want to take a stab at that one?*

Well, my point of reference is the visual arts, and I think it's safe to say that, in all the arts, at any given moment, there's a lot of bad stuff. One just hopes they are not adding to it. As far as queer work specifically, I think that many people are understandably hungry, some might say starved, for a reflection of our own experiences, and this means some writers offer that sense of audience identification. In some cases, the merit of the work begins and ends there. In some cases not. I'm not at all upset by Mr. Lowenthal's remark. Of course, he included me in a list of good writers, so I'm obviously biased. But Nabokov said that a sense of identification with a writer's content is the lowest form of understanding, because a good writer can make you identify with experiences entirely remote from your own. As a gay writer, I hope my work sparks engagement from various quarters, and as glad as I am when homosexuals like my work, I love it when heterosexuals can connect. No writer can control who responds, or how, but it seems reasonable to want to make art great enough to stir people beyond their sense of relating to the content, to touch their sense of music, and offer a glimpse into human nature that is particular to, but not limited to, a certain strain of experience.

You write so eloquently and richly and movingly about being part of a "sero-different couple." How has your relationship with Brian affected your writing life?

I'm nuts about the guy and we have sex on tap, so to speak, so I've been able to really focus on my work in the place in the world we make together. My love life is a done deal, and that has freed me up for the arduous task writing is for me. Writing about him was so hard. Writing about his health, which is always changing, was like trying to shoot a moving target. I felt such a burden of responsibility to represent him fairly, to show him as the spirited man I think he is but not to aggrandize or gloss over his suffering, to retain our privacy but bring to light the endurance of love and eroticism in the face of all obstacles. My life with him has been a miracle, yet I don't mean this boastfully; I am surprised and heartened, and can't really explain why I have this in my life, it's a form of grace, in the Catholic sense.

What's it like to be a writer in Los Angeles where, as you humorously depict in your short story "English as a Second Language," people care as much about rain on their suede as about the poetry of Auden?

Here's the kicker: Los Angeles is absolutely thriving with incredible art and writing at this point. Reading series abound, galleries and museums are springing up like weeds. And I have the luxury of being in the thick of it when I choose, or allowing the anonymity of L.A. to harbor me. I love that about this city: you can get as much culture as you can stand! Life is awfully surreal here, but in a slightly arid and existential way that I love.

What have you discovered in reusing material from your memoir pieces (like your brother's death) in your fiction? Are there transformations that occur? Are there things you can say in fiction that you can't say in memoir, and vice versa?

In *A Year Of Rhymes,* I added fictional characters, like the buoyant and skewed Marion, to see how they would effect a somewhat grim and inextricable situation. There's a level of "play" in the novel that was not in the nonfiction, where I felt more compelled to honor what had actually happened. Right now, I'm writing stories in third person, and about things that have not, for the most part, happened to me. I love the freedom of it, the fabrication of things from whole cloth—a real departure from auto-biographical writing. Through characters—a pregnant girl, for instance—I can talk about the burdens of physicality in a whole new way than I could in the novel or *Truth Serum.* Third person has opened up a new aesthetic terrain for me, just as writing directly about sex had. In the obliqueness of speaking through characters, I find that all sorts of my grievances and affections and proclivities are expressed, and even emotions that are in no way my own. I am still writing memoir, specifically a book about attending the country's most avant-garde art school, but I'm refreshed by using third person. But boy, stories are hard.

We're living in an age when hot best-sellers are being put out by very young writers: Leavitt fifteen years ago, Scott Heim and others now. You didn't publish your first book until you were almost forty. What sustained you through the years when you didn't have a book out?

Actually, I published *Maps To Anywhere* in my thirties. But wanting to be a writer took me by surprise, and since being a visual artist required, I knew, a long apprenticeship, I figured the same would be true for writing. It wasn't easy, especially since my classmates went on with the course they had set in graduate school, and there I was, changing horses midstream. By the time you're in your mid-thirties, though, it's too late to be a young hot item like my friend Scott Heim, so I suppose it wasn't worth getting upset about. I just wanted to do work that amazed, that exceeded my expectations. Of course, I would have sold my mother for a few accolades, but I've learned that no matter to what extent you're praised, there's still that very large, very blank page.

Do you see yourself as part of the confraternity of Jewish writers—the straight ones like Bellow, Roth, Ozick, and/or the gay ones like Raphael, Leavitt, Glickman, and Lowenthal?

Roth was an influence. Jewishness is more central to Lev Raphael's work than mine. I should be half as talented as Bellow (read in Jewish inflection). What I mean to say is that I'm probably more aware of subtle ethnic differences in our work rather than similarities. I do think that the collision of humor/suffering in the Jewish sensibility has really colored my outlook, and therefore my prose.

What does the term "gay writer" mean to you?

A gay writer is a writer who has sex with other men. This may or may not be central to his work. He may write with or without a quill, may want to overturn the known universe or simply pass the time. Probably, he looks at the world from some odd and unique angle, and has had to endure doubt and ridicule, which may make his voice singular and his sensibility worthwhile.

What was it like to be photographed by Robert Giard?

Photographs steal the soul. I try to avoid it. Unlike my lover, who licks his lips and straightens his posture within fifty feet of a camera. Giard was awfully nice, and the experience couldn't have been less self-conscious for me. Unlike another photographer who, when I opened the door, before he even said hello, looked at my receding hairline and asked, "Do you own a hat?" After I talked him out of the hat, he laughed this psychotic, shrill giggle before pressing the shutter. He meant to make me laugh.

How has teaching affected your writing? Do you like to teach? What do you teach?

Teaching has made me look deeply into a few texts I love and has required that I discern and articulate what precisely it is about them that ignites my awe and esteem. I've also seen a lot of folly when it comes to young people who care more about publishing and celebrity that the quality of their work. Teaching can be exhilarating as well as draining; it is a reason to take a shower and get out of my writing room once in a while. I need to do it because otherwise, I'd starve. When it goes really well, it's close to inspiration in the rush of blood and clear ideas.

What advice do you have for young gay writers?

Read everything. If you're not feeling envy toward great writers, something is wrong. It will take a long time. You must give to it your every excellence. Find another writer or two who can help you through the hard work and inevitable periods of self-doubt. Revise till you feel you need a straitjacket; then you are done. You are never done.

Michael Lowenthal

The youngest writer represented in this collection, Michael Lowenthal, was born on 9 May 1969, "just less than two months before the Stonewall riots and the man on the moon," he says. As a member of that generation of writers who grew up with a full-blown post-Stonewall gay literary heritage at their disposal, Lowenthal is emerging as an intelligent, articulate, and increasingly authoritative voice in the ongoing conversation about what constitutes gay literature and gay culture. A novelist, short story writer, essayist, editor, anthologist, and coordinator of a popular gay and lesbian reading series in Boston, he is a kind of jack-of-all-gay-literary-trades. Among his many projects, he has edited a collection of essays, *Gay Men at the Millennium*, which, in the manner of a salon, brings together a wide spectrum of ideas and perspectives.

In the introduction to *Millennium*, Lowenthal writes, "It is unclear to me, as we close in on the year 2000, whether we are speeding toward the hoped-for period in which justice will triumph, or if the backlash will be stronger and steal our ground." He goes on to note that, in fact, "there may be no such thing as *the* 'gay community.'" Lowenthal thus represents the growing number of gay writers who are embracing a sense of the plurality and diversity possible within the phenomenon we have chosen to call "gay literature." In this respect, he stands for the spirit of this book of interviews, too.

Lowenthal's work has appeared in more than fifteen anthologies, including *Best American Gay Fiction 1996, Men on Men 5, Wrestling with the Angel,* and *Friends and Lovers.* When John Preston became too sick to continue working, Lowenthal took over editing the *Flesh and the Word* series, and edited Preston's final book, *Winter's Light.*

The following conversation took place on 19 January 1998, some months before the publication of Lowenthal's debut novel, *The Same Embrace.*

Let's start with some warm-up questions: stuff like how old are you, where were you born, raised, et cetera?

I was born—significantly, I guess, in terms of my later sexual life—a month or so before the Stonewall Riots in 1969. I was born in Washington, D.C. but when I was six weeks old my family moved to Peru, where we lived till I was three. So I learned English and Spanish together, and according to my mother, was proficient in neither.

When did you start writing?

Like most people, I wrote swoony, self-important love poetry in high school, and was dumb enough to publish some of it in the high school literary journal. It was full of self-torture and all that. I was also editor-in-chief of my high school newspaper. I guess I started writing more seriously in college, where I took a couple of creative writing courses.

Who were the objects of your love poetry in high school?

Mostly the sublime soccer stars I could never get my hands on, but also, occasionally, my girlfriends. It's funny, now that I think of it—so many of my recent essays and stories are *still* about those untouchable boys.

What did you major in in college?

I did a double major in English/creative writing and comparative religion. But in truth, I didn't finish either of them—I fell one course short in each—because I spent my last year on a great program Dartmouth has called the Senior Fellowship, given to about ten students each year. You work on an independent project and don't have to take any courses or finish a major.

What was your independent project?

I wrote a novel about a verging-on-autistic backwoods Vermont farmer whose father, just before the old man dies, orders a Guatemalan mail-order bride for the kid. Then just watch the cow patties fly!

You watched the cow patties fly or your autistic farmer did?

The farmer, I guess. He really doesn't know what to make of the woman. So the story is all about how they learn to live with each other.

Jacob, the protagonist of your novel, The Same Embrace, *at one point describes himself as "'congenitally, terminally unhip.'" Does that in anyway describe you during those years in college?*

Well, like most characterizations in a novel, it's a little exaggerated. At least I hope so. But yes, that kind of describes me in college, and probably more so now. I'm always lagging about six-and-a-half steps behind the beat.

Was the cow-patty novel a way for you to circumvent gay material—I mean, a way for a gay man to write about "not knowing what to make of a woman"?

Well, yes and no. I was out of the closet by the time I wrote that project, and a very in-your-face activist on campus, so it's not like I was trying to "circumvent" gayness. I just had the idea for that story, combining this obsession I had with mail-order brides with my obsession for rural Vermont, and so I wrote it.

On the other hand, it seems awfully clear in retrospect that, yes, the story was about difficult love between societal outsiders, which certainly seems like a stand-in for gay issues. As politically active as I was at the time, I had read basically zero gay-themed literature, and so I didn't have any real sense that I could write a gay story. I only did that after I graduated from college.

As someone who came late to writing—late to the idea that I could possibly even presume to be a writer—I'm interested to know what it felt like to be twenty and embarking on, and finishing, a first novel. I'm thinking about Tony Kushner's idea that art involves enormous pretensions. What did it take to muster that kind of pretensions?

To be honest, I felt like such a fraud taking on that project that I could barely talk about it with anyone. I mean, I had only written four or five short stories before I tried that. But I guess going to an Ivy League school, you get well trained in a certain kind of confidence and presumptuousness. I proposed my project to the committee—having written only a three-page outline—because I hated taking classes and needed to do something, *anything*, to keep from dropping out of college.

You helped to found Dartmouth's first gay newspaper, right?

Dartmouth is a really conservative, isolated school, and so the small number of gay people there were kind of radicalized and banded together. So I helped some friends start a queer newspaper called *In Your Face*, with political articles and op-eds and poetry. This was in 1989 or so, right when ACT UP was huge and Queer Nation was about to start, so it was all part of that campus mood.

What effect do you think writing journalism has had on your writing career, style, et cetera?

I've never thought of myself as a journalist. I think it's an art form of its own, and to be good at it, I'd have to study it and imitate good journalists and all that, and I've never put in the effort. I guess I've published a fair amount of what would be considered journalism, but frankly, I don't think I'm very good at it. I write journalism that's too prosy or something.

Okay, but I'm thinking that your prose is very clear. The sentences feel so tightly locked into place, like each paragraph is this neat little puzzle. Does that clarity and conciseness come from journalism?

No, I think it comes more from rejection. Every time I sent out a piece of writing and it got turned down, I would go through it line by line, and cut it some more. Then I'd send it out to another place, and when it got rejected again, I went through the same process. After a while, there was kind of nowhere else for the words to go. Do you know what I mean? And by now, I do a lot of that process on my own, before anybody has a chance to reject me.

The best writing workshop I've ever had was writing a mini-essay for the back page of the *New York Times Magazine,* where the strict word limit is nine hundred words. I discovered the word-count feature on my computer, and so as I was working, I was constantly counting how many words. I wrote a two-thousand-word essay, then cut it to fifteen hundred, then to one thousand, word by word by word, seeing where I could cut every "and" and "but," till I finally got it to nine hundred. Then I sent it to some folks to critique it, and they told me all the elements I had to add, so I wrote three hundred new words, then cut three hundred more.

When I was revising *The Same Embrace,* I did the same thing. I gave myself strict limits, and ended up cutting one hundred pages from the first draft.

To get back to that point you were making about feeling like you are always "lagging six steps behind the beat," do you feel that writing is your way to "catch up," to hear the beat more clearly, to figure out what the beat is? Are you attracted to writing as a way to compensate for that feeling of lagging behind?

Well, writing fiction seems like the artistic endeavor that requires the least "hipness" or cultural acumen, because there's always a delay. It takes months or years to write a book, then more months or years to publish it, so even if you did have your finger on the pulse, you'd miss it by the time your book came out. So in a way, that seems like nice insurance for a dolt like me.

I also think that writing is a place where oddballness is largely forgiven. You can be a kind of hermetic weirdo making your little commentaries on the world, and people tolerate or even respect that, whereas if you did that in normal life, people would laugh at you and throw snowballs. Since writing happens at home, in privacy, you can be a schlump with all the wrong clothes and the wrong hair, listening to the wrong music, and it doesn't matter. So maybe writing for me is like "revenge of the nerds."

In The Same Embrace, *a friend says to the protagonist, Jacob, "'I'm trying to figure out what parts of you are just your genes, and what parts are, you know, really you.'" To what extent do you think a writer can choose to become a writer, and to what extent is he thrown to writing by innate talent, genetic makeup, et cetera?*

I don't much believe in innate writing talent. But I do think that certain genetic predispositions—say, for a kind of obsessive-compulsive behavior—can tilt you toward the writing life. And I also know that in my case, it's something I've always just kind of assumed was right for me. When I was in the second grade and we had to write what we would do when we grew up, I answered that I would play left field for the Boston Red Sox during the summer, and in the winter, be a writer. I was too much of a klutz to play ball, so I extended the writing part to full-time.

In the introduction that you wrote to John Preston's Winter's Light, *you quote him as saying that "'it is necessary to write about our lives in order to save them.'" How does that motto apply to you and your work?*

Well, this will probably sound pretentious and self-involved, but I've determined that the only time I'm sane is when I'm writing regularly. So I guess writing is the way to save myself emotionally. But the line would probably apply better for me, personally, if it said, "It is necessary to write about our lives in order to understand them."

In your novel, you include some very powerful and risky sexual situations. I'm thinking, for example, of the S and M circumcision scene between Jacob, who is a Jew, and a German; and Jacob's decision not to use a condom when he fucks; and even, I guess, the fact that Jacob's boyfriend, Danny, is only seventeen. Did any considerations about sexual self-censorship go into the drafting of your novel, or any other fiction you've written?

I try never to "censor" myself when I'm writing, but I did think to myself pretty explicitly when I was writing the novel that I wanted it to be something my mother could comfortably read. She's a huge supporter of mine, but has read less than half of my published work, by mutual agreement, because I've written some weird sexual stuff. So I conceived of a story— or thought I did—that doesn't hinge on explicit sex. In a four-hundred-plus-page manuscript, there are only three sex scenes. But now that you point it out, they are a little bit "out there." I guess I just can't help myself. My hope is that the mood of the story, and the scope, will allow people like my mother to accept the sex without freaking out.

Do you think that that kind of self-censorship—Could my mother comfortably read this?—has in any way compromised your writing?

No, if anything, I think it really sharpened my writing. In the same way as the word-count parameters I mentioned before, I think working against limits can really enhance one's work. It's a great project, for example, to try and write a really sexy scene in which you don't mention any sexual act, or describe any sexual organs, or use the usual words. This can lead to a much, much hotter piece of writing than something full of thrusts and groans.

I should also say that I never wrote something and then thought, Oh crap, Mom will have a cow, and deleted it. I'm talking more about an underlying conception of a project than a scene-by-scene kind of vetting.

Jacob's aunt Ingrid tells him at one point, "'Always speak in a voice that can be listened to.'" Have there been any situations when you're writing—I'm thinking still primarily of fiction—where you would have liked to raise the volume, so to speak, to say things that might not be immediately listened to by an audience of moms?

Absolutely, and so I *did* raise the volume, and that's why my mom, and millions of others, haven't read those stories. But for me, in fiction, the story always dictates the voice, so I don't feel I have a lot of leeway.

What was the hardest scene, sexual or otherwise, to write in your novel?

For me, writing is always, always hard, simply on a logistical, one-word-after-the-other level. So the scenes got harder and harder as I got closer to the end, and I felt the weight of all the previous scenes bearing down. I felt like I started off juggling three balls, and then with each chapter, I added another ball. By the end, I was like a crazed clown, trying to keep dozens of balls in the air.

Emotionally, one of the hardest scenes was the Passover seder, where so many of the family tensions come to a head. I had to make it intense for an extended period, while trying to avoid melodrama. It's a tough line to walk.

Speaking of complications, I thought one of the most amazing parts of the novel was the story of Josef, the protagonist's lost gay uncle. But I can also hear some critics saying that here you go, a gay man, "trumping" the Holocaust story with a story of a gay son being ousted from his Jewish family during the Nazi occupation. Did that potential criticism come to mind?

Yes, but I tried not to think about it, because the whole idea of "competing oppressions" is so distasteful and counterproductive. What I hope is that, instead of seeing the hurts and wrongs as being in competition with one another, I've helped people to see the similarities—the fact that all kinds of rejection and hatred are disastrous.

I also wondered if people might say, "How could you write about the Holocaust, since you didn't go through it?" But if we start limiting fiction writers to experiences they've personally endured, literature's going to get awfully tedious.

Besides the obvious comparison with the Biblical story of Jacob and Esau, your novel—about rival Jewish brothers, one gay and one straight; one religious, one not—also reminded me of Christopher Isherwood's somewhat neglected novel, A Meeting by the River, *about two rival brothers, one gay, one straight; one religious, one not. Did you have Isherwood in mind as you wrote your novel?*

I didn't. I'm embarrassed to admit that I hadn't heard of that novel until I was finished writing my own. And though I now have a borrowed copy on my shelf, I still haven't had a chance to read it. I will soon, though, because it sounds right up my alley.

What writers have influenced you?

Again, I feel a little bit dense, because I haven't read widely enough or deeply enough to feel I have consistent "influences." My education was very, very spotty. I read almost exclusively contemporary American writers.

One way to answer your question, though, would be to list the writers whose next book I will automatically read. Among them are: Bernard Cooper, Tim O'Brien, A. M. Homes, Michael Cunningham, Annie Proulx, Ethan Canin, David Long, Robert Olmstead, Grace Paley. Of course, my list of favorite writers is much longer, and always growing.

What about the earlier generation of gay writers—I'm thinking of the Violet Quill gang—Holleran, White, Picano, Ferro, et cetera? When you first tried your hand at gay material, had you read them? Were they at all influential?

No, I hadn't read them when I started writing, and to be totally honest, with the exception of one or two books, I still haven't. Even though I'm quite friendly with some of them. I've never had the guts to admit that to them in person.

Unlike me, you are of that generation of gay writers who, in fact, came into your reading life with hundreds of choices of gay books to read. I'm not sure what I want to ask here, but just perhaps for you to comment on that.

It's a huge generational divide, I find more and more. For me and my peers, it just can't be assumed that we've read *Dancer from the Dance* or *Faggots* or *A Boy's Own Story* or Vidal or Isherwood or whoever. That kind of "core curriculum" carries less weight. In a way it saddens me, because the commonality is diminished. On the other hand, of course, it's a sign of great political and literary progress. After a necessary period of "gay literature" being a very specific and limited thing, it's now branching out to encompass all sorts of new possibilities.

What was the first "gay book" you read?

For years I thought it was *Eighty-Sixed*, by David Feinberg, which I read when it came out, during my senior year of college. But recently I realized that the book I read a hundred times in high school—and bought used copies of to give to the boys on whom I had secret crushes—was very much a gay book. It was *The Zoo Story*, by Edward Albee.

I wonder if that by now common idea that the early generation of gay books was "limited"—I wonder if that idea hasn't been over exaggerated. I think, for instance, that Dancer *will go down as one of the great gay books of all time. Sometimes, the early works from a particular literary movement—Shakespeare for English drama, Wordsworth and Keats for romantic poetry—are the greatest. Any thoughts?*

You're absolutely right. And I didn't mean at all to imply that the early works were limited *artistically.* I only meant that what qualified as a "gay novel" seemed more clearly delineated in the late seventies and early eighties. Some of that work is fascinating, because it was really the first time in history that a contingent of gay people were writing novels with gay audiences in mind—no apologizing, no explaining.

In what ways do you see your work and the work of your fellow contemporary gay writers as a departure from the work, themes, aesthetics of the Violet Quill pack?

Well, one major point of departure might be my resistance—shared, I think, by lots of younger gay writers I know—to the idea that our work as "gay writers" necessarily even has, or should have, any connection. For example, is my work really part of any kind of "movement" with Dale Peck or Travers Scott or other thirty-and-under gay writers? I'm not convinced.

But if I were to pick out a kind of general shift, I would point to the idea that many of the Violet Quill generation's books were about leaving home, leaving the family, establishing a gay identity, often in an urban gay ghetto, that had primacy over everything else in life. Now a lot of younger gay writers are writing about finding ways to incorporate a gay identity and gay life with one's home life and family roots. Gayness isn't the be-all and end-all so much anymore.

In "Everything Possible," your essay in Friends and Lovers, *you describe your first trip to the Castro in San Francisco and how it was there "for the first time I felt gay not in theory but in practice." What has been the importance of gay communities for you and especially your sense of yourself as a writer?*

Like a lot of gay people I know, when I first came out, I thought the gay community was the answer to all my problems: Finally, a group I would fit into, and that would accept me! But then I realized, of course, that the gay community is an in-group like any other, and that my same aversion to joining and "group-think" would apply here as well. So after a period of deep immersion, I've been slowly but steadily extracting myself.

I will say, though, that the "small pond" of the gay writing world gave me some of the confidence to try writing seriously. Because the chances of success—of getting something published—were so much greater in the gay world, I felt I had a shot at it, and I went for it. In the long run, I'm not sure it was the best thing for my self-conception as a writer. It really limited me in some ways. But without it, I may never even have tried.

Where do you find the locus of "family" in your life now?

I tend to get hives whenever the concept of "family" comes up, which must mean it's of some importance to me. My actual family is important to me; they've been very supportive, and best of all, I like most of them. What I really get obsessed with is the family past, so in a way, when I think of "family," I'm thinking of people who are dead now, or who I never even knew. My friends are also incredibly important to me, but I don't need the crutch of calling them "family."

There's a wonderful image in your novel. A rabbi puts his hands on Jacob's head and Jacob says that afterwards he could "'still feel the pressure of the fingertips on [his] skull.'" To what extent do you still feel the "fingertips" of Judaism on the skull of your life and work?

To use a slightly different metaphor, for me Judaism is like being in a room with a ceiling that's too low, so you keep thinking you're about to bump your head. I never actually do bump my head—in the sense that I never believe in the religious doctrines or alter my behavior because of them—but the feeling that I *might* makes me skittish.

For example, I eat plenty of nonkosher food, but I always, always do it with an awareness that I'm eating *treyf.* And when I go to synagogue—once a year at most—I mostly go to hear the sounds and smell the smells. It's almost like a drug trip that loosens up my creative memory. But no one was more surprised than I when I started writing about Jewish topics. I fought it for a good while before I realized it was a big cookie jar full of material.

What about Judaism—religion in general—as the wellspring of happiness? Toward the end of the novel, Jonathan, Jacob's twin brother, says, "'Unhappi-

ness dismisses [God's] blessings. It's like saying the world He created isn't good enough.'" Do you retain any of that sense of the triumphalism of God's splendor in your own outlook?

I love that notion, which is why I included it in the book. But for me, the idea of God is so completely alien that I really can't relate to the statement on a literal level. Even on a metaphorical level, I have a hard time relating, because the world seems so inherently unsplendid and unhappy in so many countless ways. To be unhappy to me seems realistic, whereas happiness often seems escapist and irresponsible.

Why—other than because it's part of your background and provides great "color"—do you think you're letting the Jewish stuff into your work?

I think Judaism—like all religions, but in some unique ways, too—embodies a key theme that I seem to focus on, namely, How do we live as individuals who are always yearning to connect, but who fundamentally can't? Writing about love and sex and relationships is an obvious way to explore this theme, but so is religion: connecting with God, or some higher power. And in the specific case of Judaism, there's this attempt to connect with all Jews past and present, to imagine yourself escaping from Pharoah's Egypt, or riding a cattle car to Auschwitz. This is nonsense on one level, but it holds a tremendous power, too. I think the notion of Jews holding together their culture throughout the diaspora is heartbreaking. For what? For what? For what? Well, for *everything*, but what does that mean?

To quote once more from the novel: "Conformity terrified Jacob, but also beckoned him." How does the push-pull between conformity and nonconformity manifest itself in your work?

I've never held much truck with nonconformity for its own sake. And in artistic terms, I often have difficulty with the avant-garde, "new narrative," experimental writing, or what have you. So in some ways I'm a conformist writer. I want to write in a way that everyone can relate to. At the same time, I want to be unique. So I obsess over ways to say my own thing, in my own way, within the context of normalcy. I swear, sometimes I will spend an hour trying to find a new way to say, "He walked across the room." And the sad thing is, I only know that my effort has paid off if nobody ends up noticing it.

Your work is full of children and young people. I'm thinking of stories like "De-livery," and "The Acuteness of Desire," and of course the flashback chapters in your novel. You have observed children very well and render them perfectly on paper. How exactly do you think about your own keen attention to children and young people?

I love kids for the same reasons everyone does, I suppose: their freshness and openness. In something I'm working on now, I just wrote about kids that "their love is so urgent and unencumbered; they haven't yet learned the shame of asking for it."

I worry that my recurrent interest in kids and writing about them will sour into a clichéd kind of nostalgia. But writers have always written about childhood and always will. An interesting goal, I think, is to write about children but in a "grown-up" way. I'm not exactly sure what that means, but I'm working on it.

How do you square your involvement in what some might call less "literary" projects, like your editorship of a series of books of gay male erotica, Flesh and the Word, *with your more literary pursuits?*

On one level, I don't "square" them. I do the *Flesh and the Word* books because I stumbled into the job and it pays relatively well, which allows me to write my more "serious" fiction. And now that I have a literary novel published, I hope to let the other stuff fall away. But I try never to do anything half-assed, and so I've worked really hard to make the *Flesh and the Word* books as interesting and serious a literary experiment as possible. I've tried to prompt people to write work that tests the boundaries of the "erotic"—which is really more a marketing category than anything—and I've called upon talented literary writers like Jim Grimsley and Brian Bouldrey and Robert Glück. So in a way, I've taken what could have been a crass "money job" and tried to conform it to my own literary standards. I have no idea how well, if at all, I've succeeded.

Has your working in the "erotica" business affected your more serious literary work? Has it informed it? Opened it up? Changed it in any way?

I don't think it's affected my own personal writing, because I just write what I write, and how I write, no matter what. Where it gets published doesn't have much to do with the words that come out. So my "erotic" work has been filled with death and sickness and sexual frustration, whereas my "literary" work—like the novel, or my story published in the *Kenyon Review*—has some intense sex scenes. The only time I tried to sit down and write a specifically "erotic" story for an anthology, it was a failure, and I'm very embarrassed by that story.

Flesh and the Word 4 was a book of memoirs rather than an anthology of fiction. That was your call as editor. Does the current rage for memoir threaten to crowd out good fiction? Are memoirs more "reader friendly," easier to take in, than complex literary fiction?

I chose to limit *Flesh and the Word* to memoirs as a way of enacting the shift I was talking about earlier, toward serious literary merit. I wanted to break the cycle of dumb stroke stories and push writers to a deeper level of honesty. But that was very specific to the erotic field. In larger terms, writers are often much more honest when they're making things up. So I'm sure that after this momentary blip on the screen, people will go back to writing novels and stories. I'm not worried at all. Also, I have to say that I love memoirs, too, and some of the best books I've read in the last few years have been memoirs. Memoirs aren't inherently easier to read. They can be as easy or complex as novels—which range from boilerplate to brilliant.

It's been a little over half a year since you caused a stir within the gay writing community by publishing an essay in the Boston Phoenix *in which you said that it took "virtually zero talent to make it in gay literature, where competence is scorned as politically incorrect." Care to elaborate now?*

First, I should say that I wrote that piece in a pretty pointedly inflammatory style, hoping to provoke some discussion of topics that I thought were being ignored or suppressed. So my rhetoric was a little strong, perhaps. What I was arguing against, in that sentence you quoted, was the notion that a novel is good or valuable simply because it tells a gay story, or toes some identity-politics line. At one point in history, that might have been true. It was important simply for readers to be able to pick up a book and read about a gay character. But now it seems obvious that we're way, way past that rudimentary requirement. And so I'm more interested in evaluating books on *literary* terms: Are the characters believable? Is the prose well crafted? Are the emotions honest? This hardly seems radical to me, but many people in the gay literary community seem to resist it, because if some books are deemed good, then others must obviously be less good, and that doesn't mesh very well with a political movement that's about equality for all. I think they need to learn the difference between politics and literature.

Do literary ghettos have any justification? What about Yiddish theater in the thirties, for example?

I don't know if "justification" is an appropriate or important way to look at it. Literary ghettos arise for various social, artistic, and political reasons, and then they usually disappear. It's just the nature of the beast. These things go in cycles, and they're not good or bad, necessarily, but we shouldn't cling to them when their time has past. In the case of Yiddish theater, there are other factors involved, like the potential death of an actual language. Gay people don't have that problem.

In that article, you say that certain gay and lesbian writers, by virtue of the fact that they have also published books that focus on heterosexual characters, have thereby refused to be pigeonholed, "an indication of their maturity and artistic integrity." But what about the gay writer who—like many black writers, or Jewish writers—focuses almost exclusively on material from his primary milieu? Couldn't he be deemed to have an artistically important and wide-ranging career? What about, for example, a writer like Jane Austen, who wrote about a very narrow world, but through it examined a wide range of the human comedy?

Absolutely! Or Philip Roth, who writes almost exclusively about Jews, or Toni Morrison who writes about African Americans, or Joyce and the Irish. It's the writer's greatest challenge to write about the specific and make it universal. What I was saying in the article, though, was that gay writers shouldn't be limited to writing *only* about gay characters or themes if they don't want to. I've so often heard gay writers criticized for writing nongay books, as if they are betraying "the cause." People accuse them of selling out and just trying to get more mainstream recognition or money. And so I was saying that those gay writers I know of who've written non-gay-themed works have not done it for those reasons. They've done it because they are confident and mature enough to write about a story that compels them, even if their "own people" aren't involved. I wasn't criticizing people who *do* write only about gay themes; I was defending those who *don't*.

Okay, but isn't it something like homophobia that allows Toni Morrison and Philip Roth to have their "exclusive" say but not, well, Andrew Holleran?

I suppose it may be. Holleran gets reviewed in the *New York Times*, but straight people seem not to buy his books in mass quantities. What's keeping them from it? Homophobia, or homo-uninterest, seems a culprit. But I also think we should explore the question of what exactly it is that straight people aren't interested in. They seem to have an appetite for *some* books with gay characters and themes, which indicates to me that gayness, per se, isn't a huge hurdle anymore. Could a truly homophobic reading public have put David Sedaris and E. Lynn Harris on the bestseller list this year? And what about *Midnight in the Garden of Good and Evil*, which has now been on the *New York Times* list longer than any other book in history? Why will "the public" read some gay books, and not others? I want to work on finding the answer to that, rather than jerking our knees and shouting "homophobia!"

Well, my off-the-cuff guess is that, in part, what accounts for some gay books not becoming crossover best-sellers has less to do with the quality of writing than with sex phobia—that the books you mentioned don't present certain aspects of gay life, especially sex, in particularly graphic ways. To use your mother again, those authors—Sedaris, [John] Berendt, and others—wouldn't have to worry that they would offend your mother. But, yes, I agree with you that just screaming "homophobia" doesn't get us anywhere closer to understanding what's really going on.

I think it's not sex phobia in general, but *gay* sex phobia. Because straight books with explicit sex fly off the shelves.

Do you think your Phoenix *piece opened up the conversation about all this or just served to entrench people more deeply into their already formed opinions?*

I hope the former, but I fear the latter. Mostly, people either seemed to agree with me so much that they almost wondered why I had to articulate it, or to disagree so vehemently with parts of the argument that they dismissed all of it. But I'm encouraged by the increasing numbers of people who are looking at "gay literature" in much more open-ended terms.

What does the term "gay literature" mean to you?

To paraphrase the Supreme Court justice on pornography, I can't define it, but I know it when I see it. Truly, I'm not sure it means much at all to me in real terms, especially now that there's no "core curriculum," as we discussed earlier. Like "erotic writing," I think "gay literature" is a marketing category more than anything, with some benefits and some serious drawbacks, too.

What about the term "gay writer"? Any different response there?

How about this: A gay writer is someone who's gay, and who writes, and who doesn't work to separate those two elements of his life. I think you can be a gay writer without writing about specifically gay topics or characters, but not if you're closeted or consciously exclude the gay part of your nature.

Jacob asks his grandmother why she has a mole on her chin and she tells him "'To remind me that I must always reconcile with my blemishes.'" What writerly blemishes do you feel you need to be reconciled with?

Ouch. Do you mean, what are the weak spots in my writing?

No, not necessarily, but what things in your writing do you recoil from that you suspect you don't need to recoil from, or would like to learn not to recoil from?

My biggest fear about my own writing is slipping into sentimentality or bathos or melodrama or nostalgia—all of which I think I lean dangerously close to. I *agonized* over the fact that my novel could be said to have a happy ending, or at least an ending that points to the possibility of happiness, because I have this notion that to be serious, art has to be bleak and heartbreaking. But I also think that my writing succeeds best when it drives that cliff edge right next to sentimentality and all that stuff. In order to get my best material, I have to go there and risk toppling off.

You once beautifully described John Preston as the literary equivalent of Miles Davis. To what jazz musician or other musician would you compare yourself?

Well, I wrote that line about Preston with full knowledge that it probably applies to me as well. I'm not the most technically gifted or inventive. I guess I'd also like to compare myself to Pete Seeger, one of my absolute heroes, who was once described as sounding "as though he had corn husks stuffed down his throat," but who, through utmost sincerity, managed to be a unique and compelling voice.

Another hero of mine is Bela Fleck, who plays wicked improvisational jazz on the banjo. I love that wacky combination of elements, and I'd like to try that too: writing about gay sex after a funeral, or about sex in a yeshiva, or about "edgy" material in a very conventional narrative form, or whatever.

Speaking of sex in a yeshiva, I'm reminded of Lev Raphael's title Dancing on Tisha B'Av. *Has he been an influence at all?*

I wouldn't say he was an influence. I read his collection of stories years ago, and admire him a great deal for opening up the possibilities of writing about gayness in observant Jewish settings. But stylistically and philosophically, I think we come at things from different angles. Lev is actually an observant Jew himself, and that's very important to him. I write more from an outsider perspective, I think.

You're in a relationship with fellow writer Scott Heim. He lives in New York; you live in Boston. I'm wondering why you've chosen Boston as your town. Doesn't it make more sense, not only from a relational perspective but also from the perspective of your career as a writer, to live in New York? What's Boston's attraction for you?

I'd like to keep the relationship matters private, but as to the comparative benefits of New York versus Boston . . . I have always resented New York a tremendous amount, which probably relates to our earlier discussion of my congenital unhipness. "If you can make it there, you'll make it anywhere." Well, in a "with-it" sense, I'll never "make it there." And so it's been my goal to prove that you can make it as a writer without living in New York.

I'm also so easily distracted that I fear living in New York, because with everything going on there, I'd never get any work done. I mean, I don't even have a TV.

I also want to stay as far as possible from the competitiveness that I associate with the New York writing/publishing scene, because I think competitiveness kills good writing—at least mine.

As for Boston, it's where both sets of my grandparents lived when I was growing up, and so, although I never lived here until 1994, it feels very much like home. It's the city that most "makes sense" to me. My sister is here. The Red Sox are here. It's very comfortable. If at some point that comfort turns into stifling, I'll pack up and go.

Care to talk, even in abstract and/or general terms, about the joys and perils of being in a relationship with another writer?

Nope.

Part of your writer's life in Boston is involved with the Bromfield Street Educational Foundation. With them, you help to run a gay and lesbian reading series. Why get involved with something that must rob you of so much time from your own writing?

I love meeting writers, since they're the only people who really, really understand what my life is like. I also know how hard it is to get the public to notice good books, and so I'm committed to doing my part in trying to get the word out. I have a somewhat karmic notion of things, a very anticompetitive one, I hope, that if I help out other writers, I will eventually be helped myself. I don't expect exact reciprocity, like someone else running a series that I could read in. But I just want to support other writers and books and hope that I'll find some kindness along the way. If you and your wonderful interviewing are any indication, my karmic theory works!

Thanks. Final question: What advice do you have for young gay writers just starting out?

There are all sorts of standard responses I could give about reading—and rereading—good authors, and taking yourself seriously, and all that, but those apply to every writer. For specifically young *gay* writers? I guess I'd rephrase my definition of a "gay writer," and advise them to embrace their gayness as completely and honestly as possible, and at the same time to forget about it entirely. They should reject any kind of restriction: from straight readers or editors, from gay readers or editors, and from within themselves. They're lucky enough to be starting out in a world were the possibilities are basically boundless, and that gives them a wonderful freedom as well as a wonderful responsibility to live up to that freedom. My final advice: write books that I want to read!